In my view, the culture gap between Christians and contemporary unbelievers is *the* major impediment to effective proclamation of the gospel in America and Europe today. That culture gap is especially wide in the case of the so-called "New Age" and its adherents. What we need is some key, some point of articulation between the Christian faith and the New Age worldview. Charles Strohmer has both the experiential credentials and the intellectual skills to provide that key for us.

Strohmer's "key" is simple in conception, but rich in implications. It is this: the New Age is not simply a retreat from rationality, nor an incoherent mix of superstition and mysticism. At its bottom, it is a form of spiritual "wisdom." As such, it has a basis, an insight, and a structure of ideas about reality. And as such, it can be directly addressed by the wisdom of the gospel. Strohmer explains in depth and in detail how to apply that simple key of understanding. His book is an invaluable tool for anyone who wants to help bring the good news of Christ to the late twentieth century.

Brooks Alexander
Founder, Spiritual Counterfeits Project

This is a book about effective communication. In an age of confused spirituality, how can Christians present the gospel with clarity and zest? Charles Strohmer, who has been doing this for years, tells us how. Clearly written, amply illustrated. Follow his guidelines and expect good results!

James W. Sire, Ph.D.
Campus Lecturer, InterVarsity Christian Fellowship

This book is an outstanding example of how Christians can intelligently and sensitively reach those who are involved with New Age beliefs. Charles Strohmer's inside knowledge gives him a particular advantage when dealing with this difficult area. His "submarine" strategy provides an excellent model for apologetics and evangelism when approaching someone with any other worldview, and therefore has a much wider application than the New Age. I strongly recommend this clearly written and practical book.

Dr. Richard Winter
Associate Professor, Covenant Seminary

The Gospel and the New Spirituality is the first book I have seen that both explains clearly the New Age perspective and equips Christians in the art of engaging New Age people through rational and winsome persuasion. In addition to being imaginatively written, biblically informed, and theologically sound, this important book records a wealth of instructive, real-life encounters with New Age people. I highly recommend it to all those who want "to speak the truth in love" to those involved in the New Age.

Douglas Groothuis, Ph.D.
Author, Unmasking the New Age

What is it your neighbor believes? Do New Agers really believe in God? How has New Age thinking become so influential? To what degree can the gospel penetrate our culture? Answers to these and many more questions are found in this book. If we want to reach our friends and neighbors with the gospel, we must understand how they think and why. This book will definitely help us.

Gerald Coates
Director, Pioneer

THE GOSPEL AND THE NEW SPIRITUALITY

Charles Strohmer

THOMAS NELSON PUBLISHERS
Nashville • Atlanta • London • Vancouver

Published in Nashville, Tennessee, by Thomas Nelson, Inc., Publishers, and distributed in
Canada by Word Communications, Ltd., Richmond, British Columbia.

Published in Great Britain by Nelson Word Ltd., Milton Keynes, 1994. Original title: *Wise as
a Serpent, Harmless as a Dove.*

Unless otherwise indicated, the Bible version used in this publication is THE NEW KING
JAMES VERSION. Copyright © 1979, 1980, 1982, Thomas Nelson, Inc., Publishers. Scripture quotations noted KJV are from The King James Version of the Holy Bible. Scripture quotations noted RSV are from the Revised Standard Version of the Bible. Copyright © 1946,
1952, 1971, 1973 by the Division of Christian Education of the National Council of the
Churches of Christ in the United States of America. Scripture quotations marked NIV are
taken from the HOLY BIBLE, NEW INTERNATIONAL VERSION ®. Copyright © 1973,
1978, 1984 by International Bible Society. Used by permission of Zondervan Publishing
House. All rights reserved. Scripture quotations noted AMPLIFIED are from THE AMPLI-
FIED BIBLE: Old Testament. Copyright © 1962, 1964 by Zondervan Publishing House (used
by permission); and from THE AMPLIFIED NEW TESTAMENT. Copyright © 1958 by the
Lockman Foundation (used by permission).

Library of Congress Cataloging-in-Publication Data

Strohmer, Charles.
    The gospel and the New Spirituality / Charles Strohmer.
        p.   cm.
    Includes bibliographical references.
    ISBN 0-7852-7664-5 (pbk.)
    1. Christianity and other religions—New Age movement. 2. Spiritual life—New Age
movement. 3. Evangelistic work. 4. New Age persons. I. Title.
BR128.N48S77 1996
261.2'993—dc20   95-34580
                                                     CIP

Printed in the United States of America.

1 2 3 4 5 6 — 01 00 99 98 97 96

CONTENTS

Inter-Mission

Part Two: Harmless as a Dove

PREFACE

There is a real sense in which this book started to be written thirty years ago. It did not seem to matter that I was being raised in the American Midwest, in a stable family and a good school system; I was growing deeply disillusioned with the American Dream.

I was a sensitive teenager searching for some meaning to life in a decade when the U.S. president (in whom I'd hoped) was assassinated; when violent and bloody inner-city rioting (including in my home of Detroit) spread across the U.S. throughout four long, hot summers (1965–68); when I had to face the possibility of dying in the jungles of Vietnam (a war I did not believe in); when Bobby Kennedy and Dr. Martin Luther King, Jr. (a man of dreams like myself), were murdered in cold blood. I could go on. All of this got to me, big time. It was easy to conclude that America, and by implication the West, was morally and spiritually bankrupt. It was into this intellectual/spiritual disenchantment that a desire to find the Truth, whatever that was, cast like iron in my soul, and I made an inner vow to find it and, once found, to share it with my friends, family, and other interested seekers.

The first major consequence was the direction of my search. America was a Christian nation (so I'd been taught), so I felt that there was little point in digging deeper in Christianity for the Truth. I stopped going to church and headed East. It was easy to find the East in the West in the late 1960s. That is, in fact, when the two worlds married, and the fruit of the union is rife in the land today.

I already had some acquaintance with Eastern religious beliefs as a result of doing a massive school research paper on Brahmanism, years earlier. I hadn't thought much about it since, but now seemed the time to get reacquainted. A kind of ingenious spiritual synchronicity hung in the air. The Aquarian counterculture had dawned. Down the rabbit hole I plunged.

Now in my early twenties, astrology, meditation, visualization, "spirit guides," vegetarianism, asceticism, and psychic healing, roughly in that order—along with a spattering of other occult and so-called New Age beliefs and practices—dominated my search for Truth. It had taken eighteen years for me to become thoroughly disillusioned with the American Dream. It took only eight years for the joy that was within me to die when the "truth" of the Aquarian Dream was found to be lies. The hope of more and better lives through reincarnation disappeared. Practices like meditation no longer brought tranquillity; others lost their appeal. As a friend later said, "I was no better, I was no god." What I now know to be the power of God had smashed my Aquarian Dream.

Not knowing in what direction to turn for the Truth, I dropped into deep depression. If Truth wasn't in the West or the East, or in a metaphysical marriage of the two, just where was it? I hadn't a clue.

After several weeks of bewilderment, by God's grace I met the Truth Himself, Jesus Christ, through an unexpected and powerful encounter, which has often since seemed to me a bit like what rabbi Saul must have felt upon being knocked off his horse on the road to Damascus. I became a Christian in July 1976. What an awakening, I can tell you! And indeed I wanted to tell everyone about the Truth, Jesus Christ.

However, though I had been a spokesperson for the New Spirituality, I quickly discovered that it was terribly difficult to communicate Christianity to non-Christian spiritual seekers. I was bumping up against arcane intellectual/spiritual dynamics that frustrated Christian communication. Since I could not figure it out on my own, I dropped into some Christian bookstores, but I could discover no relevant material. I went to ministers and other Christian leaders, but they either answered my questions with a blank stare or pooh-poohed my zeal. I searched around on the periphery of the church for former seekers like myself, but the few I turned up in the late 1970s were equally at a loss about how to speak to our old friends in a way that would make sense to them.

A few years passed with only sporadic success. I got established in Christian fellowship, served in the church however I could, discovered my spiritual gifts, and went on earning a living. Yet all the while the desire to reach non-Christian seekers with the Truth steadily increased.

My serious hobby was writing, and in 1979 after much prayer and counsel, I began to transform it into a full-time occupation. I asked an increasing number of friends to pray that I would be able to write a book that spoke to spiritual seekers. Part of the vision came to pass with Tyndale House's publication of *What Your Horoscope Doesn't Tell You* in February 1988, amazingly, just three months before the Nancy Reagan "astrology in the White House" story broke.

Two years previously, I had left my job as a parts manager in a Chevrolet dealership to move to Scotland to marry a missionary and pursue full-time writing, editing, and speaking. After the release of *Horoscope*, I began traveling to teach about the New Age "movement." As I traveled the grassroots of Christendom on both sides of the Atlantic, I met increasing numbers of Christians who were asking, "How do we reach non-Christian spiritual seekers with the Truth?"

How indeed? I was meeting unexpected numbers of believers whom our Lord was raising up to reach non-Christian spiritual seekers, and there was precious little understanding about how to go about this timely and important work. The brave souls who were trying usually found themselves outwitted by the people of the New Spirituality when they were in conversation with them. This constrained me to draw together the ideas that had worked for me and to develop further ones. Eventually testimonies began to trickle in. This was in the late 1980s.

As we head into the twenty-first century, the New Spirituality, already mainstream, will become increasingly influential. Tens of millions of secular Westerners are becoming cosmic in orientation, transformed by a nonbiblical spirituality from all points East, ancient and occult. This book is prayerfully offered as part of a growing discussion by Christians everywhere as they search for ways to understand the New Spirituality and reach its seekers with the gospel of Jesus Christ.

ACKNOWLEDGMENTS

Producing a book is like building a house. In no way is it the labor of a lone individual. I was enormously helped by so many people, without whose generosity and candor this book would be lacking a great deal.

Thank you: Vic Oliver for the vision of the American edition and for coaching me through its production; John Leeper and David Booker, for turning me on to Scotty Briggs and the new parson; Dr. Richard Winter, for bringing a psychiatrist's eye to the uncharted waters of chapters 5 and 6; Joe and Melanie Adair, whose suggestions, critique, and tolerance have improved chapters 14 and 15; Jerram Barrs, whose L'Abri tapes on Christian engagement with the world scratched several of my spiritual itches; Phil White, who combined just the right mix of surrealism and humor in the artwork of the interior illustrations; Noël Halsey, Linda Finley-Day, Beth Bissett, and Win Kennedy of Nelson Word, not only for their ongoing enthusiasm about the book and for help in its preparation, but also for their patience and prayers when I was sick and for a year the project greatly slowed down; the countless anonymous but not forgotten persons whom I have met during my travels, who have shared their experiences and observations and so inspired me to keep going; the affirming special individuals who "caught the vision" and generously offered their endorsements; the ministers, leaders, principals, and other risk takers who have invited me into their churches, parachurch or mission organizations, schools, programs, and not a few ingenious settings, who gave me space to experiment, to make mistakes, to learn, and to teach on this timely and important subject (superb hospitality, too!); elders and members of Trinity Baptist Church and Trinity House Theatre and Arts Group (Livonia, Michigan), Evergreen Presbyterian Church (Sevierville, Tennessee), and Earl Soham Baptist (Woodbridge, Suffolk), for vigilance over my walk with our Lord, for intellectual stimulation, for moral challenge, for spiritual insight; the faithful and valiant souls whose prayer vigils I, my wife, and my audiences rely on so deeply (your Father, who sees what you do in secret, will reward you). All of you have given more freely than I could have hoped.

Two very special people remain, to whom "Thank you" somehow does not seem enough. One is the Reverend John Peck, an esteemed Christian thinker and a dear friend. His penetrating biblical teaching on the subject of worldview and his book *Wisdom in the Marketplace* have been inspirations to me over the years. Without them, this work would be without the essential Inter-Mission, which is not at the heart of this book by chance. Time and time again John has helped me to clarify my thoughts and has given me confidence; but even more, his selfless Christian life has shown me how to live more consistently out of a worldview whose twin foci are a manger and a cross.

And to Linda, my loving wife, I am without reservation grateful. Her suggestions and insights as a missionary have been indispensable; her prayers, encouragement, and support, unfailing; God's secret weapon from the womb of the dawn.

INTRODUCTION

This book is about the New Spirituality and what to say to the millions of people in our land who follow it. The New Spirituality is no longer a fringe element of marginal ideas or an amusing story for *Time* or *Newsweek*. It is a dominant cultural dynamic, moving leading thinkers and shading the issues that deeply touch us. Its ideas filter through TV and radio, and they are the energy behind many books, seminars, therapies, and superstars.

Who are the people of the New Spirituality? Who are its visionaries and thinkers? What do they think, and why do they think it? Where do their beliefs and practices come from? How do they feel about Christians, and how do we feel about them? But most important, how can we communicate to them in a way that really gets through?

The beliefs and practices of the New Spirituality may be as extraordinary as enduring a vision quest, hugging a tree out of brotherly affinity, or beating a buffalo drum to dissolve negative psychic energies. Usually, they're more mainstream. It may be your psychologist in Dallas proposing Neuro-Linguistic Programming as a powerful tool for achieving what you want. It may be a friend in Chicago encouraging you about feminist spirituality and Sophia worship. It may be your instructor in midwifery suggesting that pagan rituals during childbirth are just the thing. It may be your lawyer in Memphis reading Carlos Castaneda and Fritjof Capra (instead of John Grisham!).

The New Spirituality is in the foreground of Jungian psychology, holistic health care, self-help and personal growth approaches, women's issues, and the recovery movement. It is in the background of herbal remedies, dream interpretation, advertising, music, and Hollywood sci-fi movies. It is heard with praise in Bill Moyers's PBS programs about Joseph Campbell or alternative medicines. It is in good standing in Fortune 500 business management training and in the phenomenological, or experiential, or affective, approaches to education. It is in growing demand with hardworking type A personalities who did everything their parents and society demanded of them, but who still remain unfulfilled.

Millions of fed-up materialists are asking, "Is that all there is?" And they are seeking to connect with the spirit. So they're not just dressed in saffron robes meandering along California beaches or chanting "Hare Krishna" in Central Park. They style your hair at Supercuts, sell real estate through Century 21, or work alongside you at Sears. What will you say when you hear them going on about Gaia, the I Ching, wicca, feng-shui, archetypes, karma, enlightenment, Higher Self, near death experiences, or sacred cultural myths? How will you respond to your doctor when he recommends acupuncture treatment because orthodox Western medicine fails to relieve your back pain? What will you say to your child's teacher when she introduces creative visualization, or guided imagery, into the classroom?

It's not easy to know what to think about all this or to know how to respond productively. The people of the New Spirituality are disillusioned with the West's secular worldview and disenchanted with traditional, that is, patriarchal, religion. As a result, they have chosen not Christianity but a confusing swirl of beliefs and practices that form an alternate spirituality to Christianity. In this unpredictable ebb and flow of otherworldliness they seek to resolve their crisis of hope and fill their spiritual hunger. To manage this, the people of the New Spirituality mix Eastern religions with varying degrees of the occult, considerable measures of New Ageism, self-help, and pop psychology, along with a dash of Western optimism justified by whatever current scientific theories can be assumed. And, yet, despite the plethora of diverse, personal, and private agendas, these seekers are united in a common goal that a spiritual New Age for humanity should arrive in the twenty-first century. Remember? It's the dawning of the Age of Aquarius. The Christian Age is ending.

Unfortunately, it is not enough to know only this, as Christians who have tried getting through to people of the New Spirituality are discovering. It is a daunting task. Merely understanding the beliefs and practices (this has been our strong suit so far) of the New Spirituality is not enough to make us effective communicators to its adherents. Certainly, it is a beginning. But then we must take the next step and discover the intellectual/spiritual dynamics that short-circuit communication. Once we know that, we can solve the communication problems and build communication bridges.

That is the purpose of this book. It's not so much an analysis of the New Spirituality as it is something to help us understand the people of the New Spirituality and what to say to them. Realistically, our task is no different in principle from other exasperating communication headaches that the church has been called by her Lord to relieve. Even back in the years of our Lord Himself the disciples must have really been up against it, for He gave them a quite peculiar kind of guidance. And I have chosen it as our guiding light here.

When it was time for the gospel to hit the streets, Jesus warned His disciples that they were being sent out as sheep into the midst of wolves. This is understandable. Yet in the same breath, Jesus told them that they were, therefore, to be "wise as serpents, and harmless as doves" (Matthew 10:16 KJV). That is peculiar. Serpents and doves teamed up? Jesus' double simile seems contradictory. Yet to the Master it's not. To Him it is an ingenious method for producing understanding disciples who are also effective communicators. No easy feat, considering that it was such a formidable task and that it was to be done by sheep!

We, too, need a peculiar kind of guidance for moving around Christianly in the world of the New Spirituality. With that in mind, this book is divided into two parts. Part One identifies the intellectual/spiritual personality dynamics in their relation to the key beliefs of the New Spirituality and how they may frustrate Christian communication. The emphasis is on becoming as wise as a serpent. Part Two introduces both time-tested and biblical ideas for avoiding the communication barriers of these dynamics. The emphasis is on becoming as harmless as a dove. There is also an Inter-Mission, but it's not a rest break! It looks at several popular models that are used for understanding and addressing the New Spirituality and how they assist or hinder the communication process. It also raises the curtain on a fresh and, I hope, more desirable model.

PART
ONE

Wise as a Serpent

BUCK FANSHAW'S
FUNERAL

—⚉—

MARK TWAIN IN Roughing It wrote an absolutely humorous scene about making a hash of communication. The incident involves a rugged fireman and mining "rough" named Scotty Briggs who was dispatched to the new parson by a grieving Nevada mining community to make funeral arrangements for the late Buck Fanshaw, who had been a hard-living saloon keeper, bar-room brawler, foreman, miner, and political aspirant. He now needs burying, and with ceremony, having been well liked.

These early Western mining communities had "representative adventures," as Twain put it, from peoples everywhere, and they brought with them the language and slang of their nations and localities. Scotty Briggs and the new parson were cases in point. The former was a likable mining rough, the latter a "fragile, gentle, spiritual new fledgling from an Eastern theological seminary, and as yet unacquainted with the ways of the mine."

The purpose of this book is to help Christians find solutions to the baffling problems of communicating with the millions of non-Christian spiritual seekers in our land. Some will say "Well, that's easy enough. Just start talking." Others, however, will understand from experience that it is not quite so easy; some know the ways of the mine, but others do not. And some Christians have only heard rumors about the communication hassles, which others have encountered at first hand.

The following extract by Twain, it is hoped, will provide all readers with an illustration of the difficulties. It's a different context of course, set as it is in the old American West, yet its portrayal of the language muddles between the new parson and Scotty Briggs ought to be a perfect launching-off pad for us all. Here's Twain to tell it:

Being admitted to the presence [Scotty] sat down before the clergyman, placed his fire hat on an unfinished manuscript sermon under the minister's nose, took from it a red silk handkerchief, wiped his brow and heaved a sigh of dismal impressiveness, explanatory of business. He choked, and even shed tears; but with an effort he mastered his voice and said in lugubrious tones:

"Are you the duck that runs the gospel mill next door?"

"Am I the—pardon me, I believe I do not understand."

With another sigh and a half sob, Scotty rejoined:

"Why you see we are in a bit of trouble, and the boys thought maybe you would give us a lift, if we'd tackle you—that is, if I've got the rights of it, and you are the head clerk of the doxology works next door."

"I am the shepherd in charge of the flock whose fold is next door."

"The which?"

"The spiritual advisor of the little company of believers whose sanctuary adjoins these premises."

Scotty scratched his head, reflected a moment, and then said:

"You ruther hold over me, pard. I reckon I can't call that hand. Ante and pass the buck."

"How? I beg pardon. What did I understand you to say?"

"You see, one of the boys has passed in his checks and we want to give him a good send off, and so the thing I'm on now is to roust out somebody to jerk a little chin music for us and waltz him through handsome."

"My friend, I seem to grow more and more bewildered. Your observations are wholly incomprehensible to me. Cannot you simplify them in some way? At first I thought perhaps I understood you, but I grope now. Would it not expedite matters if you restricted yourself to categorical statements of fact unencumbered with obstructing accumulations of metaphor and allegory?"

Another pause, and more reflection. Then, said Scotty:

"I'll have to pass, I judge."

"How?"

"You've raised me out, pard."

"I still fail to catch your meaning."

"Why, that last lead of yours is too many for me—that's the idea. I can't neither trump nor follow suit."

The clergyman sank back in his chair perplexed. Scotty leaned his head on his hand and gave himself up to thought. Presently his face came up, sorrowful but confident.

"I've got it now, so's you can savvy," he said. "What we want is a gospel sharp, see?"

"A what?"

"Gospel sharp. Parson."

"Oh! Why did you not say so before? I am a clergyman—a parson."

"Now you talk! You see my blind and straddle it like a man. Put it there!"—extending a brawny paw, which closed over the minister's small hand and gave it a shake indicative of fraternal sympathy and fervent gratification.

"Now we're all right, pard. Let's start fresh. Don't you mind my snuffling a little—becuz we're in a power of trouble. You see, one of the boys has gone up the flume—"

"Gone where?"

"Up the flume—throwed up the sponge, you understand."

"Thrown up the sponge?"

"Yes—kicked the bucket—"

"Ah—has departed to that mysterious country from whose bourne no traveller returns."

"Return! I reckon not. Why, pard, he's dead!"

"Yes, I understand."

"Oh, you do? Well, I thought maybe you might be getting tangled some more. Yes . . . they've scooped him."

"Scooped him?"

"Yes—death has. Well, well, well, we've got to give him up. Yes indeed . . . There ain't any getting around that, I don't reckon. Now if we can get you to help plant him—"

"Preach the funeral discourse? Assist at the obsequies?"

"Obs'quies is good. Yes. That's it—that's our little game."

Well, the floundering tête-à-tête continued until the "obsequies" were all that "the boys" desired. And how well it captures something in principle of what many Christian conversations with "outsiders"—

5

too many of mine, at least—have been like. We may even have felt a slight pang of envy at seeing Scotty and the new parson wade through to some understanding! For our conversations may have resulted in confusion, offended feelings, or further alienation between parties due to our little word wars. Yet we cannot in good conscience give up.

COMMUNICATION BREAKDOWN

—ᴍᴍ—

WE LIVE IN a time when it has become a priority of Christian denominations, mission organizations, and parachurch groups everywhere to "evangelize the world for Christ." Committees brainstorm innovative global, national, regional, and local strategies to reach communities everywhere with the gospel. Conferences present both ministers and their congregations with the vision and equip them for the work. Programs are developed even to reach the churched!

It is exciting to see the emphasis on world evangelization, and this has been the reason for impressive conferences like the ones at Lausanne and Singapore, where fresh ways of reaching the world for Christ were conceived, discussed, and later implemented. Yet despite all the noise and excitement about how to reach this, that, and the other people group, there is an unfortunate silence, perhaps more of an omission, that will prove costly to us. Except for the infrequent lecture and even rarer program, we are not preparing ourselves to reach one of the fastest growing "worlds" within the one world, the world of the New Spirituality, which many have called the New Age. How, then, shall we reach the entire world for Christ if we are unable to communicate with this emerging "world"?

7

A WORLD OF ITS OWN

In becoming a world of its own, like that of *Star Wars* or *The Lord of the Rings*, the world of the New Spirituality has its own authority figures and codes to live by, myths and symbols, spiritual technologies and vocabulary. It has singular ways of looking at God, human nature, the world, education, the arts, science, industry, health care, and so forth, as well as a mystical way of inner development.

We have not seen the New Age phenomenon as a world of its own, I think, because its people usually look just like we do, that is, Western, and because as a community, they do not live apart on a desert island. Since they look like us outwardly and live among us, it is easy to assume that they are also like us inwardly. Yet, as we shall see, they have been undergoing an intellectual/spiritual transformation that has been making them increasingly unlike us inwardly and consequently foiling our naive attempts at communication.

If we begin to see the one world not all of a piece but as different worlds within the one world, and if we see the world of the New Spirituality as one of these inter-worlds, it may give us the kind of framework by which to consider seriously the problems of communication. Missionary organizations often subdivide the one world into individual worlds. It helps them develop ways of speaking, for example, to the Jewish world, which would be significantly different from how they approached the Muslim or Hindu world. When Jesus commanded His disciples to "go into all the world and preach the gospel" (Mark 16:15), and later named several target communities—Jerusalem, Judea, Samaria, and the ends of the earth (Acts 1:8)—surely He knew that the different worlds would have to be approached with His message in different ways.

The apostle Paul was skilled at making use of these subdivisions and in approaching the different worlds in ways that actually communicated to each one. He is explicit about this in 1 Corinthians 9:19–23, where he says that he becomes like those to whom he is sent, wherever he travels, that "by all means" he might gain converts. To the Jews, he was as a Jew; to those under the law, he was as one under the law; to uneducated rural pagans, he spoke their largely unreligious language; to philosophers, he spoke their educated language. "This I do," he says, "for the gospel's sake." He is ready to understand them as far as it is necessary to gain them for his Lord.

8

How large is the world of the New Spirituality? How many adherents are there, and how culturally influential are they? With no membership lists or even a coherent philosophy, such questions are difficult to answer. In every major American and European city, an increasing number of enthusiasts are seeking the transpersonal and the transcendent through New Age rather than Christian perspectives. In some areas in the United States, researchers indicate that New Agers constitute as much as 12 to 15 percent of the population, which certainly rivals church growth programs!

The extent of influence is also difficult to determine, but some clues exist. The circulation of the popular magazine *New Age Journal* increased from 65,000 in 1983 to 165,000 in 1989. Bantam increased its list of New Age titles tenfold in the 1980s. Between 1985 and 1989, the number of New Age bookstores in the United States doubled to 4,000. Total sales of New Age titles exceeded $100 million a year at the beginning of the 1990s.

New Age music and audio- and videotapes for mind expansion and such were selling at $300 million a year in 1990, and in the same year corporations were spending a massive $4 billion on New Age consultants. (Figures and statistics are from *Megatrends 2000*, by John Naisbitt and Patricia Aburdene.)

In the high-powered, influential world of publishing, the new spin in the 1990s is on spirituality, according to the May 16, 1994, issue of *Publishers Weekly*. Bob McCullough writes that there is a pent-up demand for books that address soul issues or spirituality. He cites a "burgeoning spiritual restlessness among authors and readers," and he notes that publishers are following suit by making spirituality themes address topics such as personal growth, the recovery movement, women's issues, abusive relationships, twelve-step programs, the meaning of life, the purpose of suffering, and other subjects that apply to everyday life.[1] These books offer ten thousand ways of opening the gates to one's inner world—it is said to be a higher world, a spiritual world, a world of enlightenment, growth, liberation, and infinite resources—where a vital presence takes over and takes one deeper still. Enthusiasts would say that this is another major step toward a completely spiritual culture on the earth in the twenty-first century.

In Great Britain, the media have raised the profile of the New Spirituality markedly. Every weekend for several months in 1989 the popular *Guardian* newspaper ran a "New Age Page," which usually carried one article on a popular New Age topic or place and a shorter piece about a leading British New Ager. On March 4, 1990, the weekend London supplement of *The Times* featured a cover story on the New Age, and also that year Channel 4 ran a six-part series that featured forty New Age leaders from around the world, including David Spangler and Sir George Trevelyan. The programs had no guests who could provide a critical view. On August 4, 1991, the *Sunday Express* carried an article listing the names and phone numbers of New Age therapists. There are also numerous healing arts and alternative health-care exhibitions that are held frequently and attract thousands, the most popular probably being the Body, Mind, Spirit Festival held in London every spring, which is similar to the Whole Life Expo held in San Francisco—a three-day event attended by 25,000 people every year.

As in the United States, many alternate spiritualities influence industry and education in Great Britain. The computer giant Digital, the South Scottish Electricity Board, British Telecom, and other corporations have run training seminars that are more than cosmetically New Age. The new national curriculum sees an influx of religious education methods with motifs decidedly from the New Spirituality. The degree to which these methods now influence the British national curriculum may be unlawful. The Education Reform Act of 1988, dealing with religious education and collective worship, states that "new locally agreed syllabuses must reflect the fact that religious traditions in the country are *in the main Christian*" and that "the collective worship in county schools must be *wholly or mainly of a broadly Christian character*" and that "acts of worship in a term *must be broadly Christian.*"[2]

THAT WORLD NEXT DOOR

As the world of the New Spirituality increasingly emerges, the means by which we learn how to communicate with its followers—our neighbors, employers, fellow employees, children's teachers, health-care professionals—becomes a burning question. About the only thing resolved so far is that ways of presenting apologetics and evangelizing among other kinds of non-Christians are not working with these non-Christians. We need, therefore, to unlearn inappropriate ways of communicating with people of the New Spirituality and develop relevant and effective approaches.

It's not as if Christians are not trying. In fact, it may surprise some to know that the number one topic of concern as I travel and speak in this field is "effective communication with people of the New Spirituality." I have lost count of the number of stories Christians have told me, on both sides of the Atlantic, of failure in this area. These tales are being told not only by novices but by Christians who are well versed in the faith and practiced at apologetics or evangelization. People are asking, "What can we do about this communication breakdown?"

"My boyfriend's mother is an astrologer," said a young woman in her early twenties. "She's pressing me to let her read my horoscope and compare it to her son's, to see if we're compatible. I'm trying to explain to her why I don't want her to do that, but it's so frustrating because I know I'm not getting anywhere with her. She believes we're entering the Age of Aquarius and that the Christian era is ending. She also thinks the Bible endorses astrology. When I talk to her, I think she only pretends to be listening to me, and the last time we ended up in a big argument. What can I do?"

"I have an aunt who's a spiritualist," a young man told me. "She thinks her spiritual gifts are the same as the ones mentioned in 1 Corinthians 12. I know she's mistaken, and I've tried to discuss it with her. But she doesn't see the sense of what I'm saying, and she confuses me with her spiritualist views of the supernatural. What can I do?"

"I went with several friends," said a woman in her forties, "to a festival to witness, but we didn't do too well. We had read up on the New Age and had been in prayer, but the conversations we had didn't seem to do much good. I'm more puzzled than ever now. What can we do?"

"There's a psychic up the road from us," another said. "She likes to predict things over the neighborhood children. The parents think it's amusing, and so now she's inviting them over to have their palms read. I finally got up the nerve to talk to her about this. It was incredible! She told me that I had negative psychic fears—whatever those are—and refuses to talk to me now. What can I do?"

"My aunt," another said, "goes for treatment to a New Age acupuncturist. She's been telling me about body meridians and bal-

11

ancing her life energies. I hadn't a clue as to what she was talking about, so I bought a book on holistic health. This gave me a Christian understanding of what she way saying, but now even when I try to talk to her about some of her problems, I'm not getting through to her. What can I do?"

Many stories are coming in from the increasing number of Christians who are trying their best to speak to non-Christian spiritual seekers. Christians are quietly discovering friends, acquaintances, fellow employees, or even family members who are open to the New Spirituality. It has been a big encouragement to all of us that we are not isolated in this particular work, but that we are part of the larger picture of evangelizing the world for Christ. It is becoming more common to meet people who want to pool their resources, form small groups under church leadership, and network in their shared vision to reach people of the New Spirituality with a Christian message. And the emphasis of their training, they now say, must be on communication.

THREE AREAS OF INSIGHT

As a former insider who is now a Christian and called to teach, I have a great desire to help us find some answers to this communication problem, and reports of breakthroughs are coming in (see Chapter 3).

As I have understood it, we need insight in three areas. First, we must gain some understanding of the New Spirituality's beliefs and practices and how they are influencing our culture. This has been our strong suit so far. However, the problem is that communication still goes haywire even after we have read the books. We remain outfoxed in conversations, not infrequently argumentative, or even speechless! It seems that knowing what these people believe is not enough.

This brings us to the two chief concerns of this book. One will take us into the area of understanding not only the beliefs but the intellectual/spiritual dynamics within non-Christian spiritual seekers, to show how they disrupt Christian communication. (Insights will be offered in Part Two concerning dynamics within Christians that also contribute to this disruption.) The other area offers caring ways to outwit these disrupting dynamics.

In summary, besides knowing what the people of the New Spirituality believe, we must identify prevailing intellectual/spiritual dynamics that foil a Christian witness, and then discover ways of overcoming these dynamics.

Though some of the following material of necessity overlaps, the basic plan is as follows. In Part One, the subject will be identifying the dynamics that jam Christian communication frequencies, with the emphasis on becoming "wise as a serpent" in understanding. During the Inter-Mission, we pause to consider a variety of popular models for seeing the New Age phenomenon. The focus here is that some ways of seeing the New Spirituality are not conducive to effective communication. And then Part Two will cover overcoming these dynamics, with the emphasis on becoming "harmless as a dove" in communication.

3

MEET SUCCESS AND FAILURE

—⚉—

BRENDAN AND DAVID

THE ROYAL PAVILION at Brighton, England—a striking symbol of Eastern influence in a Western nation, with its huge Oriental-looking onion domes ballooning the waterfront—was an apt background for what had been taking place around me there one evening in the late autumn. It was wet and cool, and the three of us were sitting cross-legged on the thinly carpeted floor of Brendan's two-room apartment, warming by the fire, sipping hot tea, and talking about spiritual things. The multicolored phantasmagorical artwork of several Eastern religious posters pinned on otherwise bare walls corresponded to the intellectual/spiritual confusion that hung in the air as we talked. And we had talked for hours.

Brendan and I were new friends, and he had invited me to his apartment to talk to his friend David about the occult, New Age ideas, and Christianity. David was as earnest a spiritual seeker as I have ever met, and he was steeped in Eastern religious metaphysics. The lengthy give-and-take of ideas that evening covered most of life's big questions. What is God like? Is He impersonal energy or personal Being? Is life after death about reincarnation or resurrection? Are suffering and evil the result of everyone's bad karma or sin? Is Jesus Christ merely a god-man akin to Buddha, Krishna, and Rama, or is He the unique Son of God? Are all religions ultimately leading to the same place but with different outward expressions, or do the fundamental ideas of Christianity preclude that? Why should the Bible be preferred over other religious books like the Bhagavad Gita?

I'm not sure how much help I was to David. Clearly, the gospel did not penetrate his heart, and I probably should have prayed more ahead of time. I felt discouraged when David left after midnight to drive home. Not only because I had not been successful, but because in the back of my mind that evening another scene had been playing.

A few months earlier in June, I had visited the English L'Abri Centre to do some research. It was there that I first met Brendan, who was among the twenty other guests who had arrived to study during L'Abri's summer term. Amid sundry activities around the manor house and grounds, Brendan and I struck up conversations and discovered our similar spiritual backgrounds. Yet I soon realized that Brendan's search had not ended; he had not met Christ. He was trying to become a Christ, which had also been one of my goals. He had spent a decade as a devotee of Indian mysticism and had even been on pilgrimage to India a few times seeking enlightenment. I was deeply moved by the sincerity of his search for truth. As I had done years earlier, he had given up just about everything to find it. Now here he was, a serious non-Christian spiritual seeker in a Christian environment, alongside me.

I was determined to use my testimony as best I could. Years earlier, before my conversion, I had been advised by a teacher of the occult to read the Bible as yet another means of unearthing the esoteric wisdom of the ancients. That did not make a lot of sense to me, even at the time, but I respected the advice. I got a Bible and went excavating for a year, cover to cover. It was a long, demanding dig, and I got little out of it.

Brendan was in a Christian environment merely at someone's suggestion, and I did not want the same thing to happen to him. He was making yet another stopover in his spiritual wanderings, and so I prayed, along with the L'Abri workers, that his search would end. It did. Near the end of my two-week visit to L'Abri[1] I was privileged to help Brendan, through deep repentance, to meet the Savior.

Back home, Brendan had been trying to express the Christian faith to his good friend David. But as a lot of us have discovered, it is not always easy for new Christians to share their newfound faith, and so Brendan had invited me to talk to David.

15

TERRI

Having heard these two stories, you might be tempted to think that I am always level-headed in my discussions. Don't fool yourself. I've made some terrible mistakes. Once a friend asked me to "talk some sense" into her sister (I think it was) who believed the Aquarian views about Jesus Christ.

Do you remember the so-called eighteen silent years of Christ's life in the Gospels? To account for this missing piece of Jesus' life, several popular books suggest that when Jesus was twelve years old, He traveled from Israel to India, where He lived for eighteen years at the feet of gurus and through enlightenment discovered His godhood status. He then traveled back to Israel when He was thirty to preach not the gospel but Christ-consciousness to the Hebrews.[2] Well, Terri (not her real name) believed this Aquarian gospel, and it was a disaster when I was taken to her home to talk about it.

I thought I was prepared, but when Terri hauled out books and articles to support her position, I knew that I was in over my head. Instead of applying some of the possibilities for effective communication that you will read about in the following chapters, I was reduced to making ridiculous remarks like, "That can't possibly be true," without being able to say why. I have rarely seen a conversation deteriorate so fast. What Terri felt I can only imagine. I felt embarrassed and threatened and could not control my indignation. Within minutes I was making heated remarks, and soon we were both antagonistic. Even when a third party tried to clear the air, we could still feel the hostility in the room. It was pointless to continue, and I fled, suffering an onslaught of guilt for days.

Of the three stories above, which ones were successes, which failures? I think you will agree that Brendan represents a success, Terri a failure. But what about my time with David? I used to look at that as a failure, but I have changed my view. The conversation lasted for hours because it was nonargumentative, and I learned many things listening to David. Furthermore, he got some clarity about the incompatibility of Christian and Eastern religious answers to life's big questions. It was David's acknowledgment of these incompatibilities, I have concluded, that made the conversation a success.

With some people, conversations like this will be enough for the time being. People of the New Spirituality must come to grips with the incompatibility of their wisdom and Christian wisdom in order to make sense of the gospel later. After all, within the New Spirituality it is customary to think (though they're a bit embarrassed about it) that Christianity is somehow a part of the oneness of all things, albeit an outdated religion for the lesser-evolved. David, therefore, first had to see the fundamental dissimilarities and then be challenged by their significance. We could call this a preevangelistic conversation, and within that framework the time spent was successful. The only failure was my time with Terri.

Another occurrence that I am tempted to call a failure is when we unexpectedly find ourselves talking to people of the New Spirituality and have nothing to say. Many Christians still have not read up on the New Spirituality and so get caught short if they happen to bump into a follower. Suddenly an opportunity has arisen, but just as suddenly it passes. Or in trying to be polite, we may find ourselves nodding our heads in agreement with the silliest spiritual ideas.

But most likely we may keep silent because we don't know much about it, or because we think it requires expert handling. The day, however, of the Christian expert who handles this for us has ended. That world is just too big now.

PAM AND LINDA

With so many opportunities arising, we want to be able to hold conversations. And there are many ways to speak effectively without first having to be an expert.

This is the purpose, in part of the "Submarine Communication Model" that is developed later in the book. We do not need to have communication failures even if we have not read up on the alternate spiritualities. We do not need to avoid conversations because we do not know enough about it. This is a great relief, overall, as Pam and Linda discovered.

Pam unexpectedly had a captive audience "who was dressed a trifle funny" sitting by her on a flight from San Francisco to Dallas. They had not begun the flight side by side, however. Soon after the seatbelt sign had been switched off, a middle-aged woman, beaded and fringed, with long hair, glided down the narrow aisle to Pam and asked if she could sit by her, explaining that she was unhappy with her assigned seat. Pam yielded up the seat next to her, and the woman settled in, rummaging through the flight bag at her feet. It then

17

dawned on Pam that the curious aroma attending this 1960s apparition was generously escaping from that bag.

"Sorry 'bout that," the Californian said. "The incense bottle leaked all over the bottom of my bag."

She then brought out a New Age music cassette and a Shirley MacLaine book, and Pam did not need Columbo to help her figure out all the clues!

"She did not become a Christian," Pam told me. "But what excited me was that I was able to talk to her about her beliefs during the whole flight even though I don't know a lot about them. If this had happened to me before I became acquainted with the 'Submarine Communication Model,' I wouldn't have known what to say. I would have had to sit there passively for two hours listening to her preach about the New Age. What an ordeal that would have been! As it was, I think I was able to communicate in a way that really got her thinking. Even though it was hard to bite back my words whenever I wanted to demand that she get rid of that foul-smelling incense!"

Linda is another Christian who found herself with an unexpected opportunity and was not caught unprepared. She spent much of her six-hour train journey talking to a university student, who was curious about the so-called white witchcraft (wicca, at times) that was being practiced in her dorm.

"She was seeing," Linda said, "that there was a certain power behind it, but she hadn't made up her mind about what that power was. I knew I had an opening. Using some of your material, I found it was easy enough to show her what kind of power her friends were dealing with. I knew from what she said as she got off the train that she had had a change of mind."

"I'm going to explain all this to my friends at the university," she said. "That business is not good. We don't want to be a part of something like that."

We can have good impromptu conversations with non-Christian spiritual seekers. Opportunities do not have to be lost. Much of this book will help us discover how to do this.

LAYING GROUND FOR UNDERSTANDING

Some may wonder, *What's the point? Why not just jump right in with the gospel? Isn't that what Jesus, Paul, Peter, and the other apostles did?* Yes, but they often spent time beforehand preparing people for the gospel. In most cases, we will need to do the same for the following important reason. People of the New Spirituality live in a world in which the gospel seems improbable, unthinkable, unimaginable. Because of what they believe, the gospel simply does not make sense to them, and many of them are not being converted as a result. Should some of them make a confession of faith in this condition, they could easily backslide, not understanding the message to begin with. A large part of our efforts must be spent first on helping these people to come into a way of seeing life in which the gospel seems probable, believable, credible. *Then* the gospel will make sense to them.

Jesus spoke of this as people who understand what they hear. In Matthew 13:11–23, Jesus taught that only those who hear *and understand* the message of the kingdom produce a crop. Those who hear but do not understand have the seed of the Word snatched away by the evil one, for there is no ground, or basis, for understanding. The effective communicator establishes grounds that help people understand what they are hearing.

Call it what you will; the task of moving these non-Christians from the improbable to the probable, from the unimaginable to the imaginable, from the unthinkable to the believable, is inescapable. It is about cultivating a certain frame of mind in our relationships. It is about presenting ideas that make the gospel become acceptable in people's imaginations, so moving them closer to saving faith and gaining them for Christ in the long run. It is not difficult to do this.

The Californian, the university student, David; all represent conversations no less successful than the two weeks I spent with Brendan. It is a false pressure, and unsupported by the Bible, to think that every conversation with a non-Christian spiritual seeker must be about giving them the gospel immediately. Not a few Christians, however, labor under this burden, and their lives are guilt-ridden because it is impossible to live up to expectations.

Worse still, this state of mind generates gunslinger evangelism. People are reduced to the status of mere objects—souls—to be notched on our gospel guns. Having become "things" upon which we "do" our evangelization projects, they are no longer persons with whom we can have a variety of relationships. This is one of the chief complaints from people about Christians. It keeps them from listening, from understanding, and from opening up. After all, it is difficult to appear interested, sensitive, and personable with a smoking gun in the hand.

4

ENTERING THE INTER-WORLD

—〰—

"SON OF MAN," God said, "eat this scroll, and go, speak."

After the repast, the prophet is then told, "Go to the house of Israel and speak with My words to them. For you are not sent to a people of unfamiliar speech and of hard language, . . . whose words you cannot understand. Surely, had I sent you to them, they would have listened."

This selection from Ezekiel (3:1–6) seems apropos of the church's commission to people of the New Spirituality, but with a twist, for we are being sent to a people of unfamiliar speech and hard (difficult) language, *even though* we all speak English. But look at the promise: they will listen. They will listen, that is, if we masticate the scroll, which for us means identifying and, I think, chewing over the intellectual/spiritual dynamics that have created the communication barrier. And we will now turn to identify these dynamics for the remainder of Part One.

INVERSION

In Lewis Carroll's *Through the Looking Glass*, Alice finds everything backward in Looking-glass House and its countryside. The words in books go the wrong way, seemingly straight paths have sharp corners to them, very dry cookies are eaten to quench thirst, however

20

fast Alice runs she never passes anything, and to meet someone you walk in the opposite direction! This situation is terribly confusing to poor Alice, and all the more so when she discovers from the Red Queen and other Looking-glass characters that they consider that their way of seeing life is normal, proper, and sensible. She does try to set things right, but it's tiring. And when she has to deal with the Looking-glass perspective in her conversations, it's at best *"rather hard to understand"* and at its worst "nonsense."

The conversations we take part in and the things we encounter in the world of the New Spirituality can be just as astonishing because the perspective there is often radically different from that of Christianity. Because it's similar to what Alice found, let's call it the dynamic, or principle, of inversion. Things are the wrong way around. A passage in Isaiah (5:20) reflects this, speaking as it does about

> *Those who call evil good, and good evil;*
> *Who put darkness for light, and light for darkness;*
> *Who put bitter for sweet, and sweet for bitter!*

This principle of inversion is very bewildering because it brings *us* face-to-face with the unbelievable, the unthinkable, and the unimaginable, and I have always thought that even an initial understanding of what it is like would be invaluable for our work among non-Christian spiritual seekers. I found a compelling analogy in the book *Peace Child* by Don Richardson. It's in a different context—set as it is among cannibals and headhunters—but as a description of the inversion principle, it is unforgettable, as well as being helpful in preparing us for what we face.

In 1962, Don and Carol Richardson moved from North America to the western half of the island of New Guinea, called Irian Jaya Indonesia, just north of Australia. The Sawi people lived here, and the Richardsons settled in to learn their language and customs. Life among the cannibals and headhunters was difficult, complicated further by warring tribes; but eventually the Richardsons had learned enough to begin communicating the gospel and Don Richardson began to meet with the Sawi men in the "manhouse" to do just that. Though Richardson presented the gospel story carefully building line upon line, the Sawi men just stared unresponsively day after day. That is, until the day came for the portrayal of Jesus' betrayal, when a curious amusement and excitement arose among the Sawi men.

From that moment the men were deeply interested in the gospel story, but for a most unexpected and wrong reason. Here is Richardson's account of his startling discovery:

> On subsequent visits [to the manhouse] I expanded further on the life and ministry of Jesus, trying to establish His reality and relevance to their lives, but without apparent success. The Sawi were not accustomed to projecting their minds into cultures and settings so forbiddingly dissimilar to their own.
>
> Only once did my presentation win a ringing response from them. I was describing Judas Iscariot's betrayal of the Son of God. About halfway through the description I noticed they were all listening intently. They noticed all the details: for three years Judas had kept close company with Jesus, sharing the same food, traveling the same road. That any associate of Jesus would have conceived the idea of betraying such an impressive figure was highly unlikely. And if anyone *had* conceived the idea, one of Jesus' inner circle of trusted disciples would have been the least likely to choose such a course. And yet Judas, one of Jesus' disciples, had chosen to betray Him and carried out the dreadful act alone, without any of the other disciples suspecting his plot.
>
> At the climax of the story, Maum whistled a birdcall of admiration. Kani and several others touched their fingertips to their chests in awe. Still others chuckled. Then the realization broke through. *They were acclaiming Judas as the hero of the story* [his emphasis]! Yes, Judas, the one whom I had portrayed as the satanically motivated enemy of truth and goodness! A feeling of coldness gripped my spine. I tried to protest that Jesus was good. He was the Son of God, the Savior. It was evil to betray Him. But nothing I said could erase that gleam of savage enjoyment from their eyes.[1]

What do you do? The Sawi admired Judas! An unthinkable principle of inversion influenced their way of seeing. How do you put the thing the right way around? For Don Richardson, it meant discovering why Judas, not Jesus, was the hero. In private conversations with one or two Sawi men, Richardson dug up the appalling fact that treachery was highly esteemed among the Sawi men. It was therefore natural for the men to admire a betrayer, especially Judas whom they saw as the archetypal quisling.

"The Sawi honored cruelty," Richardson wrote.

Their highest pleasure depended upon the misery and despair of others. *Judas was the super-Sawi* [his emphasis]! And Christ, the object of Judas' treachery, meant nothing to the men in the manhouse. My task was to reverse the situation totally.[2]

Unbelievable? Unthinkable? Yes. And though Judas may not be the hero of the story in the world of the New Spirituality, we will be encountering unimaginable and unthinkable perspectives there, each of which presents its own fundamental difficulty in communication that must be overcome. Part of our work, then, will be similar to Richardson's: to reverse the situation.

But how could one man and his wife reverse the worldview of an entire people, a worldview which had been entrenched in their collective psyche for perhaps a thousand years? I wanted to win *this* generation of Sawi. And I wanted to win them on their own ground and by their own fireplaces. If the gospel could not win men like Mahaen, Kani, Hato and Kigi, it was not the message it claimed to be. I was game, but I was also stymied. I didn't know how to tackle a cultural enigma like this. I headed home for lunch groaning inwardly, "Lord, in all of time and space, has Your message ever encountered a worldview more opposite . . . to the gospel? And has anyone ever faced a communication problem bigger than this one You've assigned me?"[3]

Does this sound familiar? I have wondered before God, groaning over exactly this. Yet one man and his wife in the wisdom and power of God cracked the code. We serve the same God. Shall He not also enable us to solve the communication riddle we face?

THE CLOSED MIND

At least the Sawi men were willing to listen. But what about those who do not want to listen to us? We meet them. And here we encounter the intellectual/spiritual dynamic of the closed mind.

23

When my wife and I lived in Paisley, Scotland, we liked to take the train to Edinburgh for a break from our hectic schedules. Strolling through the beautiful and nearly year-round gardens along Princes Street, visiting museums, or simply seeing sights like Edinburgh Castle, we found time to relax. And after meandering around, we had a habit of stopping in the Waverley Market for a cup of coffee and something sweet.

Many of those times were slightly marred for me, however, by the sight of a numerologist who worked the Waverley Market. He had been granted permission to set up a small table, folding chairs, and a poster that announced numerology readings. For more than a year I saw him set up in the same conspicuous spot inside the Waverley Market where he would be dispensing numerology charts, giving readings, and collecting small fees from a steady stream of people. Nearly every time I was there, he was there. Whether coincidental or not, I don't know. But the more I realized the number of people he was influencing, the more grieved I got, until one day I summoned up enough nerve to speak to him.

I waited off to the side until he had a free moment. I knew I would need to be brief, whatever I said, because the interested would begin lining up again. As I was waiting, I pondered what I would say and how to do it in the short time I figured I would have. Since I had some copies of *What Your Horoscope Doesn't Tell You* with me in my briefcase, I decided that it was probably best just to get that book into his hands. *It won't take long to do that,* I thought, *and then he can read it at his leisure and discover what we don't have time to discuss here.*

I walked up and carefully asked if I could have a quick word with him.

"What about?" he said.

"I used to do readings for people similar to what you're doing. I've got a different perspective on it now and was wondering if during your break here you might like to hear about that."

"No. I'm not interested."

"Could I give you a book, then, that you could read in your spare time?"

"No."

"Oh, well, why not? The book's free."

"Because I know what I'm doing. I've been doing this for twenty years, and it's not what people think."

24

"But I've got a book here in my briefcase I'd like to give you. Wouldn't you like it?"

"No," he said with the finality of a judge.

I took the hint, rose from the chair, and said a polite good-bye. Similar experiences have taught me that pressing harder for a hearing when up against a closed mind usually degenerates into a heated argument. Even though I was being as circumspect as I knew how, the numerologist had shut down any avenues of approach. I had not used any religious language or words such as *occult, New Age,* and *Christian* because they might easily make him lose interest in what I wanted to say and deter him from accepting the book. I had not even told him it was my book! In plain English, the guy was closed. I had encountered the closed mind.

It's ironic. People of the New Spirituality claim to be very open-minded. And indeed they are open-minded to virtually anything and everything *except* traditional Judeo-Christian perspectives. Agonizing though this may be, we must allow them their choice; unwise though it may be, they are free to make it. Arguing will probably entrench them deeper in their position and so further alienate them from the only true Hope. When we get the cold shoulder, it may be best to disengage ourselves from the conversation as graciously as possible. A closed mind is a shut door. This is not our fault. We have not failed. If someone does not wish to hear us, that is the choice we must allow the person to make.

Yet even walking away from a shut door graciously can be redemptive. The person may respect you for allowing him the freedom of his choice. This might seem inconsequential, but not when the God of grace can work with it. It may just be that in walking away graciously, rather than in a huff or staying to argue, you make a favorable impression on the person. It may even have been the first favorable impression he has ever received from a Christian. This, then, could pave the way for you to have a conversation with the person later, or perhaps the person will speak with another Christian at another time. Let us never underestimate the redemptive potential of our actions.

5

THE STORM OF
THE IRRATIONAL

—❦—

THERE IS A story about the absentminded professors who were gathered for a leisurely day in the country. When invited by their host to spend the night because a storm had arisen, they went home to get their toothbrushes!

It's amusing, yet we cannot help wondering what in the world was going on in their minds. We may face similar bewilderment during some of our conversations with non-Christian spiritual enthusiasts. It needs to be seen as irrationality, which, due to the nature of the beast, is hard to pin down. Never mind how real it is, or how annoying; it is by nature ambiguous and therefore incapable of being nailed down by airtight definitions. At least by me. Nevertheless, storms of irrationality have been known to blow in unexpectedly and shipwreck an effective Christian conversation. Consequently, we need to take a look at it as best we can.

SAILING IN STORMS

I have sailed into these storms more than once. On one occasion it happened during a live interview on a British radio program as I was going up against astrologer Marjorie Orr. I had been seated with a presenter in a soundproof studio in Scotland, Orr was in a London studio. The program had begun with me trying to reason with Orr about glaring contradictions within the rationale of astrology.

The subject of the supernatural eventually came up, and I mentioned that it was one of the things wrong with astrology at its deepest level because of the frightening supernatural experiences it could give people. I cited one of mine as a case in point.

"I would kindly like to suggest," Orr said, "that it was Mr. Strohmer's psyche that produced these things rather than the astrology itself. I mean, astrology certainly comes out of the realm of the irrational, but that's no reason to be frightened by it."

When I then tried to reason with her about this, she tried interrupting me and shouting me down several times. I had to concentrate very hard to drive through her agitation and finish what I had to say. The presenter tried switching the topic "to more practical matters," but unsuccessfully. Orr was speaking of irrelevancies, and I tried to pin her down to the question and our need for a reasonable discussion of the matter.

I don't think Orr liked hearing about the necessity for rational thinking. She caught her breath and said that "the rational" was the real problem, "similar to what we have at the moment with Islamic fundamentalists" (who were that week making world headlines by pronouncing their death sentence against Salman Rushdie for his "blasphemous" book *Satanic Verses*). I wasn't happy about being placed alongside such infamy, and the presenter saw the illogic herself and rolled up her eyes in disbelief. Orr would not be stopped. She rattled on explaining "the irrational" in terms of Mrs. Thatcher (then prime minister) living out the Athena myth.

That must have been enough even for the presenter who quipped that she wasn't convinced that Mrs. Thatcher sprang from the head of Zeus, and then she promptly ended the "interview." I have a suspicion that even the presenter was tired of dealing with the irrational during this "conversation." Yet no doubt the dust-up that morning was great for the program's ratings!

The Bible challenges people: " 'Come now, and let us reason together,' says the LORD" (Isa. 1:18), and the picture is from the law court: the arguing of cases, frank confrontation, and the use of evidence and good and sufficient reasons. That is what Job would have liked in his case (Job 23:7)!

SUPPRESSING THE RATIONAL

Part of the trouble in storms like this is that the irrational has little or no tolerance for the rational. It takes issue with reasoned argument, especially the kind that discloses its inconsistencies. In extreme cases the irrational gets behind the wheel and then bullies the rational into taking a dusty seat at the back of the bus.

Also, irrationality creates an intellectual/spiritual climate in which non-Christian spiritual seekers begin to feel comfortable bedding down with contradictory beliefs and values. Such people may not only appear diffident when a reasoned analysis discloses inconsistencies; they may even be proud of them, for in the world of the New Spirituality the rational is understood to be a hindrance to reaching enlightenment, expanding consciousness, and spiritual evolution. This will be understood by Christians who have heard seekers say, "I don't care if that seems illogical to you. We must escape the confines and limitations of rational, black-and-white thinking. Our society has placed too much emphasis on the analytical left side of the brain. It's time to develop the intuitive, creative right brain. We must get beyond the rational."

According to this way of thinking, in order to get beyond the rational, a person must first have let the irrational subdue the rational. A striking yet typical illustration of this curious process is found in *Dancing in the Light*, Shirley MacLaine's best-selling second New Age autobiography.

MacLaine has traveled to "a very evolved spiritual community" in Santa Fe, New Mexico, to visit Chris, a woman who "is a very experienced acupuncturist in psychic therapy." MacLaine writes that she will receive "psychic therapy" sessions from Chris, who (like MacLaine, we are told) has her own "spirit guides" who will assist her during the sessions in which MacLaine will be "administered past-life recall treatments through . . . acupuncture." The sessions take place daily, with MacLaine resting in deep meditation while lying face up on an acupuncture table with "needles quivering from various areas of [her] body." Here is an example of how subduing the rational is a dynamic within the New Spirituality.

"Now relax," said Chris. "Let your mind go. Don't evaluate, and don't let the left brain judge what you are thinking. Give your right brain more space. As a matter of fact, don't think."

As MacLaine submits, she feels her mind "drift away from its own consciousness . . . into blankness." It then occurs to her, "I lay there wishing there were words in the English language which could more aptly describe the experience . . . the whole process of measurement and evaluation was an exercise in futility unconsciously designed to keep us in the muck and mire of our own limited thinking."

The rational mind, however, was created not to be set aside but to think, and whenever a meditation technique attempts to outwit this, the rational mind fights back. MacLaine discovered this the moment the "spirit guides" began giving her mental pictures of her supposed past lives. She slipped and began evaluating.

"It's nothing," she says to Chris.

"No," said Chris. "Wait a minute. Something *is* happening. Stop judging and evaluating what you're getting. Leave your mind out of this. Just get out of your intellectual way."[1]

And what happens is that the more MacLaine "gets out of her intellectual way," the more the irrational "pictures" come into her mind.

That is typical of the way in which the New Spirituality is intolerant of things rational. This may seem unthinkable to Christians, and we will talk more about this during the Inter-Mission. For many spiritual enthusiasts the promised goal makes it all seem worthwhile. For irrationality, it is said, holds the key to upward spiritual mobility, the way to discover one's godhood. (The sickly sweet fruit of the wrong tree still tempts.)

In *Understanding the New Age*, Russell Chandler quotes psychologist Maxine Negri about obtaining godhood, New Age style:

One only has to rid oneself of the limitations imposed by the human brain's left hemisphere's reasoning which Western culture, by way of its technological advances, holds in such high esteem. The pathway to godhood lies not in the left hemisphere's logic but in the right hemisphere's intuitive knowing and creativeness.[2]

The inevitable results, however, run in the opposite direction: further decline into irrationality, and this intellectual/spiritual dynamic plays havoc with Christian communication. By denying the rational, the spiritual seeker permits the irrational to reach a place of ascendance where there will be a marked intolerance for things rational and reasonable, like the gospel message.

29

CONTRADICTIONS OF BELIEF

Yet this is not the end of the story. It only identifies a condition. There is a symptom of this condition that needs bringing to light, and that is the contradictoriness of certain presuppositions and beliefs that are held by many people of the New Spirituality, who may even be unaware of them. The contradictory nature of the presuppositions can present a troublesome roadblock to effective communication. Yet when identified and properly handled, they can be used to help people pause and consider.

In his book *Confronting the New Age*, Douglas Groothuis discloses the problem and how it can be handled by recounting part of a conversation between an East Indian Christian, Vishal Mangalwadi, and a Hindu:

> VISHAL: Is . . . universal consciousness personal or impersonal?
> HINDU: It is impersonal and infinite.
> VISHAL: Is personality higher than impersonality?
> HINDU: Of course!
> VISHAL: Then why do you want to become lower and merge into impersonal consciousness?
> HINDU: Well, no, personality is actually lower than impersonality.
> VISHAL: Why do you then use the term evolution? You should say that we devolved out of the impersonal. Then you should really respect this grass on which we are sitting. Being impersonal, it is higher than us, and you should not walk on it.
> HINDU: This is confusing.[3]

I frequently point out another example during my seminars. The "universal consciousness" cited above has many shades of expression within the New Spirituality's way of seeing life. For our purposes, we may simply deal with the presupposition that the ultimate nature of the universe is an invisible spiritual energy, which is *impersonal*. After doing some teaching on this, I then move on to discuss another prominent New Age belief, karma and reincarnation, a nonbiblical view of the next life. *Karma* is an old Sanskrit word meaning "deeds," "works," or "actions." *Reincarnation* means "to come again in the flesh." The belief is that at the end of each lifetime a person's good and bad deeds are weighed in a sort of cosmic scale of justice, and the balance between them determines the quality of the next life. Mother Teresa, therefore, is doing quite well, but Hitler is in a lot of hot water!

Invariably during a seminar someone will say, "But you've just told us that in the New Age view the universe is ultimately an impersonal energy. How then can an impersonal energy make value judgments about good and bad deeds?"

Obviously it cannot, and part of our efforts as effective communicators will be to help the seeker discover such inconsistencies of belief.

André Kole has a humorous though astute illustration that clearly sums up what we are up against here. He calls it Fire Engine Logic, and it's a story about why fire engines are red:

> Fire engines are red because they have two firemen. Two firemen
> have four feet. Three feet from four feet leaves one foot. One foot is a
> ruler. Queen Mary was a ruler. Queen Mary ruled the seven seas.
> The seven seas have fish. Fish have fins. The Finns were conquered
> by the Russians. Russians are red. Fire engines are always rushin'.
> And that's why fire engines are red.[4]

This, I think, epitomizes many presuppositions of the New Spirituality.

PERSONAL AND CULTURAL CONDITIONING

Christians usually wonder how on earth spiritual seekers can be satisfied with illogical positions. But there are reasons for this that are quite significant as far as understanding the communication breakdown. Here I am thinking of prior personal and cultural conditioning.

By "personal conditioning" I am thinking of the many years during which non-Christians live making bad, unwise, or immoral choices. Thus they become accustomed to existing in a state that is by degrees increasingly inconsistent with the way God made the universe and made them as moral and rational beings.

And then there is the "neglect of rational thought," as *Reader's Digest* put it, saying that children today "can't apply reasonable thought to everyday situations" and the problem is similar with adults. *Reader's Digest* asks,

How do Americans come to neglect rational thought? The answer is complicated, but one explanation is depressingly obvious. Thinking is hard work, demanding rigor and discipline. But those virtues went out the window when we let children in the 1960s and 1970s "do their own thing." Television reinforced this by encouraging children to sit passively with their minds on idle. [And] in too many classrooms too little was demanded.[5]

By "cultural conditioning" I have in mind what Dr. Francis Schaeffer called the "escape from reason" that is characteristic of our age, as it seeks to free itself from the box of philosophical rationalism in which it has been suffocating. Rationalism became entrenched in the West during the eighteenth and nineteenth centuries, a period during which Western people were dismissing the knowledge that God could act in human history and speak to them.

Rationalism holds that by reason and human intellect alone people are capable of discerning all that can be known. It therefore takes issue with religion and fundamentally rejects the claims of faith. The increasing knowledge of the sciences helped stir popular support for rationalism. Both God and the Bible had less and less authority in the minds of Western people, who then had only reason to turn to and to depend on. This brought a tremendous change in the thought forms of Western culture in the area of how people came to *know* things about themselves and the universe. It was during this period that the secularization of our culture and society advanced momentously.

Several decades ago, however, people began admitting to the deficiencies of rationalism, and a great disillusionment set in. The limits of human reason were becoming only too evident. Rationalism had left people without meaning, without a way of coping with the problems of life's big questions, for example, about God, human freedom, morals, immorality, and so on. This provoked another radical change in the thought forms of Western peoples, who shook off rationalism (not completely but to a great extent) to search for meaning in an escape from reason. "The worship of science and the rational to a great extent [was] thrown over for a revival that specifically value[d] the emotional and the non-rational."[6] They sought for what would transcend reason in order to discover the meaning of life.

Yet where did they escape to? God? No. To them He is dead. There was no point in looking "outside" to God. This left them with two choices. They could look for life's meaning either in something in the universe or within themselves. In our day, this search for meaning has usually meant "going within." Thus people are swinging from reason alone to intuition alone as the source for spiritual insight. Rationalistic man is being replaced by intuitive man. The flight from reason prepared the way for a kind of gut mysticism.

The language of the intuitive, therefore, is in no short supply in the world of the New Spirituality. Terms that contextualize it include *right brain, self-exploration, going within, centering, stilling, meditation, grounding, enlightenment, inner self, Higher Self, self-realization, mystical experience, altered states, cosmic consciousness, transcendence, psychoactive drug experience, the irrational, the nonlogical, and the nonrational.*

There is some justification for the swing from reason to intuition. There are limits to human reason, and there is an intuitive dimension to humankind. People are reawakening to something that is true about themselves, which was suppressed by rationalism. We must not dismiss this but redeem the truth of it in a Christian context, or a whole aspect of what it means to be human may be lost.

Christians should submit the intuitive, as they do all else about themselves, to the lordship of Jesus Christ, and within this context the intuitive does not stand against reason but has a proper relation to the world of the rational. Also, under Christ's lordship it can be renewed. The problem is that non-Christians make an idolatry of the intuitive when they divorce it from reason and God in Christ.

Many non-Christian spiritual seekers look to the intuitive for the "final experience," which is so big that it answers for them the question of life's meaning and provides them with spiritual enlightenment. Yet this adventure with the intuitive will fail because all answers and mystical experiences are relative to the person who receives them.

Here is another communication headache posed by the irrational. Mystical experiences cannot be explained. People of the New Spirituality can usually live contentedly with themselves and others even when their experiences, views, and lifestyles are personally or mutually contradictory. Nothing is absolutely true for them. So truth is merely whatever happens to the seeker, whatever he or she happens to like intuitively. If you sweep away reason and rationality from life's big questions, you no longer need to be responsible for truly knowing if you are right or wrong. You just leap into your experience.

Such seekers have no way—no Book, no God, no absolutes—by which to verify an answer or a mystical experience as final or even true because no certainty about anything exists in intuition alone. Everything is relative to the individual. Thus the search for life's meaning and for enlightenment will go on ad nauseam and never be experienced. It will be pursued even on the deathbed, which is exactly what happened to longtime LSD experimenter Aldous Huxley, who on his deathbed invited Timothy Leary to assist him in taking LSD in a last desperate attempt to receive the final experience.

FINAL OBSERVATIONS

There are two kinds of irrational, namely, what merely *looks* irrational and what *is* irrational. By the use of the term *irrational* in this chapter, I do not mean what only looks so to the one perceiving it. Such would be the case if the thing under consideration simply did not seem possible to someone. A long time ago I asked my grandparents what they would have thought as teenagers—this would have been before the First World War—if someone had told them that a man would be walking on the moon during their lifetime. "Such an idea was unthinkable," they replied. "It was preposterous. We would never have believed it." Yet it happened in their lifetime. What *seemed* irrational to them eventually became possible.

This is not what I mean by irrational. I have in mind what is by nature irrational because it stands against, and is contrary to, the way God has ordered the universe and the way things ought to be; therefore, it will *never* be true. I also have in mind the antirational, as the demonic world is thought to be. Perhaps it is when the demonic realm interferes with the human realm that things turn irrational, which may provide a clue as to why the irrational as a spiritual/intellectual dynamic within the world of the New Spirituality can pose all sorts of communication difficulties. The advantage we have, however, is that even the non-Christian spiritual seeker, because he or she was created in the image of God, has certain God-given inner characteristics by which to apprehend and understand truth. All is not lost.

Also, in saying that spiritual seekers trust in the irrational, I in no way mean that they are thoroughly irrational. For instance, they realize that the bills must be paid and so they work. They don't leave their car windows down when it's raining. They will not break the law if they want to stay out of prison. One plus one still equals two, at least in their checkbooks! In some areas they live rationally. Indeed many of them seek a balanced development of intellect and intuition, seeing the two as complementary.

Yet for some, their intuition may have become the only criterion for critical thinking. It is not that such people lose their critical or rational faculty entirely; rather, this faculty may be framed by intuition alone, which then becomes their single means of discriminating right from wrong, especially in the area of spiritual experiences or life's meaning. The individual is then left with her private interpretation or understanding of things, apart from any outside authority, except perhaps for that of the world of the New Spirituality itself. She may look for confirmation from a spiritualist minister, a transpersonal psychologist, or even a "spirit guide," but her rational analysis about how to process the information and apply it, or ignore it, may be framed entirely by her personal, intuitive way of seeing life.

Thus Christians will find these people discussing values and standards, but not often in the way we are used to. For example, some New Age spokespersons argue for "setting standards" in "channeling" to stop what they consider abuses. Now how could they set standards apart from using their critical faculty to discriminate between good and bad channeling? Their reasoning, however, will be framed by their personal intuition on the subject. Helen Palmer, a New Age psychic with strong leanings toward channeling and transpersonal psychology, states it clearly, "The task remains yours to evaluate what you receive in terms of your own experience, your inner world and the world at large."[7]

Also, in communicating what is reasonable and rational we must not give the impression that the Christian faith has reason as its core principle or God. Let us not be seen as rationalists. This is important for two reasons. One is that some non-Christian spiritual seekers recognize a glaring contradiction within Western Christianity: that we will fight tooth and nail to affirm the miracles of the New Testament but deny the supernatural today. Thus they see the church as rationalistic today, and they're not interested. The other thing we want to be careful of is not to disagree that there are some very real limits to human reason. The mind certainly is limited. What we want to do is help the persons see that reason and rationality have a much higher and consistent place in the ultimate scheme of things than they may have thought. We want to help them see that when Christians look outside themselves to God in Jesus Christ for meaning and salvation, it is not an unreasonable or nonrational mysticism. This does not mean that suddenly there are no more question marks; rather, though mystery and paradox remain, we know that they are ultimately resolved in the person of Jesus Christ. And so we can rest spiritually, knowing contentment amidst the very real limitations of our human reason.

This significant distinction may be worth mentioning to followers of the New Spirituality. Whereas enlightenment stands opposed to reason and rationality, due to its subjective reliance on intuition, Christian salvation rests consistent with the world of the rational when it looks outside to a supernatural God as He is known in Christ Jesus.

Let us, therefore, be wise when working in the world of the New Spirituality. We will meet people in whom the irrational is to be desired. Most of them will have been led toward it by both personal and cultural conditioning. And as an intellectual/spiritual dynamic, the irrational (usually occult in nature) plays havoc with Christian communication.

6

THE CALM OF
PASSIVITY

—✺—

CLOSELY ALLIED TO the escape from reason into intuition, and
its attendant the irrational, is the intellectual/spiritual dynamic of
passivity of mind. It is another communication foiler, and it is probably
easiest to understand in the context of meditation. In fact, it is difficult
to separate passivity of mind from most popular forms of meditation
within the New Spirituality. They are like halves of a pair of scissors;
if you had only one half, you would wonder how the thing worked.

It is the rare non-Christian spiritual seeker who does not practice
some form of meditation (which includes visualization), and therefore
it is likely that we will meet spiritual enthusiasts who have become
accustomed to degrees of passivity. Insofar as it hinders our Christian
witness, an understanding of how it develops will give us an advantage. Also, as we saw with irrationality, passivity of mind is hard to
define conclusively. But we will make an attempt here.

RESTRICTING AWARENESS

Spiritual passivity of mind may be understood by analogy with the
inactivity of the body and the sensory insolation that usually precedes
the individual's entering a meditative state. The person deliberately
separates himself for a short time, often about twenty minutes, from
people and daily activities. A quiet room is recommended, where one

can be alone. External sources of stimulation, including sensory ones, should be eliminated or kept to a minimum to avoid distractions. Emphasis may also be placed upon maintaining a specific posture to keep body movements to a minimum.

By these means, everything about the person becomes still and quiet—except for the activity of the mind, which is noisy with all kinds of thoughts. However, with the body at rest and the senses largely inactive, the mind can be made to follow suit. To still the mind one's attention is focused for as long as possible on a single object such as the flame of a candle, the picture of one's guru, perhaps a sound called a mantra, a color, or a symbol like a mandala. Concentrating on one object, source, or idea helps push all other thoughts aside. This is essential for achieving stillness (passivity) of mind and for entering a meditative state. Because it restricts awareness to a single source for a definite period of time, focusing acts as a sort of quieting device for all other thoughts, pushing them aside.

This active restriction of awareness to a single source and the withdrawal of attention from conscious thought is the common element in most forms of meditation.[1] It's no secret that meditation has always been on a collision course with conscious rational thought. Because the exercise of meditation does not involve reason, stilling the conscious mind of thought (passivity) is unavoidable before a meditative state can be entered. The meditator, therefore, becomes involved in a process of restraining, subduing, and inhibiting the rational faculty and conscious thought.

To the Eastern religious person, meditation is the obverse of rational thought, being concerned not with intellectual but with intuitive knowledge, which is frequently called inner knowledge, or self-knowledge. Meditative techniques and styles, including yoga, necessitate a shift away from conscious rational mental activity to intuitive knowing and are designed to produce a corresponding alteration in consciousness by going within. One is supposed to shut down perceptions of the external world and tune in to the internal, and it is a meditational axiom that this cannot be accomplished actively, only passively. Passivity therefore becomes the passage to temporary suspension of conscious thought while in a waking state, a key for entrance into meditation and intuitiveness.

Some meditators, like the ancient mystic St. John of the Cross, are militant about forbidding conscious thought. St. John of the Cross, it is said, demanded of meditators that the soul must "strip and void itself" of all "forms and manners of knowledge," including memory.[2] This tyranny of passivity over conscious thought offers meditators a goal that is variously described as an open mind, emptying the mind, a blank page, a clear state, the void, emptiness, ignoring thought, silencing the mind, turning off the active-verbal mode, and the like. However it is stated, the effect is a vow of mental silence, and however this is interpreted, it equals passivity of mind.

TOM'S TECHNIQUE

Let us now move the discussion from the theoretical to the practical. Imagine thirty participants—ordinary persons, university students, single parents, secretaries, businessmen, taxi drivers, some unemployed people—gathered in the conference room of a suburban hotel. We are in the middle of a weekend "Mind Development" course, which I later discovered was very similar to "Silva Mind Control." It is a bright Saturday afternoon, and for the next session the thick tan curtains have been drawn across the floor-to-ceiling windows. Some of the fluorescent lighting is now being switched off as we listen, keenly attentive like students before exams, to Tom, a forty-five-year-old silver-haired retired marine, who is our instructor for the weekend.

"So that you won't distract your neighbor," he said, "for this next session separate your chairs about three or four feet apart."

We slid the cushioned, straight-backed chairs apart and reseated ourselves. Tom then gently asked us to become quiet.

"Get as comfortable as you can, too," he said. "That's it. Now relax. Take several deep breaths, slowly, and relax. Now I want you to close your eyes and try to relax even more."

It grew very quiet, and as Tom's voice, deftly modulated, became the only sound in the room, it began to occupy our thoughts fully.

"You're doing fine," Tom continued. "Try not to let yourself be distracted by anything. Even try to let the sound of the air-conditioning disappear. Now you'll begin by focusing your attention on a single area of your body when I name it. Follow my voice. Try to block out all other thoughts. We'll start with the toes. Concentrate upon your toes."

After a brief pause he said, "Now focus on your entire foot."

A short pause, and then, "Now concentrate on your calf."

About thirty seconds later he continued, "Now on your knee. Try to see it in your mind's eye. Ignore all other thoughts that arise."

A pause, and then, "Now move the focus from your knee to your upper leg. Try to forget about the other body areas as I lead you on to the next one. Hear only my voice. Focus only on the area I mention. Try to keep your memory out of this, as well as thoughts about tomorrow."

A longer pause, and then, "Now concentrate on your hip."

This procedure continued until we had covered the entire anatomy from toe to head. It took about fifteen minutes.

"Continue with your eyes closed as we move to a deeper level. Remain relaxed and place your hands on your laps, palms up. Now rest your thumbtips lightly on the tips of your index and middle fingers. That's it. Try to remain as comfortable as you can. I'll pause momentarily to let you get used to this new position."

Tom's voice was compelling but without coercion, which produced a desire in me to obey it, perhaps because of my dislike of being forced into something. I decided to follow the voice into the next level, whatever that meant.

"Now I want those of you who can," Tom continued, "to move with me beyond relaxation and into meditation. To accomplish this, you will need to quiet your minds of all thoughts. This will be difficult for some of you at first. So to help you, without opening your eyes, I want you to recall the symbols I had on display during the previous session. Some of those symbols will have impressed themselves on your mind. I want you now to focus your attention on the one, and one only, that now comes to mind. It will be a different one for each of you. Push all other thoughts away and concentrate on the one symbol. See its color, its shape, its lines. Try to discover its meaning for you. But remember to block out all other thoughts. I'm now going to leave you in quietness to experiment with this for several minutes. Meditate on your symbol."

I do not recall hearing any noises in the insulated and dimly lit room as I practiced this, my first ever contact with meditation, which occurred more than twenty years ago. After several minutes Tom spoke again.

"Now with eyes still closed, I want all of you to take your minds off your symbol and gradually become aware of this room again. Hear its sounds. Feel the air-conditioning. Now slowly open your eyes and become fully conscious of this room. Good. Some of you had trouble stilling your minds. Don't be too concerned about it. You will soon be able to master it. You may stand up and move around now. We'll take a short break, and then come back and talk about your experiences in a moment."

From the comments that followed, it was evident that many of us did a poor job shutting down our conscious thoughts while trying to remain awake. If someone wasn't thinking about the coming summer holiday, it was the unpaid bills, the fight with a spouse, roses, the dental appointment, or the recent funeral . . . Tom knew we would have trouble stilling. After all, the mind has been created by God to think. Attempt to shut it down and it fights back.

"Your stories," Tom said, "sound so familiar. I used to have the same difficulty. But there are ways around this. So if you're willing, we'll pick up where we left off before the break. Get comfortable in your chairs again, and I'll give you some tips to help you quiet your minds. Then we'll try practicing them. After you have mastered them, which may take a few weeks, you should be able to move in and out of meditative states easily. But this is not something I can do for you. You must learn to do it for yourselves."

During the next session, Tom instructed us in the use of various mental techniques, that is quieting devices, by which to outwit conscious thought and still the mind. This is not the book to take you through the slough of details describing them. They entail imaginative uses of symbols, sounds, objects, colors, Zen koans, breathing exercises, even crystals, and with practice these become mental trigger mechanisms by which to outwit conscious thought and slip into meditation.

CHANGING WAVELENGTHS

How, then, is the use of this technique able to counter an effective Christian witness? The answer lies in its *aftereffect*. After a season of practicing this kind of meditation, the person has been party to a shift of consciousness from the rational mode of receiving spiritual knowledge to receiving from the intuitive, mystical mode. He is less interested in comprehensible spiritual knowledge and more interested in the incomprehensible, the ineffable. Meditative passivity has actually reduced the range of sources of spiritual knowledge available to that person. It has become a narrower band, and a kind of spiritual antenna signals the person to receive things New Age, for example, but there is no longer much of a frequency or carrier wave to receive things that are not of the New Spirituality. This transformation produces a temper of mind that increasingly guards itself against traditional spiritual answers. Such a person has a heightened resistance to whatever he perceives as spiritually foreign to the meditative, mystical, intuitive way of life.

What happens, then, when a Christian talks to a meditator about comprehensible spiritual knowledge? The meditator sees it as outside the range of what she has been conditioned to accept. Refusals to listen to Christians are therefore not uncommon. There may even be antagonism to the Christian message.

SPIRITUAL INTERFERENCE

One other aspect of this dynamic needs mentioning here, and that is the potential for demonic activity in the meditator that will impede Christian communication. The continual practice of Eastern meditation produces an open mind through passivity. We need to ask the question: To what is the mind open during states of passivity? It may be open to new ideas because prejudices have been cast off, which in itself may not be wrong. The danger, however, is that the meditator's mind sooner or later opens to contact with the spirit world.

This is certainly no secret in the world of the New Spirituality, though its adherents would not admit that the nature of their "spirit guides" is demonic. A host of spirit entities, with names such as Mafu, Ramtha, Lazaris, Seth, John, McPherson, Raphael, and Michael, have been popularized by several film stars and leading channelers. Yet even ordinary meditators may have their personal spirit entities.

I ended up with several myself, having been taught how to contact them in the subsequent "Mind Development" sessions that followed the one described above. I was told that in deep meditation my mind would open up to powerful forces and voices in the spirit realm, and that these spirit beings live in a "belt in the air" that surrounds the earth (echoes of Eph. 2:2?). Through meditation I could contact them. The object was to discover their individual names and characteristics and find out in what areas of my life they could be of help. I was taught how to contact these spirits by using visualization techniques to construct a spiritual room, or workshop, in my imagination, which would be the place of communion with the "spirit guides." I merely had to invite them in. And the more open I became, the easier it would be to receive them.

I submitted to this for reasons that are common to most meditators. The spirits, I had been taught, were not demonic but former human beings who had lived many previous lifetimes. They had reincarnated so often that they were spiritually evolved; they no longer had to return in their earth suits anymore because they had paid off all their bad karma with good karma and were therefore entitled to be highly evolved spirit beings. If I contacted them, they would instruct me and entrust me with all the esoteric wisdom that they had gained during their, possibly thousands of, incarnations. In this way my spiritual evolution would advance by leaps and bounds. This is a common deception.

When a regular pattern of contacting "spirit guides" develops, a meditator can become oppressed, possessed, or in some way influenced by demonic powers, which can impede another's communication with him. This was my experience more than once when I was a meditator. And I was clearly delivered from the evil spirits that I thought were "spirit guides" the evening of my conversion to Christ. The wise communicator will want to be alert to the possible problems, and some solutions are discussed in Part Two.

SUMMARY

The way of seeing the intellectual/spiritual dynamics that I have described in this and the previous chapter has helped me a great deal, though I do not claim that it is etched in stone. I hope that the following summary will help readers to whom the idea is new. It ties both chapters together.

God created the rational mind to think, reason, and analyze. Spiritual irrationality, however, slips into the driver's seat after relegating the rational to the back of the bus. The rational mind, however, dislikes the passivity and scrambles its way back into the driver's seat time after time. Quieting devices are then instituted—to outwit and suppress the rational mind. Eventually, meditators are conditioned to accept passivity of mind as a way into the intuitive, mystical mode of perceiving life and of receiving incomprehensible mystical experiences. This becomes a chief vehicle of spiritual development in the alternate spiritualities, and along the way irrationality rationalizes the illogical and the adherent then feels comfortable bedding down with contradictory beliefs and values.

7

THE GENESIS OF DECEPTION

—⚬—

THE BIBLE IS a book with many literary images. They are important because they embellish the realities that they represent with depth of meaning. Take the Holy Spirit as an example. Some images in the Bible, especially as used by Jesus, depict the Holy Spirit's nature as personal. Other images do not, such as fire, dove, and wind. Each image of the Holy Spirit has its own nuance that contributes to a fuller understanding of the third person of the Trinity.

OF DRAGONS AND SERPENTS

This holds true throughout the Bible; its literary images ornament the things they are naming with significant features that we would otherwise be unaware of. In this chapter we will look at one particular biblical image, that of the serpent, which is one of the ways the Bible depicts certain clear characteristics of the "hidden things of darkness" (1 Cor. 4:5).

Other images of darkness may be more difficult to understand, such as the dragon mentioned in the book of Revelation. As a rule, the dragon image represents multinational or international evil. Then there is the devil. Why is the devil not given the image of a dragon in Matthew's gospel? Simply because it is not international evil but temptation that the Bible wants to convey here.

Another image of darkness is found in the book of Job: Satan, or *the* Satan, as the Hebrew has it, signifying an enemy or accuser. In the first two chapters of Job we see Satan leveling accusations against Job. Here the Bible enlarges our understanding of the hidden things of darkness by showing us a characteristic we can liken to a prosecuting attorney. From it we get the familiar biblical doctrine that Satan is the "accuser of the brethren."

This is merely hermeneutics simplified: the dragon, for international evil; the devil, for temptation; the Satan, for accusation. Associated, overlapping, or parallel features are often found among the images. Let us, therefore, not be simplistic about this. Yet neither let us ignore discussion about the hidden things of darkness because we may have been bothered by the raw handling given them by some people. At times it is necessary to do some study in this area.

So now we move from Revelation to Matthew to Job to the beginning of the Bible, where we read about the serpent. As a rule, the image of the serpent portrays deception and the treachery of the deceiver. It reminds me of pirates who sailed under false colors in order to get alongside merchant ships without arousing opposition; but once alongside they hoisted their true colors, the Jolly Roger, and it was too late for their prey.

Deception is a strong word and ought not to be used lightly; nevertheless, it brings us to another intellectual/spiritual dynamic that can cripple Christian communication. And the Bible is certainly not silent about deception and its ramifications. In fact, in the image of the serpent, deception is the first characteristic of the kingdom of darkness that is mentioned in the Bible. Here is a working definition we will use; it has many implications for us as communicators, and it is what I take to be its chief feature biblically: deception is about the deliberate misrepresentation of facts or truth to purposely lead someone astray.

Let us look at the biblical setting and see how it relates to our work with non-Christian spiritual seekers:

Now the serpent was more cunning than any beast of the field which the LORD God had made. And he said to the woman, "Has God indeed said, 'You shall not eat of every tree of the garden'?" And the woman said to the serpent, "We may eat the fruit of the trees of the garden;

45

but of the fruit of the tree which is in the midst of the garden, God has said, 'You shall not eat it, nor shall you touch it, lest you die.'" Then the serpent said to the woman, "You will not surely die. For God knows that in the day you eat of it your eyes will be opened, and you will be like God, knowing good and evil." So when the woman saw that the tree was good for food, that it was pleasant to the eyes, and a tree desirable to make one wise, she took of its fruit and ate. She also gave to her husband with her, and he ate. Then the eyes of both of them were opened, and they knew [not that they were "like God," but] that they were naked [quite a distinction]; and they sewed fig leaves together and made themselves coverings (Gen. 3:1–7).

Note that deception begins with the deceiver's introduction of facts or truth into the conversation. These are then later distorted, perhaps when a degree of fascination in them is expressed by the listener, in the hope that the listener will then act in obedience to the distortion. In an effort to see how deception led the primary human family astray, let's do a little time traveling. Can you pretend with me that you are secluded in Eden's lush, beautiful foliage watching the incident unfold?

To clarify some of the points, let us pretend that Eve is five feet ten inches tall and adorned with long dark hair. Here she is, then, a beautiful tall brunette standing alongside a certain tree, and she appears to be talking to it. No, wait a moment. She is talking not to the tree but to the serpent.

Notice that the serpent does not open the conversation with a bold-faced lie, saying, for instance, "You're lookin' good today, Eve. I always did like short blondes." This sounds silly, but after all, he is the father of lies (John 8:44), so why not begin with an outright lie? Obviously, if the serpent had begun by lying, Eve would have brushed him off immediately. If he could not get even the simplest facts right, she would not have bothered to listen further. But if he starts with certain facts or truths, he can appear credible and so hold Eve's attention. Thus he begins with something that Eve knows to be true about herself: God has been speaking to her about the trees. And around this fact the serpent will then camouflage his deception at the point in the conversation where Eve is becoming fascinated by his hidden (occult) spiritual knowledge.

Still with me in Eden? If so, let's supplement the conversation and imagine the following exchange between Eve and the serpent in an effort to get a fuller understanding of the nature of deception.

SERPENT: Afternoon, Eve. Don't be startled. No need to be afraid. Here, over here. Yes, I am a bit difficult to see, but don't let that worry you. Lovely weather today, eh? By the way, I hear that God has been talking to you.

EVE: What? Who said that? Who's speaking?

SERPENT: Oh, there's no need for introductions. It's not important who I am. What's important is that I know who you are and that God has been talking to you. God talks to me, too, you know. I also know what He's been talking to you about . . . the trees, right?

EVE: That's right. But how do you know God has been talking to me? I don't recall seeing you around here before.

SERPENT: Like I said, it's not important who I am or how I know these things. What's important is that I do.

EVE: Well, you've certainly got your facts straight.

SERPENT: Good. But that being so, I'm more than somewhat puzzled about your well-being. If God is so good, as you believe, why has He withheld spiritual advancement from you?

EVE: Now you're puzzling me.

SERPENT: What I mean is, why has God forbidden you to eat from *any* tree in the Garden? Sounds as if He's withholding some higher good from you.

EVE: No. There you're mistaken.

SERPENT: Oh?

EVE: You're right in saying that God has been speaking to us about the trees, but you're wrong in thinking that we can't eat from *any* of them.

SERPENT: Sorry, I probably wasn't paying attention when I should have been. But I really would like some clarity on the point then. Sure you've got it right?

EVE: There's no doubt in my mind about that! God said we could eat from all the trees in the Garden. Except one, that is. In fact, it's this tree right here!

SERPENT: Imagine that. What a coincidence! Still, I think it's harsh of God to forbid you to eat from such a splendid tree.

EVE: Not in the least. He doesn't want us to die. And if we eat from this tree, we will die.

Suddenly, the coup de grâce.

SERPENT: You will not surely die. For God knows that in the day you eat of it your eyes will be opened, and you will be like God, knowing good and evil.

Before Eve had time to collect her thoughts, the serpent had shown himself a master of innuendo and undermined what God had said.

EVE: There must be some mistake!
SERPENT: No. Not in the least. There's no doubt about it. I'm not kidding. I'm deadly serious. Trust me. I've got my facts straight, right?

And the rest is history. Fascination with the forbidden is too much for Eve to handle, and the way of the curse is substituted for the way to blessing.

Here, then, is an unmistakable process; the deliberate misrepresentation of facts and truth to lead someone away from what God had said. The initial introduction of facts (one, God has been speaking; two, about trees) catches the listener's attention and then holds it and gains credibility for the speaker. As the listener becomes more interested, the speaker can then distort the truth in the hope of soliciting the listener's obedience to what is now a lie. This is the process of deception. Through the subtle and misleading use of facts, which in and of themselves cannot be disputed, disobedience to God and obedience to serpentine enlightenment are realized. If the speaker has his facts straight, the listener is likely to assume that the interpretation of those facts will be right. Trust is gained, and the hidden knowledge is then adopted for guidance.

FROM EDEN TO HOLLYWOOD

Let's now leave Eden and return to the present to look at a sample of this dynamic in context of the New Spirituality. The following illustration is from Shirley MacLaine's best-selling book *Dancing in the Light*. The excerpt is taken from a lengthy conversation that MacLaine says she had with a "spirit guide" called John, who speaks through channeler Kevin Ryerson.

MACLAINE (to John): I guess my first question is, is there a real need on our earth for spiritual enlightenment? I mean, would it decrease human suffering if more people understood the spiritual dimensions of themselves?

JOHN: That is correct. The collective consciousness of the entire human race manifests the reality of your earth plane. The influence of the mind of man creates disturbances in nature and of course in your human activities.

MACLAINE: You mean the mind of man can influence nature, like earthquakes and flooding and things?

JOHN: That is correct. Gravitational influences and planetary harmony are affected by the minds of beings on every planet. You are experiencing natural disturbances on your planet because the consciousness of the human race needs raising.

MACLAINE: Is that why spiritual enlightenment is necessary?

JOHN: Yes, the mind of man is more powerful than nature. You are suffering from your state of mind, which is influencing the patterns of nature on your plane.

MACLAINE: Okay. With all the bad stuff that's happening in the world today, would you say there is a negative force operating here that is equal to the God-force? I mean, is evil a part of God also?

JOHN: You are speaking of satanic influences?

MACLAINE: Yes.

JOHN: The concept of Satan as interpreted in your Bible has its origins as follows: Adam and Eve stood symbolically for the creation of souls. They were created originally as pure spiritual soul energy, as everyone was. When they became captivated by the material plane, or the earth plane as you know it, they found themselves incarnated in the bodies of the lower primates because they were seduced by the attractions of physical existence. Because of their fall from grace, they activated the law of karma. Their spiritual and divine origins were only dimly remembered because of the confined restrictions of their physical bodies. The struggle back towards original divinity is what your Bible means by Satan. . . . What you term as Satan is merely the force of your lower consciousness as you engage in the struggle to return and know God, which was your origin. The feeling of what you term evil is the struggle with self.

MACLAINE: Well, how could we have gone so far wrong about this subject?

JOHN: The struggle for self-knowledge would not be a struggle if one

49

loved God with all one's heart and soul and one's neighbor as one's self. For one's neighbor is one's self. But mankind set up the dualities of good and evil in order to judge others rather than to discover self. Therefore, it was even possible to make war on one another. Out of a lack of knowledge of God came the concept of evil. But when mankind understands that it itself is a collective being representing the God-force, it is impossible to make war on the self. Is this to your understanding?

MACLAINE: Yes.[1]

This piece from *Dancing* is indicative of a galaxy of occult ideas that fill MacLaine's New Age autobiographies, which have influenced millions. It also takes us to the source of many ideas and beliefs, that is, the countless spirit-channeling sessions (channeling being a sort of quantum leap from the old spirit-mediumship phenomenon) that now dot the map of the New Spirituality. Topics will vary from the big questions of life's meaning to small mundane matters. We might be tempted to dismiss it as just so much bilge. Yet what the entities are saying is being ingested and acted upon because lie is blended with truth in the spiritual chalice from which an increasing number of seekers are drinking.

UNSCRAMBLING AN EGG

As Christian communicators, we will want to help the spiritual seeker unscramble the truth from the deception, so let us examine the exchange between MacLaine and John to see the similarities with what occurred between Eve and the serpent. It begins for MacLaine, as it did for Eve, by becoming interested in forbidden spiritual knowledge, which places her on the threshold of deception. John then loads the conversation with facts and affirmations by which he gains credibility and keeps the dialogue running. Throughout the conversation, the facts and truths are distorted, and like Eve, MacLaine reaches a point where she acquiesces to the forbidden knowledge.

The conversation opens with the facts of human suffering, pain, and the spiritual dimension (things true enough), and soon includes the question of evil. These John does not deny but affirms. In fact, he loads the conversation with Bible words: *Satan, Adam and Eve, fall from grace.* John may have pitched the conversation in this direction because such images would carry obvious connotations for MacLaine as they connected with her childhood Christian (such as it was) memories. John has his facts and he has a listener; now he can distort them as much as he wants.

Earthquakes and floods become the result of low human consciousness. Suffering becomes merely a state of mind. Satan becomes the struggle within human beings to get back to original divinity, and it is implied that Satan is an equal opposite to God. And I admit I am slightly impressed by John's craftiest sleight of mind in the passage. Right on the heels of the truth that one ought to love God with all one's heart and one's neighbor as one's self, John tells his listener why: because "one's neighbor is one's self." This, however, is sheer monism.[2] (I wonder if John in some curious way inspired the popular Beatles' line, "I am he, as you are me, and we are all together"?)

The image of the serpent also gives us an instructive point about how mediumship and channeling hook listeners. It is as true today as it was in Eden. There is an element of truth in what adherents hear from the "spirit guides." This is an important principle because it means that some New Age beliefs may be only partially false. I will have much more to say about this in Part Two. A lie or a deception would have no power to fascinate and mislead people on its own. It would have no power to solicit obedience in an epistemological vacuum. A lie or a deception derives its power because there is such a thing as truth. It is not the other way around.

Christian communicators will want to be conscious of the dynamic of deception when we are in conversation with non-Christian spiritual seekers. We will want to be informed and sensitive to the truth behind the distortions. In Part Two, we will try to discover ways to rectify the distortions and thereby redeem the truth of the matter. The habit some of us have had of throwing out the baby with the bathwater has been about as helpful as a screen door on a submarine. Deal with the dirty bathwater by all means. But let us not flush the truth out with it.

8

IDENTIFYING
DISTORTIONS

—⚒—

"*GET YOUR FACTS* first," Mark Twain wrote, "then you can distort them as much as you want."

This and the next chapter look at several areas where truth becomes distorted in the world of the New Spirituality, in such a way as to hinder Christian communication.

We have touched upon the phenomenon of channeling. It provides enthusiasts with communication from a "higher power" that becomes a spiritual authority figure. Channeling also helps the seeker break free from the strictures of reason and rational explanations. These and other features of the phenomenon are meeting some spiritual needs, at least temporarily, of many seekers. Thus famous channelers like J. Z. Knight, Kevin Ryerson, and Jach Pursel can pack auditoriums in city after city with people who are longing for "a tender word to come and tell them who they are." Channelers and their "spirit guides," therefore, take the place of prayer, counsel, comfort, and the authority that people ought to be receiving from the *Holy* Spirit.

Yet the New Spirituality is meeting another need, and that is by offering answers to life's big questions. We will now look at what it has to say about some of the big questions and see how distortions of truth occur. Please note that the following material will barely scratch the surface and is meant merely to get us thinking from this point of view. The recommended reading list at the end of this book includes titles and brief reviews that cover these topics more thoroughly.

GOD

Most people of the New Spirituality take the truth of God's existence seriously. Unlike atheists and agnostics, they are convinced of a reality called God. But then, all who grapple with this big question must come to some conclusion about God's nature. Is God a He or an It? A personal Being or an impersonal energy or force? Is He or It good, evil, or some combination of the two? The answer to these questions will influence how we relate to Him or It.

The Bible reveals that though God is Spirit, He is also personal in nature. Though the New Age way of seeing assents to the truth that there is God, it then distorts the nature of God, who becomes strictly It, an impersonal energy or life force. It is the "God" typified by the Luke Skywalker mentality in *Star Wars*: the Force be with you. In the biblical view, God makes moral demands and is known through the person of Jesus Christ. In the New Age view, "God," being impersonal, makes no moral demands and can be accessed and utilized like electricity by anyone who knows how to plug in to it. In another view, God is what is both good and evil, darkness and light. Or, in another, beyond good and evil.

DEATH

Seekers also take the truth of death seriously, and they grapple with its nature and meaning. The Bible, of course, teaches that death is the judgment of God upon the human race as a result of our sin. Also, death is seen as an enemy that is faced once. Christ defeated it through His resurrection, and believers in Christ are passed from death to life.

In Eastern religions, however, death is redefined as a transition from body to body through thousands of lifetimes, that is, reincarnations. It is not thought of as an enemy but more like a succession of invisible archways through which one passes between periods of physical existence, wandering the long and winding road of spiritual evolution in search of perfection, enlightenment, the discovery of one's status as a god, and so on. Death is therefore seen as the result not of sin, or as an enemy, but of one's bad karma, which can be paid off, sooner or later, by accruing mountains of good karma during future incarnations, of which there may be thousands.

THE UNIVERSE

Concepts about the nature of the universe abound within the New Spirituality. The Bible teaches that the universe and its countless material things are real and not illusory. They are real because the Reality who created them is real. Perhaps we could call God "Creating Reality" and material things "created reality," which might help us understand that both are real but not the same reality. Furthermore, the Bible teaches that when God created things, He created them distinct from Himself and also from each other. We may take as examples: day/night; land/water; the inanimate/the animate; a mineral kingdom, a vegetable kingdom, a human kingdom, an angelic kingdom. We also learn that within the vegetable and animal kingdoms, things are brought forth "after their kind," which is another mark of distinction. In other words, separately created realities are distinct from each other and not a part of God. This does not mean that there is not an interconnectedness to life, which we will see shortly.

In what may be the dominant presupposition of the New Spirituality, the universe is scrambled up with "God" to become the distortion: pantheistic monism.[1] In another view, the universe and its things are thought of as an illusion, not necessarily in the sense that they are nonexistent but unreal the way a dream is unreal. This ancient view from Hinduism has been adapted to the New Spirituality's way of seeing. In Hinduism, one encounters millions of gods, but there is also an important trinity representing three aspects of "the Supreme": Brahma(n), the creator; Vishnu, the sustainer; Siva (Shiva), the destroyer. In this metaphysic, the world is the Dream of the creator, Brahma. Thus the things of the world, including individual souls, are parts of the Dream.

There is an element of truth in this dream metaphor that is close to a biblical view, for there would be no world without Brahma, and Brahma's existence does not depend upon the appearance of the world. However, Hinduism parts company with the Bible with ideas that in the Dream World the senses are deceived by *maya*, which prevents us from realizing the dream nature, or illusory quality, of the world and the universe. Also, the human mind is said to be deceived by *maya* into attributing much more reality to the world than it possesses.

ONENESS

There is an interconnectedness and interdependence, or whole-ness and unity, to the things of creation. Yet Christians know that the unity is found only in God through the Agent of His creation, Jesus Christ in union with the Holy Spirit (Heb. 11:3; Col. 1:17). In no way, however, do you lose the reality of the existence of the things that God has made or their fundamental distinctions (see "Universe" above). A true interdependence would mean, for instance, that you could quite rightly talk about the dependence of the butcher upon the cow for his livelihood; the cow upon the grass for its continued life; the grass upon the soil for its existence. It is an interdependence in which the grass takes up from the soil the minerals it needs, the cow takes up from the grass the nourishment it needs, and the butcher takes from the cow what he needs. A striking example of dependence is that of the human body upon the dust of the earth for its existence. There is, therefore, a kind of interconnectedness and interdepen-dence among the distinct things of God's creation.

The New Spirituality's way of seeing distorts the biblical picture of unity. It relies heavily on Eastern religious wisdoms. In these views—chiefly expressed in Hinduism, Buddhism, and Taoism—one certainly loses the distinction between things and their realness and that, then, becomes the Oneness of all. The world is said merely to be seen as separate objects (and events), not because it is a funda-mental feature of reality, but because we have so categorized it to help us deal with everyday life. This is why most leading Eastern mystics are uninterested in explaining things and much more intent on intui-tive experiences, whereby things lose their distinctions and they perceive the Oneness of all.

We have room for one example. *Maya* is one of the most difficult words in Hinduism to understand. Earlier, it was seen that *maya* prevents the senses from recognizing the dream nature of the world. It is also said to prevent the recognition that reality is one and indivisible because nothing else really exists except Brahma. *Maya,* therefore, is generally understood (at the least) to be the quality of illusion, or the illusory structure, of the empirical world that makes the One appear as many independent things. When a person perceives he is a part of the Dream, which he may do intuitively through ascetic practice, contemplation, meditation, yoga, and so on, oneness with Self, that is, with all else, becomes the deception. This is the Oneness that many, if not most, non-Christian spiritual seekers reach for, and it is a far cry from the answer to Jesus' prayer in John 17.

JESUS CHRIST

Interest in the person and nature of Jesus Christ runs high in the New Spirituality. The Bible reveals that Jesus Christ is God the Son, the Incarnate One, Lord and Savior, and it discloses many other characteristics that mark Him off as uniquely different from any other religious teacher or holy man.

Within the New Spirituality, however, Jesus is usually seen as one of several special holy men who have walked the earth. He is considered an "ascended master," "christ," or "avatar," that is, one who attained perfection and divinity through enlightenment. Here Jesus is immortalized in a select constellation of spiritual teachers such as Rama, Buddha, and Krishna, who were considered god-men.

There are many variations on this theme. Gnosticism, theosophy, anthroposophy, the "I AM" movement, Unity, George Trevelyan, David Spangler, Annie Besant, Benjamin Creme, Levi Dowling, and a host of other schools and teachers have produced distortions about the person and nature of Jesus Christ. The New Spirituality may lift Jesus higher than most mortals but not nearly high enough.

THE HUMAN BEING

The nature of what it means to be human is another big question addressed by the New Spirituality. The Bible teaches that we have been created by God, that we are finite and limited in potential and power, and that we are beings separate from God. Having been created in the likeness of God, who is personal, we are each unique in that we are *persons* and not mere animals or things, or illusory souls in a dream state.

Within the New Spirituality's way of seeing, human nature is exalted to the status of God or as being part of God, or in some sense divine. In *Dancing in the Light*, a "spirit guide" tells Shirley MacLaine, "You each need to become masters of your own souls, which is to say, the realization of yourselves as God." This belief is taken from Hindu pantheism, updated and adapted. Thus many spiritual seekers now believe in their unlimited self-potential. Alternatively, in Deep Ecology's biocentrism, each living organism has the same level of value and uniqueness, which makes human beings, as far as worth goes, on a par with animals or a Brazilian rain forest.[2]

In the world of the New Spirituality, a human being is unique, which is true. But in that world, a human being is unique not because he is made in God's image, but because he is God. That is the distortion.

UNION WITH GOD

The Bible reveals that we are separated from God because of sin, and that we are utterly unable to save ourselves from the consequences of this. Union with God, as the Bible teaches, is more of a reunion. We are reconciled to God through the cross of Christ as our moral guilt is removed, and this access to God is through the Cross.

The New Spirituality's views about our connection with "God" are many and varied and difficult to state succinctly. Gnosticism holds that our union with the Supreme Creator is achieved through escape from this present material world, which is said to be evil, into life in the sphere of pure spirit. Hinduism holds that Brahma(n), the all-pervading "God," is not separate from the world, so we are never really separate from "God." Some adaptation of the Gnostic and Hindu views is found throughout the New Spirituality. In the former, access to God is attained through knowledge (*gnosis*). In the latter, we reach God through karma (good deeds) and the metaphysics of reincarnation. Either is thought to liberate us from the limiting, confining world of time and physical existence and release us into the invisible world of the eternal and infinite. In these and other nonbiblical views, we are never really separate from God. We have merely forgotten our true state; we are unaware that we are already divine. It is therefore merely a matter of going within in an effort to receive that special intuitive experience, which ends all doubt about being part of God.

What these and other views have in common is that they are all doctrines of self-salvation in various forms. They are all Cross-less forms of salvation. This, of course, is incompatible with the biblical doctrine of salvation, which is the gift of God through the cross of Christ.

SUFFERING AND EVIL

The Bible teaches that suffering and evil are in the world because of our sin and disobedience to our Creator, and because the mystery of iniquity is at work, that is, Satan and his demonic host's interference in human affairs. In the New Spirituality, there are several schools of thought on this. Suffering and evil, it is said in one view, are merely perceived as such. If people would change their perception, there would be no suffering and evil. This is the chief motif of *A Course in Miracles*, which is a high-profile book of channeled material in the New Age community.

Another view makes suffering and evil a matter of ignorance. If people were enlightened that "All is (also morally) one," the problem would be solved. Or as in Gnosticism, matter is seen as evil, with people suffering in contact with it. Or as in the view of karma, suffering and evil result from everyone's bad karma. In yet another school of thought, that of Zoroastrian dualism, suffering and evil are regarded as the result of the perpetual conflict between two equally powerful and opposite principles or gods, for example, darkness and light.

THE SUPERNATURAL

The supernatural world is a frequent topic of discussion in the world of the New Spirituality. The Bible teaches that the supernatural has two distinct realms (not two sides of a coin, as may unwittingly be thought), and that God is the ultimate authority over both. These two realms are two angelic kingdoms; one comprises angels, the other devils. The former obey God and cooperate with Him in fulfilling His purposes, even in human affairs. The latter have disobeyed and rebelled against God and in so doing have become demonic. They have been thrust from God's presence and work against the purposes of God, even within human affairs. We are not taught in the Bible to contact angels, though they may be sent by God to contact us at special times. We are strictly forbidden to develop any kind of relationship with the demonic realm.

The New Spirituality generally sees the nature of the supernatural as one realm comprising innumerable "spirit guides," ascended masters, entities, forces, and so on whose natures, with rare exceptions, are not considered evil or demonic. Seekers are often encouraged by many means—meditation, visualization, guided imagery, sensory deprivation tanks, the use of crystals or pyramids, and more—to contact such spirit beings.

SUPERNATURAL EXPERIENCE

If a person actually has a supernatural experience, the Bible reveals that it will have originated from one of two sources: God through Jesus Christ, in which I would include the sending of an angel; or the demonic realm. It is important to realize that both sources are *personal* in nature.

Many seekers are eager for supernatural experiences because they are dissatisfied with the prevailing reductionist philosophies so rampant in the West, in which the supernatural world and mystical experience are said to be virtually nonexistent, or the product of delusions. In the New Spirituality, however, the source of the power is mistaken, which in turn affects how the seeker understands the nature of the experience. The source of the power, which produces various mystical experiences, is thought to be the *impersonal* life energy or god force, and this is the case whether the mystical experience originates from the seeker's lone use of crystals, pyramids, meditation, and so forth, or whether it originates through the intermediary of a guru or a spirit being.

This misunderstanding has far-reaching ramifications. If the ultimate source of mystical experience is impersonal, supernatural experience is off-limits to no one. Anyone who is willing to employ the various psychospiritual technologies can tap in to this supernatural force and receive an experience. The whole thing becomes like a kind of massive metaphysical wholesale warehouse, full of mystical experiences and available to whomsoever wills.

Because the biblical teaching about the power source and the nature of spirit beings is not believed by non-Christian spiritual seekers, and because they do at times have mystical experiences, they must have some explanation for them. The foregoing explanation is convenient because it accounts for the source and the power without having to involve the seeker in moral choices.

THE ULTIMATE GOAL OF LIFE

The Bible teaches that the whole creation is moving toward a climax, a consummation, a goal, which means that life has a purpose. It is not meaningless but caught up in the purposes of God. The creation then is not, as some have been tempted to think, ultimately subjected to the law of entropy. If it were, life would be ultimately meaningless. The Bible, however, asserts that the overriding law of the universe is one that includes purpose, aim, goal, and therefore a meaning in terms of the future. Thus nothing in the whole of creation, whether seen or unseen, can escape God's ultimate purposes.

But what are the purposes of God for us, for life, and for the universe? The goal is not an ideal or even a state such as the kingdom of heaven, which, though important, is not comprehensible enough to be the ultimate purpose. The Bible identifies the goal of life and creation as God, but even more specifically as a person, Jesus Christ (Rom. 11:36; Eph. 1:10; Col. 1:20). Everything, the individual as well as the whole creation, the seen as well as the unseen, will be summed up in Jesus Christ.

Because of the present situation with sin and evil, this summing up is seen as a rescue operation in which all things are reconciled in Christ (Col. 1:20). Through reconciliation in Christ, everything gets organized and ordered into its proper place at the end; also evil and wickedness and sin and self-will go into their proper nonplace, so to speak. This is reconciliation.

> The idea is that there are elements in creation which have become disjointed, alienated, disordered and meaningless in relation to Christ. And in relation to Jesus Christ they are going to be restored to order and meaning and a proper inter-relationship.[3]

Also—and this is amazing to consider—Christians are not merely moving along with the flow of the summing up; they are a part of the machinery at the end that directs the flow because Christ lives in them.

This is a far cry from any teleology I have seen formulated in the New Spirituality. In fact, as far as I am aware, there is no ultimate purpose envisaged in that way of seeing. Yet this is not surprising because much of that spirituality takes its cues from Eastern religion, which does not understand the world in terms of purpose. As someone rightly said, there are "movement and change without involving the idea of purpose."[4]

It seems then that *ultimate* purpose has no place in the New Spirituality. What one finds in its place are almost countless expressions of individual purposes. This may shed some light on the popular New Age platitude "we create our own realities," which provides seekers with a way out of meaninglessness by allowing them to assign at least a personal, individual, relative meaning to movement and change. Being made in the image of God, non-Christian spiritual seekers cannot escape the God-given drive for purpose, and so they will have to create purpose for themselves.

This they do in almost countless ways, and so the goal of seeking becomes to escape the confines of the material plane; to move through the metaphysics of reincarnation up the ladder of spiritual evolution; to process endless cycles of creation, life, and destruction; to become subsumed with all other personalities into the impersonal force of cosmic life energy; to live in a state of bliss in *this* life; to expand consciousness, become enlightened, realize one's godhood status; or to transform self, society, and the world. There are probably as many goals as there are seekers who, like so many others, desire to be the architects of their own futures, creating their realities as they go.

About the only goal that seems similar to that of the Christian's, at least in its language, is that of transforming self, society, and the world. But the transformation in mind derives from a spirituality that is incompatible with God's divine purposes, which means that it is not directed toward the purpose or end for which all things exist.

Some readers may wonder how the above survey could help them, since the folk they talk to are merely dabbling with practices, such as astrology, tarot, the I Ching, meditation, yoga, or crystals. Yet these people are dabbling with derivatives, or the fruit, of the above distortions. And most likely, they may never have thought of the false beliefs behind what they are into. If a friend ever says to you, "What's wrong with such and such?" you are being given an opportunity to use the information in the above survey, which shows some of the spiritual soil out of which the practices grow.

CONCLUSION

I want to stress that the above survey only scratches the surface of several non-Christian positions on these matters. There are many, many more aspects to these complex topics.

For example, Eastern views of reincarnation have been greatly modified by optimistic-minded Westerners. There is a marked dissimilarity between the depressing Oriental and the flowery Western anticipation toward reincarnation. In the East it is seen as a lamentable fact of life, an overwhelmingly dreary burden to be endured. It is called *samsara*; the eternal cycle of birth, suffering, death, rebirth. In the idiom of the West, *samsara* means "more hard times." Yet in the alchemy of Western, especially American, positivism and New Age optimism, the believer's attachment to *samsara* becomes bright and sunny. (Shirley MacLaine nearly gave *Out on a Limb* the title *Many Happy Returns*.) For bored Westerners who continually run out of new toys, *samsara* becomes a sort of cosmic playground, in anticipation not only of more and better lives but of reruns through past-life recall.

So let the Christian communicator be wise. There are areas within the above topics that have not been covered, and these may come up in conversation. Know your limitations. What I have tried to do is to reveal areas that will often come up for discussion and to show the principle that these areas are distortions of truth. Nevertheless, we do not need exhaustive knowledge of the New Spirituality to become effective communicators. This will become clear as we develop the "Submarine Communications Model" in Part Two. I find this a great relief. I do not need to be an expert on the subject. In Part Two we will learn how to use effectively in our conversations the ideas we have discussed here. I would also again direct your attention to the recommended reading list.

9

PREDICTING
PROBLEMS

—ɱ—

ANOTHER COMMON COMMUNICATION headache is the person who thinks that astrologers, psychics, or seers like Nostradamus have the ability to predict the future. This widespread deception gets many people involved in occult activities. There seems to be no stopping the influence of palm or crystal readers, clairvoyants, mediums, and others who claim to offer their clients a knowledge of the future. And an intellectual/spiritual dynamic at play here can frustrate Christian communication.

ROGER AND ROSE

Here is a typical illustration of how the error flourishes and how the dynamic frustrates communication. Roger and Rose have had a stormy marriage in which they have raised three children, who are no longer living at home. The cement of this marriage has been an earlier decision by the parents to put off getting a divorce until the children were grown and independent.

Roger, however, now refuses to initiate divorce proceedings because he has discovered that his father-in-law will then cut him out of a sizable inheritance. Rose is at her wits' end because of her husband's marital infidelity. Yet she is reluctant to initiate divorce because of her father's intolerance of it. It would be far easier on her if Roger would simply make it official. After several more months of misery and bewilderment, Rose decides, "I may have to take the risk and file for divorce myself, even if Dad misunderstands." She then calls a lawyer and goes for an initial consultation, but afterward still leaves things up in the air.

A few weeks later, Rose attends a psychic house party, and her friends needle her into getting a reading. After some small talk with the psychic, Rose consents. The psychic examines Rose's palm and asks, "Have you raised several children?" (As with Eve, a fact gets Rose's attention.) She raises an eyebrow and confirms this for the psychic, who continues by saying, "I'm also wondering if you're not bewildered about a very important decision you're trying to make." When she hears this, Rose thinks of her visit to the lawyer, and with a tentative smile she broaches the subject with the psychic. They chat for several minutes, and finally Rose sighs, "I just don't know what to do. I'm so confused. Do you see anything ahead for me?"

"It's not my place to give you advice about your marriage," the psychic replies, "or to make decisions for you. But I do see a man in your future. An interesting man. He's tall and attractive and has a full beard. He understands you. I think he's a businessman. Does this sound like your husband?"

"No, it's not Roger," Rose responds.

But she has "seen" enough. She rises, thanks the psychic, and moves off to talk to her friends about the reading. Afterward, she cannot shake off the fact that her husband is short, clean-shaven, and works as a car mechanic. She is a little confused but also a little interested.

A SLIP OF THE TONGUE

A week later a friend named Ann is talking to someone at the school where they both work. "I have a friend named Rose," Ann says, "and we went to a psychic house party last week. A psychic told Rose that she had three children and that she was going to get a divorce. Well, Rose does have three children, and she told me she was thinking seriously about getting a divorce. How did the psychic know that?"

Time passes. Two years later a divorced Rose is having lunch with Ann and mentions that she wants to consult a psychic.

"Whatever for?" Ann asks.

"Remember that psychic reading I had a couple of years ago?"

"Yes."

"Well, that psychic told me that I had three children, that I would get a divorce, and that I'd be loved by an understanding man. She said he would be a tall businessman with a beard."

"I remember now. I even told Martha about it. So why the sudden interest in seeing a psychic again?"

"Now that I'm divorced, I'm wondering what's ahead. I mean, how do I meet this man anyway?"

Do you see what has occurred? Rose and Ann have put words into the psychic's mouth. The psychic had actually said (and in the form of a question, which leaves a nonembarrassing way out if wrong), "Have you raised *several* children?" Yet when Rose tells it, it has become *three* children. The psychic had also said, "I'm wondering if you're not bewildered about a very important decision." Yet when Rose tells her friends about this part of the reading, it is, "The psychic told me I would be getting a divorce." The psychic had also said, "I see a man in your future . . . ," but when Rose tells it, it is "The psychic told me I would be loved by . . ."

It is essential for the effective communicator to see what is going on here and help people like Rose to recognize it. What the psychic actually said was either ignored or forgotten. Rose has taken specific incidents from her life and tucked them into the psychic reading as if they were the psychic's actual words. The original statements were ambiguous, equivocal, and merely suggestive, yet they became *specific* events in Rose's mind by association, which becomes the story she tells. This sleight of mind occurs frequently to the undiscerning, who then think that future events have been foretold.

Without thinking—this is the problem—the average person is not aware that an astrologer, psychic, palm reader, or even a Nostradamus merely makes clever use of ambiguous language. Expensive, glossy, full-color books are printed about Nostradamus's "prophetic" quatrains in an effort to reveal how he predicted twentieth-century events in the sixteenth century from a bowl of water! Yet his "predictions" are ambiguous and can, and have been made to, mean almost anything. Whether it is a Nostradamus or a local psychic, people have a penchant for placing words and events into the mouths of seers and then telling friends that something specific was known or foretold.

The most frequent way in which people get tripped up like this is through the vague and ambiguous advice of newspaper or magazine horoscope columns. Let us say that Gillian is sipping her morning coffee and reading in the paper under her sign Aries: "Expect domestic troubles this week." Two days later, Armageddon erupts: with her teenager, Ian, who storms out of the house, drives off with the family car, and is not heard from for two days. While playing bridge the next month with friends, Gillian complains, "A few weeks ago, Ian and I had a terrible argument. I don't know what I am going to do with him. He drove off in my car and was gone two days. It gave me and Colin a horrible scare. But what's really amazing is that my horoscope that week predicted the whole thing!"

Again, words were put into the horoscope's "mouth." Like psychics, horoscope columns employ ambiguous language that may be interpreted in many specific ways, and then astrology is credited with the power to predict the future. What is really amazing is that people are so gullible. Unfortunately, in this way astrology has gained a reputation for accuracy over the years that in itself is quite amazing. And the extremes people will go to, to bolster its reputation for accuracy can get comical.

I am reminded of one of Don Quixote's humorous incidents. This famous knight errant had his share of hallucinations, to say the least, but on occasion his discernment was striking. Take for instance the time he was educating the ever-faithful Sancho about the illogical conclusions people draw from astrological forecasts.

> "I know of a lady," Don Quixote tells Sancho, "who asked one of these horoscope-casters whether a little lap dog bitch she had would fall with pup and bear, and how many pups she would have and of what colour. To which Master Astrologer replied, after he had cast the figure, that the bitch would fall and bear three puppies, one green, one scarlet and one speckled. . . . And what happened was that two days later the bitch died of overeating, and Master Astrologer gained a reputation in the town of being a very accurate caster of a horoscope, a reputation which they mostly have."[1]

The wise communicator will want to help the person to see the ambiguity of a psychic prediction and how specific events are later made to refer to it as if that was what was originally said. This way of ascribing specificity to ambiguity is rife within the world of the New

Spirituality, and it is often used as proof that astrology, numerology, crystal readings, psychics, and so on have future-telling power. For people who are unwilling to trust in God and His grace day after day no matter what happens, this can be appealing. It gives them the hope of being able to know about tomorrow. The future, however, comes only one day at a time.

COLD READINGS

Another dynamic may be at work in psychic readings. I have in mind here what is called "cold reading," which gives these practices a semblance of a power far beyond that of mortals. I am not going to go into great detail because an excellent job has been done on this in Dan Korem's book *Powers: Testing the Psychic and the Supernatural*. What I will do here is mention how some principles of cold reading could have been employed by Rose's psychic.

In *Powers*, Korem lists six principles of cold reading: (1) the Barnum effect; (2) identifying the psychological profile of the client; (3) observing physical features and microexpressions; (4) accessing specific information; (5) loading the language; (6) the educated guess. The first is about general comments that can relate to whoever is sitting for a reading. It is a kind of stock sketch of personality that is sufficiently ambiguous so that the client could easily apply his specific characteristics to it. The second is about "partially pinpointing [the client's] personality type," for example choleric, sanguine, phlegmatic, melancholic, introvert, or extrovert. If the psychic reader is familiar with the characteristics of each type and has seen a few hundred clients, he will probably be able to identify a client's personality type quickly. And if he also knows the person's occupation, the psychic would not find it difficult, for example, to predict the client's likes and dislikes. Using the third principle of cold reading, the psychic looks "for clues that can be detected primarily by three senses: touch, sight and hearing." The look of the skin, something said by a client that he does not recall later, feeling the resistance or yieldedness of the client's hand when touched, and the sight of clothes, body posture, and so forth all assist the psychic with his readings.

The fourth principle actually includes eavesdropping or doing research on a client ahead of time. The fifth "refers to statements that can be interpreted in more than one way." Korem says that when this technique is combined with the others, it can give the appearance of infallibility. The sixth principle is the educated guess and is based upon knowing percentages, for example, of the most common jobs held by different personality types, or the most common forms of recreation, and so on.

The psychic who did Rose's reading could have used many of these principles. For example, at the psychic house party before the readings began, everyone present could have been mingling and chatting about this and that, including the psychic, who could have heard Rose mention her children. Later during the reading, the psychic may then have identified Rose as a phlegmatic temperament (often prone to indecision) and noticed that she was very unhappy or uneasy. The psychic would have known that the divorce rate is high today and so decided to risk an educated guess in that direction, but without mentioning the subject directly, which would leave the psychic a way out, such as to move the conversation into another area if Rose did not take the bait.

The principles of cold reading are used, whether consciously or not, by astrologers, psychics, and other seers. When I used to give horoscope readings to people, I found myself using them without having been taught them. I picked them up through common sense. There is always a bit of small talk going on between a psychic and a client before a reading. I used to listen for people to mention areas of interest that they had or how their jobs were going or what special problems they faced. I frequently did the readings in their homes, where I would pick up further clues.

Many of the readings I did were for hippies, rock musicians and their wives, and 1960s counterculture people in general. I was one myself and so knew the ins and outs of it. For example, I could drop a whole category of information from the readings that I did for such folk. This meant that I never needed to worry about getting it wrong. And this meant that I could save myself from a lot of potentially embarrassing mistakes. That is, I never needed to mention the things that concerned a normal lifestyle (except perhaps in a negative light!) because most of my clients were not living it. In keeping my readings confined to the categories of a countercultural lifestyle, and by including any tidbits I had overheard, I could usually keep the interest of such folk, some of whom returned for more readings.

So it is not only specificity substituted for ambiguity but also cold readings that give certain New Age practices and their spokespersons a semblance of having the power to predict the future. We can use this information in our discussions.

WHAT ABOUT THE FUTURE?

I am often stopped at this point by Christians who ask, "Are you really saying that psychics can't see into the future? What about the devil? Can he see into the future?" The answer to the first question is yes, that is what I'm saying; and to the second, no. As I understand biblical theology, the devil cannot see specifically into the future. He is not omniscient, like God. He cannot know a person's free moral choices before they have been made. He cannot know whether God may intervene in a certain situation. He cannot know the "time and chance" that happen to us all (Eccles. 9:11).

The analogy of a chess match between two chess masters has helped me to understand the only manner in which I believe it is possible for the spirit world to have even a slim knowledge of the future, and that *only* of the immediate future. After each chess master has made several opening moves, he is expert enough to know what probabilities exist for his opponent's upcoming moves for the next few plays. There are only so many subsequent combinations of moves, and each chess master will know what those are, following, as they do, as consequences of the prior moves. Because each chess master will know what these are, he will, shall we say, have specific insight into the future. This anticipation of probabilities seems to me to be the only way a psychic or the spirit world can see into the future, very shortsightedly at that. And it still boils down to making an educated guess, for even the chess master cannot know with certainty which one of the chessmen his opponent will move next.

This principle applies either to a cold reading or to a psychic who is actually receiving information from the spirit world, which could have been the case with Rose's psychic reading. The Bible is clear that evil spirits exist, that they are knowledgeable, and that they are able to communicate what they know to people who have the means of getting in touch with them. From what I understand, both from the Bible and from my experiences as a former astrologist, the psychic acts as a kind of satellite dish, receiving information from the spirit world to send to a client. If the "familiar spirit" is privy to some facts about the client, as was the serpent with Eve, it could feed this information to its spokesperson, who in turn would reveal it to his client.[2]

With Rose, the psychic could have been receiving impressions from a spirit about "children" and "divorce." The former has nothing to do with a prediction; it is merely a fact used to get Rose's attention. The children already exist. The latter, at the time of the psychic reading, was not yet a fact but an educated guess based upon a fact: that Rose had gone to see a lawyer about a divorce. It is history, and the spirit could have known it. The probability, then, was there for a move toward divorce. The psychic could have had this "impression" and hedged it within the ambiguous statement about Rose's bewilderment concerning an important decision.

I want to stress that this ability to perceive probabilities and make educated guesses about them is the only way I can see either a human being or a spirit having the power to tell the future. In either case the seeing into the future boils down to a guess, however educated. In no way could it be called a prediction, even if the thing came to pass, for that meant only that the spokesperson guessed right. Neither the psychic nor the spirit is omniscient. It could even have occurred that, sometime after the psychic reading, Roger and Rose became Christians and God healed their marriage. So we also have the sovereignty of God to consider.

Biblical prophecy is of an entirely different nature, resultant as it is from an omniscient God, the One with the power to accomplish what He says He will. Biblical prophecy, therefore, is about predicting events of which there are *no* apparent probabilities, the occurrences of which depend upon innumerable contingencies involving the history of things and the volitions of persons who may not even exist yet. Other characteristics of biblical prophecy are that it announces suitably ahead of time the event it foretells; it has a particular and exact agreement with that event when it comes to pass; no human wisdom or foresight could produce it; it has a moral element to it (this is always missing from New Age "prophecies"); and it is delivered by someone under the inspiration of God almighty.

Clients of astrologers and psychics, however, as well as the general public, are often oblivious to all of this, and the Christian communicator will want to rectify this.

10

DARKNESS
AS LIGHT

—⚡—

WE HAVE BEEN addressing a number of questions about irrationality, passivity, deception, distortions of truth, and other intellectual/spiritual dynamics that can foil an effective Christian witness to enthusiasts of the New Spirituality. These are people just like you and me, and they have not become enmeshed in these dynamics by taking some premeditated giant step. Quite the contrary. The progression is much more like the slow, almost imperceptible swelling of the pregnant womb. As Jeremiah says,

> *The heart is deceitful above all things,*
> *And desperately wicked;*
> *Who can know it?* (17:9)

That is to say, who can see what is happening? Deception is like that.

This should give us some compassion for non-Christian spiritual seekers. Indeed, I think that if we Christians examine our own non-Christian pasts, we will see that we did not set out intentionally to go astray. I know that I did not. It was a gradual process, and it had its genesis in my determination to search for Truth and the meaning of life. This holds true for most non-Christian spiritual seekers; they begin with a good enough motive, but having little or no interest in a

71

biblical way of seeing, they then move into the wrong paths when looking for spiritual answers.

I used to think that some of the conversations I have had with spiritual seekers were just so much silly hairsplitting, but now I see the sense of them. It has occurred to me that error begins like two persons diverging along slowly widening lines from the point of a very acute angle. Each person began at the same point with the same motive, but a different way of seeing life informed each person's search. Person A began his walk along the line of truth; person B began her walk on the line of error. And because it is a very acute angle, there may be a time in which both persons appear to be in agreement, as if they were walking side by side on the same path. It is not until the lines of the angle are extended far enough that the incompatibility of each person's walk with the other becomes obvious. The disparity existed with the first steps but may have gone unnoticed until some distance down the road precisely because there was no silly hairsplitting at the start.

This brings us to another intellectual/spiritual dynamic that can frustrate communication, and I would like to illustrate it from a statement by Jesus Himself. It is a rather puzzling statement for those of us who live twenty centuries this side of Calvary, the Master's meaning being obscured through the veil of ages. It is found in Matthew 6:23 where, almost as an aside, Jesus declares, "If therefore the light that is in you is darkness, how great is that darkness!"

This is not a question; it's an exclamation, a cry filled with emotion. Today He might have exclaimed, "Don't be surprised that people who walk in darkness write books called *Dancing in the Light*!" What's Jesus talking about here? How can people be walking the path of spiritual darkness and think that it is the "light"?

We can ferret out the Master's meaning from a nightly phenomenon with which we are all familiar. That is, if you are like me when it is time to go to sleep at night! You change your clothes for bed, slip in under the covers, perhaps read for a while, and then switch off the bedside lamp and close your eyes. The room has been plunged into darkness and you fall asleep. But what would it be like in the room if you were to keep your eyes open immediately after switching off the light? Would you be able to see anything? Not likely. (I'm assuming there's not a streetlight outside your window!)

But if you were to keep your eyes open for several minutes after switching off the light, what would happen? Of course, we have all experienced this; at first it is quite dark; but then it gets a bit lighter in the room and you can see, not clearly, but enough to detect the shadowy appearances of furnishings, picture frames, and so on. It's dim, but if you had to dash suddenly from bed to answer the telephone in another room, as you sprang from the bedroom you could avoid smacking your shin on the lower dresser drawer that accidentally was left open. Try hurrying from the room immediately after switching off the light and you might not be so fortunate!

This illustration may help us grasp the Master's meaning in Matthew 6:23. And I ask you to forgive me for a little literary playfulness here. To highlight the subtlety of the process, I led you slightly up the garden path in the previous paragraph to enable you to appreciate the ease with which people get tripped up. Take a moment to reread the previous paragraph to discover where I "deceived" you. Some readers may have noticed it already. Look at the wording carefully. I'll wait here for you . . .

So, what mischief did I make? It is in the phrase "It gets a bit lighter in the room." Of course, it does not get any lighter in the room; it merely *appears* to get lighter. What would actually happen, of course, is that your eyes would become accustomed to the darkness, which slowly begins to look like light. Those who walk in darkness (1 John 2:11) have had the "eyes of [their] understanding" (Eph. 1:18) acclimatized to a shadowy world that gets mistaken for light. This is a strong delusion. So much so that Jesus cries, "Look how great it is!"—which may be an echo of Isaiah 5:20, where the prophet speaks of the misfortune upon those "who put darkness for light."

Let's extend the analogy further. I suppose all people, at one time or another, have been startled awake from a nightmare and opened their eyes in the darkness only to receive a good scare from what they thought was in the room with them. They saw an indistinct shape and perhaps mistook it for an intruder. Later it became something to laugh about. "How silly we were," they tell friends, "to think that the coat extending from a hanger over the closet door had broken into the house!"

This state of affairs exists within much of the New Spirituality, but with this significant difference: *it never becomes clear what the object really is*. If people are not in a covenant relationship with the

Light of the World, the light of day never comes to them, and they walk around in a shadowy world in which they know that *something* is there, but just what it is, is never clear. The real truth about it is unknown.

And because it cannot be denied that they are seeing something, explanations are offered. Thus, God becomes an impersonal energy; a human being becomes God; death becomes a door to many future lives; evil spirits are mistaken for "spirit guides"; sin becomes bad karma or merely one's perception of evil; and so on. It is only in Christ that the truth of these matters is clarified in the light of day.

For those who walk in darkness, the things of creation, and God Himself, are seen out of character. Darkness shrouds a proper understanding, evaluation, and interpretation of what is seen or discerned; the coat always seems to be an intruder. This condition, though it does not develop overnight, may not go completely unnoticed by the person. When I was becoming a New Age adherent and was taught, for instance, that reincarnation followed death, or that the "spirit guides" were not demonic, I recall being slightly startled. Something about those explanations seemed suspect, at least initially. I do not think that I could have articulated why that was, but it certainly was how I felt early on. Some sort of early warning system within me sounded when I opened my eyes in the darkness.

This did not disturb me for long, however, because my continued fellowship with New Age teaching rationalized the disquiet, and the eyes of my understanding acclimatized to the darkness. The longer I trafficked in the shadowy world, the more accepting and established I became in its way of seeing. Eventually, a fully justified rationale existed in my mind that the coat was an intruder, and there were few doubts that I was wrong. That rationale led me on like that until several years had passed and I became a Christian.

CHANGING THE NOUNS OF THE GAME

I believe that this principle of darkness as light accounts for the New Spirituality's penchant for renaming and redefining many of the things of life and reality. This is an important area, one in which we shall need to work hard within our conversations with spiritual thinkers as they become more and more outspoken about it.

"Use the language of diplomacy," Anne Carson advises in her book *Spiritual Parenting in the New Age*. She goes on:

> Say *prayer*, not *magic* or *spell*. . . . Say *ceremony*, not *ritual*. This way, I can tell my aunt that we had a blessing ceremony for our infant daughter under the auspices of a Dutch Reformed minister, leaving out the invocation to the four elements, the sprinkling of corn meal and the bestowing of a spirit name.

Most of all, Carson urges, fudge on the word *pagan*. "Using the word *pagan* tends to make people think that you are a) an atheist, b) a flake, c) joking."[1]

This is what I call "changing the nouns of the game." It is a deception that often strips occult or mystical connotations from the New Spirituality by substituting the old offensive terms with new nonreligious, psychological, or scientific-sounding ones. *Therapeutic Touch* is a case in point. This popular health-care technique has been popularized by Dolores Krieger, R.N., Ph.D., who teaches it chiefly to nurses throughout the United States. Upon researching it, I discovered that Therapeutic Touch is virtually the same thing, almost step by step, as what I learned as psychic healing in the early 1970s.

Other examples of changing the nouns of the game are numerous. *Centering, grounding,* and *stilling* are a few of the new names for Eastern meditation. *Astrograph* is slowly becoming a euphemism for astrology, and channeler is already locked in place for the old spirit medium.

There are all kinds of these semantic distortions in the New Spirituality. They present a whole range of problems for the Christian communicator, which we will look at in Part Two. What needs saying here is that changing the nouns of the game in no way changes the nature of the game. No less a pillar of the New Spirituality's psychological thought than Carl Jung was unequivocal on this point.

Jung (1875–1961), a complex man, became disillusioned with Christianity at an early age and delved into occultism several times. He also became an authority on alchemy, Gnosticism, and religious myth. But his pièce de résistance is his analytical psychology, which is the name he gave his life's work as a psychologist and psychiatrist to distinguish it from Freud's psychoanalysis and Adler's individual psychology. Through this psychology Jung made some contributions that may merit further study in a biblical context, for example, his theories of personality types and his elaboration of the university of symbols. He also brought needed adjustments to what at the time was the highly rationalistic and reductionist field of psychology. He placed much more emphasis on human responsibility and choice. He warned against the dangers of arid dogmatism. He saw religion positively—as a necessity, in fact—and bore witness to the supernatural realm. Yet in this latter area Jung did much mischief.

To develop many of the concepts and categories of thought for analytical psychology, Jung changed the nouns of religion, spiritualism, and occultism into those of psychology. He gave as his reason for this that as a psychologist, he needed to use the terms of his own discipline and not borrow those of the theologian. We can understand this, but nevertheless it has obscured the demonic nature of some of Jung's "unconscious contents." For example, one of the terms Jung popularized was *archetype*, the nature of which is difficult to pin down even in Jung's voluminous writings. In short, archetypes are about the universality of symbols of the human race *and* the "unconscious dynamisms" or "activating points" behind the symbols and images.

Of these unconscious dynamisms, Jung wrote that they had a life of their own, purpose, and that they could be composers of dreams. In his autobiography, Jung discloses the name of four archetypes that appeared and spoke to him during seasons of deep occult experimentation.[2] He also writes about the days in which his "whole house [was] filled as if there was a crowd present, crammed full of spirits. They were packed right up to the door, and the air was so thick it was scarcely possible to breathe."[3] Jung took copious notes whenever any spirits were in contact with him. And he frequently called these spirits "the dead" or "unconscious contents," and his contact with them his "fantasies."

Late in life, Jung had this to say about such times:

These conversations with the dead formed a kind prelude to what I had to communicate to the world about the unconscious.[4]

Today I can say that I never lost touch with my initial experiences. All my works, all my creative activity, have come from those initial fantasies and dreams which began in 1912. . . . Everything I accomplished later in life was already contained in them.[5]

It has taken me nearly forty-five years to distill within the vessel of my scientific work the things that I experienced and wrote down at that time.[6]

Though he used a psychological vocabulary for speaking about demons, Jung felt that people were stupidly gullible if they thought that changing the nouns of the game in any way changed the nature of the game:

I did all in my power to convey to my intimates a new way of seeing.[7]

[If] by employing the concept of archetype, we attempt to define more closely the point at which the daimon grips us, we have not abolished anything.[8]

The concept of them as demonia is therefore quite in accord with their nature. If anyone is inclined to believe that any aspect of the *nature* [his emphasis] of things is changed by such formulations, he is being extremely credulous about words. The real facts do not change, whatever names we give them. . . . [T]he change of a name has removed nothing at all from reality.[9]

But the real mischief is that Jung did not believe that the nature of the demonia was demonic and evil in the biblical sense. Jung could not deny that he was seeing and encountering something, but since he had rejected Christianity, he was walking in darkness as to the right explanation for what he was experiencing. He thought that the demonia had a kind of neutrality or perhaps dualistic nature, and that led Jung to conclude that they could be either the gravest danger *or* the most redeeming power.

This is a fatal attraction for many spiritual enthusiasts today, who see Jung's archetypes in terms of helpful "spirit guides."[10] This is only one of the disastrous ramifications of seeing the coat as an intruder. As Christian communicators, we will want to help these seekers come to some understandings about their spiritual eyesight. This may take some work on our part, but with God's help, as we endeavor to become wise as serpents in understanding the problems of communication, we can get through to New Age people. We can offer them the truth, and then it is up to them. God has placed within every person, perhaps as a feature of His image, a capacity for recognizing the truth. This is a part of what it means to be human; were it not so, how could we ever recognize the truth of Christ—or any truth, for that matter—and accept Him? Even those who walk in gross darkness can therefore recognize the truth. Whether or not they accept it is another story. The task, then, of the Christian communicator is to express the truth about God and Life in a way that makes sense to people. We are called to untangle the lie from the truth and to make the crooked ways straight.

SUMMARY

To help you sustain your knowledge of the intellectual/spiritual dynamics that frustrate Christian communication in the world of the New Spirituality, here is a list of those characteristics in brief, summarized from chapters 4 to 10:

- The principle of inversion. Things are the wrong way around, as Alice saw in Looking-glass House, or as the Richardsons discovered with the Sawi men who saw Judas Iscariot as the hero of the gospel story.
- The closed mind. Here is the person like the Waverley Market numerologist, who was absolutely "not interested."
- The irrational. This dynamic has little or no tolerance for reason or for the rational. It conditions the spiritual seeker to feel comfortable about holding to contradictory beliefs and values. It gives a context in which to receive intuitive mystical experiences.
- Passivity. This widespread dynamic is found in many meditators. It trains them temporarily to suspend conscious thought while in a waking state, which in turn opens them up to the spirit world.
- Deception. This is the deliberate misrepresentation of facts or truth in order to purposely lead someone astray. (Also see distortions of truth, Chapter 8.)
- Assigning too much power to the spirit world. Here people think that psychics, mediums, channelers, astrologers, and so forth have power to predict the future.
- Darkness as light. The non-Christian spiritual seeker lives amidst a shadowy world that is mistaken for light. In this world,

the person knows that "something" is there, but the real truth of the thing is unknown to him or her.

- Changing the nouns of the game. This involves renaming and redefining reality according to the New Spirituality's way of seeing.

As far as I know, these areas encapsulate most of the communication problems Christians will encounter in the world of the New Spirituality. After the Inter-Mission (it's not really a rest break!), we will discover how to reckon with them.

Inter-Mission

11

MODELS OR
MUDDLES?

—⊸⊶—

TWO CHRISTIANS WERE arguing and the subject was a hot one. Jenny was saying that we must not overreact to the New Age phenomenon. To this, Tim responded, saying, "Yes, but . . . ," and the exaggerations that then shot from his mouth clearly betrayed overreaction. Jenny then tried a different tack. She said to Tim that we had to be careful not to throw out the baby with the bathwater. Here the tête-à-tête heated up because Tim evidently saw nothing of value about the New Age. Jenny then said that Tim might change his mind about this if he had a heart-to-heart talk with some seekers. But when Jenny suggested that she and Tim have lunch with a couple that she knew, Tim was turned off by the idea.

Later, Tim had great doubts about Jenny. *Maybe she's not even a Christian*, he thought. *Maybe she's a New Ager*. As he was feeling suspicious of Jenny, she was praying, "Lord, forgive me for upsetting Tim. Help both of us to see the situation more clearly, so that we may reach New Age people with the gospel."

This rupture between Christians occurs more often than you may think. The discomposure and variance that this rift has produced is evident in most of the audiences I meet. It happens chiefly because we do not really understand each other's positions, although we think we do. Ask yourself whether you could express Jenny's position to her in a manner that would convince her that you really understand it. If not, what right do you have to think that her perspective ought to bow to yours? This pride holds us at arm's length from brothers and sisters in Christ, and we find ourselves unwilling or hesitant to learn from them. If Christians themselves cannot have dialogue with each other about the New Spirituality, how will we be able to hold effective conversations with its adherents?

A WAY OF SEEING

Both Tim and Jenny are Christians, so the real problem lies elsewhere. It is found, as Jenny prayed, in the crucial area of seeing. Tim and Jenny see the situation somewhat differently. It is not that one sees it biblically and the other nonbiblically. Rather, each has different biblical categories of thought for analyzing, evaluating, interpreting, and understanding the New Spirituality. The way Tim sees it, he fears that Jenny's view is a compromise that will open floodgates of deception and demonic activity into the church. Yet if Tim had not gotten so uptight, he could have discussed this with Jenny and discovered her firm stand against occultism. He would also have had his mind set at rest when he learned from Jenny that she was uncompromising in essential biblical beliefs. When he had settled such questions, Tim would have been in a position to learn from Jenny. She had been hoping to communicate to Tim a biblical perspective that she finds helpful.

This is not to say that Jenny's view is flawless, or that she can say to a member of Christ's body, "I have no need of you." We all approach this topic as disciples, that is, as learners. Unfortunately, experience teaches that the Tims of Christendom usually refuse to learn much from the Jennys, while the latter tend to underestimate and even disregard the former. But there is a more serious consequence. Experience has indicated to me that the Tims outnumber the Jennys in the work of trying to reach non-Christian spiritual seekers with Christ's gospel. This may mean that the majority of Christian workers in the world of the New Spirituality have a manner of communicating that is not as conducive to that end as it could be.

It is not that Tim does not try. He does, and he does his best. Yet he finds seekers argumentative or dismissive of him. It would probably surprise Tim to learn that they see him as uncompassionate, prejudiced, shallow, hypercritical, even boring, or threatening. In a word, irrelevant. I realize that we may not like the case put so plainly, but how are we ever going to be able to break down the stone walls that separate these people from the gospel if we do not first know what they may be thinking of us, the messengers of the gospel? Worse still, in many cases there is justification for the ways in which they describe us. Talk about a communication barrier!

Tim may never have seen himself in this light. When people brush him off, he may think that they are rejecting Jesus and that he is suffering for the gospel. In a sense this is true. But it is probably more to the point that they are rejecting the messenger and that he is suffering because of his own mistakes. Tim may not be the best "epistle" to be read by people that he could be. Feeling discouraged, he may pass up opportunities, and the Lord has one less minister to the world of the New Spirituality.

Much of the problem here centers on *how* we see the New Spirituality. How we see it not only affects our evaluation of it; it also greatly influences how we communicate with its adherents. Of course, how we see it is largely the product of how we were taught to see it. One difficulty here is that we may have accepted some untenable and specious arguments, opinions, and conclusions. Much of what we think we know about the New Spirituality has not emerged from what we ourselves have researched, investigated, thought, and prayed through. Rather, we have taken for granted the arguments, opinions, and conclusions of one or two Christian books, for example, on the New Age, or what our friends have told us about it. Many of us may have given very little personal thought, if any, to what is actually being taught in such books or being done to verify research and conclusions.

Another difficulty is *how* it is being said. An unhelpful spirit or tone may have rubbed off on us as we read certain books. Frankly, speaking as a former insider, I have to say that several widely read Christian books on the New Age are so far off the mark that New Age people would not recognize themselves in the pages. You could never give a book like that to most seekers. There is also an arrogant tone to some of these books, suggesting, "If you don't agree with my evaluation down to the last jot and tittle, then you, too, are part of the problem, Christian or not." I have seen this contribute to an attitude in Christians that builds a barrier between brothers and sisters in Christ who see the phenomenon differently. Maybe the authors are not aware of this. But brothers and sisters, we cannot afford to be closed to each other. We need to learn from each other.

The shrill tone, the emotional hyperventilating, and the mischievous use of selected research facts leave us a long way from being equipped to reach the seeking *person*. Then there is the sensationalism that surrounds some books. This often produces in many readers an unhealthy fear of the non-Christian spiritual seeker. All this results in Christians being generally alienated from the very people they should have been equipped to help.[1]

We may, then, need to make some significant adjustments in the way we see the New Spirituality. We will need humility about what we think we know of it and its people. Somehow we have to overcome any personal arrogance we may have and repent of it. This should result in a big stride toward mutual understanding and cooperation among us as Christians and enhance our communication with others.

CHANGING PERSPECTIVES

I once heard someone say "Humility of mind produces a teachable spirit." I like that. In his book *The Practice of Godliness*, Navigator Jerry Bridges clearly puts the case for developing humility of mind in the context of modifying our views:

> We evangelicals are not noted for our humility about our doctrines— our beliefs about what the Bible teaches in various areas of theology. Whatever position we take . . . we tend to feel our position is airtight, and that anyone holding a different view is altogether wrong. We tend to be quite impatient with anyone who differs from us. . . . It is one thing to be persuaded that what we believe is correct as we understand the Scriptures; it is quite another to believe that our views are *always* [his emphasis] correct. Twice in my life I have had to make significant changes in my doctrines as a result of additional understanding of the Scriptures. . . . We must remind ourselves that God has not made our minds, or even a particular church, the depository of the sum total of his teachings.[2]

Although Bridges is writing to a different audience and in a different context, may we not say "Amen" to this? I think this will require, at the least, setting aside attitudes like that of one high-profile

Christian who, in a letter I have on file, accuses a respectable Christian book on the New Age as being "atrocious," "abominable," and "monstrous" and demands its withdrawal from bookstores. I do not say that everything in the book in question, or in this book either, is the gospel truth. Only one Book is that. But if this brother really has a leg to stand on, I wonder if the best way to use it is to kick the authors of the book in question in the stomach. It is one thing to see an issue differently; it is quite another thing to see it differently in humility of mind.

If we want to have a united witness, we shall have to start going the extra mile, or two, with our brothers and sisters in Christ who may see the New Spirituality differently from the way we do. And it will have to be done in love, truth, and sincerity. I have had to make significant adjustments since becoming a Christian in how I see it, yet still I do not think that I have the best apprehension of it that it is possible to have. I see through a glass darkly.

It is never easy for me when going through significant changes of perspective. It grates against what I think I know. It means my thinking has been found wanting in certain areas. Changing is difficult because the foundations, structures, and ideas of what we believe to be true are not so easily reorganized. One reason for this is that they usually sit comfortably within the views represented by our group, congregation, denomination, and so on. And as someone has said, if we suspect that by changing our perspective we may run afoul of the opinions of our group, we may be unwilling to do so.

There is a real blessedness, however, in running the risk (humbly!) because it opens us to new biblical horizons and fresh possibilities. There are, then, other biblical perspectives besides ours, other Christian ways of seeing a subject. We may want to make some adjustments. We owe it to each other, to spiritual seekers, and to our Lord to really listen to the reasons other Christians have for holding to their various views. We may discover that their perspectives are more biblical than we thought. Humility of mind will keep us teachable, and it will grace us with a godly pliability. Being intractable may be the fruit of a stubbornness whose root is idolatry (1 Sam. 15:23).

It really is silly how uptight and defensive we can get about this, considering that adjustments of perspectives have been taking place in us since childhood. Children may for a season think that babies are bought at the hospital or that gifts arrive on December 25 from Santa

Claus. Someday, however, these views change with the discovery and acceptance of a "better" way of seeing. And we would think a teenager quite odd who held to childish views that had run their course.

Please note: in saying that we may have an occasion to change a perspective, I am not suggesting that we compromise sound doctrine or the gospel, or that we relinquish orthodoxy. I merely wish to encourage us to be willing to reorganize our perspectives if there are good and sufficient reasons to believe that our thinking has been found wanting. I have a love/hate relationship with myself whenever some facts or truths present themselves to my way of seeing and so require a change in perspective.

A friend of mine once had a professor tell him, "Jeff, if the facts don't fit your theology, change your theology." However, I dislike doing this because it shows up some inadequacy in my thinking, often in an area where I thought my understanding was sufficient. On the other hand, I like changing because I realize I have been blessed to know more of the mind of the Master, and yet again comes the force of 1 Corinthians 8:2: "If anyone thinks that he knows anything, he knows nothing yet as he ought to know."

What really ruffles me, though, are not so much the times when a Christian's influence modifies my view, but when it happens as a result of talking, for example, to a non-Christian spiritual seeker. It is difficult eating humble pie then, I can tell you! Yet if we have a fundamental respect for the truth, we will relinquish our pride and change. Will we not receive correction from whatever source it comes? It strikes me as amusing, the sudden and unlooked-for change of perspective Balaam must have gone through after hearing the truth of the matter from a donkey! (See Num. 22:21–33.) So if we come across a spiritual seeker who complains about the fragmentation of society and longs for community, or who speaks out for a health-care system that would include the spiritual dimension of people, or who assesses the dangers of long-term environmental abuse, or who takes issue with the Western church for being rationalistic, how can we turn a deaf ear? It is all true.

When the person is right, we will want to agree. We need this humility of mind before God and our fellow human beings in order to become effective communicators. As Christians, we are in a covenant relationship with, and a respecter of, the Truth Himself. Therefore we ought to be glad and rejoice whenever anyone points out what is true. We can agree with it. This does not mean that we may be able to agree with the person's full evaluation, analysis, interpretation, or solution suggested for each matter. He may, for example, define *community, holistic health care, the supernatural,* and so on differently from the way the Bible does. This is an entirely different matter. So we may have to say, "Yes, you are right about such and such, but your definition is amiss; therefore your response is inadequate."

TOWARD A FRESH WAY OF SEEING

How, then, should we see the so-called New Age phenomenon? In this book, at the publisher's request, I am calling it the "New Spirituality." More on this in a moment. Actually there are several ways of seeing it, with some being more helpful than others. A person's model for understanding a highly complex social and religious phenomenon, like the New Spirituality, cannot be taken lightly, and it will greatly influence at least three areas:

- How we use or misuse the Bible to interpret the New Age
- How we deal with it or ignore it in our own lives
- How we speak to others about it (or see no need to)

I want us to look at the third point here.

The Christian's model for understanding the New Spirituality may be a bridge or a barrier to the communication process. Some models easily short-circuit effective communication. Take the "fad" model. To someone who has invested years of time, study, effort, and money into New Age spirituality, it is certainly not a fad. The Christian who labels it as such has no communication bridge into that world.

Another example of a communication barrier is the "demon-monger" model. It lumps the whole world of the New Spirituality and all of its people together as promoters of occultism. If this is a Christian's model, how can there be conversation with people of the New Spirituality who have no interest in occultism? Talking about demons may indeed make such people frightened—of us!

The view that the New Spirituality is thoroughly occult is far from exact. Clearly, occultism runs throughout the landscape, and I am not soft about this problem. I have understood and experienced occult deception and demonic bondage at first hand. Nevertheless, the occult is but one realm of the New Spirituality. Have you ever run your hand over the coat of a dog whose hair is wadded in large mats? The New Spirituality is somewhat like that, a tangle of complexity, diversification, and even contradictions. Some of the strands are nonoccult, and if our model is the demon-monger, how can we communicate with spiritual seekers who are uninterested in the occult? Even when the demon-monger model is used in the context of occultism, it generally compounds rather than eases the communication difficulties because it lacks a certain tact.

There is also the "conspiracy" model. This has been a fairly well-received Christian way of seeing the New Age phenomenon in particular. In many ways, the conspiracy model sees the New Age as a tightly organized global collusion to install a totalitarian one-world government that would establish its own world religion to usher in the Antichrist. I do not make light of this model or even say here that it is totally wrong, but perhaps ad-lib coordination or laissez-faire cooperation is a better way to describe the corporate efforts of some New Age leaders.

One problem with the conspiracy model is that it oversimplifies. It is like the tale of the three blind men who reported their encounters with an elephant. One had come upon a leg and so reported that the elephant was like a stout tree trunk. The second man had experienced the elephant's trunk and reported that the elephant was a long flexible tube. The third man felt an ear and said, "You're both wrong. It's like a massive leathery leaf." The oversimplification of the New Age phenomenon has contributed to the sensationalism surrounding it. Taught that it is an occult conspiracy, Christians get worried. And again, the sensationalism generates an unhealthy fear that tends to keep us from the very people we are called to reach. (From counseling many Christians who have had this unhealthy fear, I have been able to identify what I think is the core problem: they have failed to understand and appreciate that their inheritance in Christ includes authority over the powers of darkness. I will say more about this in the Epilogue.)

An understanding of the "mystery of iniquity" (2 Thess. 2:7 KJV) may be helpful here. When the Bible speaks of satanic or demonic evil working itself out in human affairs, it uses the image "mystery of iniquity." This means that there are many silences on God's part to us about how and when Satan's purposes are going to be fleshed out in the earth. It's a mystery. There are some things that, in God's wisdom, we are not going to know. In this, we must be content.

Another failing of the conspiracy model is that it does not help Christians to speak to the spiritual seekers who are opposed to one-worldism. To have a one-world government, there must be a centralization of global political power, in the hands of one person or an elite group of world governors. Many New Age leaders, however, argue strongly for decentralization, being fully aware of the totalitarian dangers inherent in a sovereign global federation of political powers. Decentralization seems to be especially liked by Green New Agers (I do not say all Greens are New Age). The Christian who sees all New Age people advocating a one-world government or religion may be hard-pressed for anything to say to a Green New Ager. All in all, the conspiracy model, when it comes to the communication process, is a rickety bridge.

One's model, therefore, determines the categories of thought that are brought to a conversation, and these in turn influence communication because they limit or expand the scope of what can be said and how it will be said. Two other Christian models are worth mentioning. One is to see the New Spirituality as a "philosophically united confederacy"; the other is to see it as a "metanetwork," that is, a network of networks. Both of these are more to the point and therefore more user friendly; they carry some solid bridge-building equipment.

There are also the models that the New Spirituality uses to describe itself. One is that of a "paradigm shift in consciousness"; another, that of "personal, social, and global transformation"; another, that of a "quantum leap in the spiritual evolution of the planet." These models, and others, conceptualize how these seekers see their world and how they shape the categories of thought from which to discuss what they are into, both among themselves and with outsiders.

Several models have also arisen from secular points of view. It may be helpful to consider the progression of several secular labels that have been put upon spiritual trends during the past two centuries. In the late eighteenth century, notoriety about the so-called new invisible "mind powers" arose when Anton Mesmer popularized a healing technique he called "animal magnetism." Though it had a stormy history, it caught on under the name "mesmerism" and later "hypnotism." During the mid- to late nineteenth century, the interest in spiritualism revived, led by the now discredited Fox sisters. This kept the interest in latent mind powers alive in the media, as did the Society for Psychical Research.

Also in the nineteenth century, mind powers and mental healing received further secular recognition as an increasing number of small independent groups met to discuss new revelations. People such as Phineas Parkhurst Quimby, Mary Baker Eddy (Christian Science), and Charles and Myrtle Fillmore (Unity) caused quite a stir. Just before the turn of the century, this rising spiritual mix was given the name "New Thought." The New Thought movement is one of the seedbeds in which part of what we call "New Age" was planted.

By the mid-twentieth century, the New Thought model was no longer able to carry the weight of explanation needed to describe, analyze, and interpret a growing spiritual trend, and the label "Human Potential" movement largely displaced it. This became the new secular model for identifying the supposedly latent but vital forces of untapped human potential—but without reference to any kind of "God" or spirits. The label quickly became a Western buzz phrase and rallying point, depicting the ideology of people who believed in sheer human ability to transform self and society. It, too, is a discernible seedbed of today's New Spirituality.[3]

From mind powers to New Thought to Human Potential to what? To the mid- to late 1960s and the Age of Aquarius, which is an astrological motif about the supposed dawning of two thousand years of peace and harmony on the earth. Then after regrouping in cultural backwaters during most of the 1970s, the Age of Aquarius was quietly relaunched in the 1980s as the New Age movement, which still may be the most ubiquitous model for trying to understand the phenomenon.

The "movement" model for depicting the New Age is certainly the most familiar one, both to Christians and to non-Christians. Yet is the "movement" model big enough to hold all the information we now know about the New Age phenomenon? Is it truth-full enough to carry the weight of explanation, evaluation, and interpretation that is now needed to characterize the New Age? Perhaps it was, once upon a time. But given the New Age's wide-ranging sweep and deepening penetration throughout virtually every cultural discipline today, the "movement" model seems passé. A movement usually depicts one particular ideology, its agenda, and the accompanying group of activists who labor to promote its goals, generally within one strata of society—for example, the student or civil rights movements of the 1960s. Perhaps it was once fitting to use the "movement" model as a label for the New Age, but today, with its complexities, diversification, and even contradictions, the "movement" model seems behind the times and therefore not conducive for constructive conversation.

If we want to discuss movements, it would be nearer the mark to speak of the movements within the world of the New Spirituality. Gaia consciousness, goddess worship, myth revival, holistic health care, earth stewardship, transpersonal education, New Age business management, and others are all designations that can be properly identified and discussed as movements within the New Age world.

Today in the 1990s it is popular to call it the "New Spirituality." That's not a bad name because it gives us a framework to think of alternate spiritualities, a universe of non-Christian beliefs and practices, and it brings more consistency to the discussion than does "movement." But it, too, has its limitations, which will become evident in the next two chapters. Furthermore, what model will we use when New Spirituality becomes passé?

The question is: Is there a model that will do justice to the entire phenomenon? If there is such a model, it will be foundational enough to carry the weight of all the complexities, diversification, and contrariety, and not only today but also tomorrow. So far it has been rather like trying to explain the size and weight of the Great Pyramid of Egypt from the foundation of a beach house. Furthermore, we need a model that will give us not only a faithful understanding but an effective way by which to communicate to its adherents.

I am not sure that I know the answer to that question, but in the next chapter I am going to suggest a model, a way of seeing that seems to be comprehensive enough for the task we face. So if you are ready, we will plunge in.

1 2

WISDOM IN THE MARKETPLACE

—ɯ—

HAVE YOU EVER wondered what motivates people to do what they do, or what accounts for the decisions they make? Take voting as an example. Some people vote Democratic, others Republican, others Independent. People can be quite inflexible about their political alliances. Or take the question of education. Many parents send their children to public schools. Other parents cannot stand that idea and place their children in various sorts of private or Christian schools, and yet other parents believe in home schooling. Why do people make the various choices that they do? What influences people in different directions, not only at the voting booth and in the choice of a classroom but in the decisions they make across the spectrum of life?

Also, have you ever wondered why some non-Christian spiritual seekers seem to be capable of doing such apparently silly things at times? Silly to Christians, that is. I'm not thinking of the more believable things like having a horoscope read, meditating, or visiting a psychic. I'm thinking of things that seem unthinkable, unimaginable, to a Christian, such as sitting cross-legged inside a custom-built pyramid in order to sharpen your senses, immobilizing yourself in six inches of water while in a state of trance within the stark blackness of a sensory deprivation tank, or wearing electronic mind massagers or brain machines around the eyes and ears that flash psychedelic light patterns onto the retina to an accompanying sound track. This would

94

be unthinkable behavior for Christians but not for many non-Christian spiritual adherents, for whom it would be as sensible as voting for their favorite political party.

Or take the "laying on of stones." Some spiritual seekers like to have crystals, and the right ones, in the bathtub with them. Others like to wear crystals, and the proper colors, too, as earrings or jewelry for healing or consciousness raising. Others, however, lay small colorful crystals and stones of diverse sizes and shapes on various areas of the body. The person, usually in a meditative state, will be stretched out flat on her back, arms slightly extended from her sides, palms up. Small crystals will have been placed upon the forehead, shoulders, upper chest area, the open palms, the navel area, and perhaps at selected points along each arm or in a straight line from the navel to the neck. Why does the person do this? To the Christian, it seems unthinkable, even foolish. But don't worry. New Age people return the favor. They generally consider our Christian practices as unthinkable and foolish, for example, prayer, the Lord's Table, confession of sin, preaching the gospel. Why is this?

PERSONAL WISDOM

The answer is found, ultimately, in each person's wisdom. Yes, superficial reasons for various behaviors—peer pressure, experimentation, amusement—could be cited, but these are not our concern here. The deeper answer for the serious choices we make is found in the kind of wisdom for life that each of us has.

Wisdom is the subject of Paul's first letter to the Corinthians, chapters 1 and 2, where he speaks not only about the futility of human wisdom but also about the blessedness of God's wisdom. The apostle's point is occasionally overlooked or dismissed by Christians. Not *all* wisdom is futile. There is the wisdom of God as it is known in Jesus Christ, which is the "message of wisdom" Christians speak, and there is futile, worldly wisdom. The passage, therefore, teaches that all people have a wisdom for life, be they atheist, agnostic, humanist, a bar-room brawler, a mother of four, a prime minister, or a New Ager. And when you become a Christian and are in Christ, your wisdom changes radically. You become a part of a wisdom that the world does not know. The point of the passage is Paul's contrast of the two wisdoms.

But what is wisdom? In his thought-provoking and groundbreaking book *Wisdom in the Marketplace*, English theologian and philosopher John Peck brings out its biblical meaning in a contemporary way. Writing as someone who teaches both Hebrew and Greek, Peck states that in the Bible, "Wisdom is a word about the sort of sense you make of creation in order to live in it effectively (and it will affect what you think is effective living too)."[1] Or, "Wisdom is a way of seeing life and behaving in it."[2]

TWO ASPECTS OF WISDOM

Wisdom, therefore, is not mere head knowledge. According to the Bible, it brings theory and practice together—it is a way of making sense *and* living, a way of seeing *and* behaving. Perhaps it could be said that wisdom is applied knowledge, and this seems to be how it is used in the Old Testament. In the book of Exodus, for instance, whenever God gave wisdom to a man or a woman, that person was both a teacher *and* craftsperson (hearer *and* doer). These people not only taught others how to make the priestly garments, the tabernacle curtains, the altar, the laver, the utensils, and so on; they also got their hands dirty doing it. In so doing, they were said to have God's wisdom which brings belief or theory and practice together. (See Exod. 28; 31; 35; 36.)

Paul was steeped in Old Testament understanding. His is a Hebrew mind. He knows that wisdom relates theory to practice. So he says that non-Christians make sense of the creation and live in it according to human or worldly wisdom, and that Christians see life and behave in it according to the wisdom of God in Christ. I do not want to be so presumptuous as to speak for the apostle to the Gentiles, but this is probably what Paul meant in the passage in his first letter to the Corinthians.

And the apostle is quick to recognize that between different wisdoms there will be communication difficulties. This is implied in his statements that different wisdoms look like "foolishness" to each other (1 Cor. 1:18, 20, 25). One wisdom looks at the beliefs, values, assumptions, practices, and lifestyle of another wisdom and ridicules them. But the other wisdom returns the compliment!

NEW AGE WISDOM

Perhaps you can see what I am leading up to. I promised you a model for understanding the New Age spirituality phenomenon. This is the "wisdom" model. People of the New Spirituality, like everyone else, have a way of making sense of the creation in order to live in it effectively. They have a way of seeing life that influences their actions. That is, they have a certain wisdom for life.

Christian writers of the New Spirituality such as Douglas Groothuis, Elliot Miller, Vishal Mangalwadi, James Sire, Brooks Alexander, and several others have spoken of this in terms of a worldview. Ronald Enroth, for example, has said, "Rather than a cult or a movement, the New Age is a philosophy, a worldview, a way of defining reality."[3] The idea of worldview is similar to what the Bible means by wisdom.

Let's see this in action with the laying on of stones. The person who does this is usually a meditator, who sees the universe as a sort of uncircumscribed metaphysical supply depot of invisible and impersonal spiritual life energies that can be tapped in to through meditation. This is a belief in the New Age meditator's wisdom, and it influences behavior. The person meditates in the hope of accessing the life energy and generating inner peace and harmony, enlightenment, healing, and so on. What, then, is the purpose of the stones and crystals? Crystals are laid on the body as a kind of spiritual power booster, to amplify the desired effects between the meditator and the cosmic energy. The procedure may perhaps be likened to the difference in reaction time and intensity between the oral and the intravenous administration of a drug.

The idea is that the crystals enhance the body's ability to tap the healing potential of the life energy. The scope of what is promised by way of getting rid of "dis-ease," as they often call it, is quite amazing. Crystal therapy purports to eliminate repressed memories, resolve mental conflicts, change attitudes, cleanse the body's auric energy field, sharpen psychic powers, direct telepathic messages, replace sadness and depression with joy and enthusiasm, provide transpersonal experiences, and much more. Crystals are also said to store memory, to be programmable by the human mind, and to teach. This is another part of New Age wisdom, and it influences behavior. Why meditate under your own steam if crystals will energize the process?

Here is a typical way in which this wisdom is expressed by an expert in the field. Katrina Raphaell has been working with crystals for twenty years. In her book *Crystal Enlightenment*, she describes the transforming properties of crystals and healing stones:

> Now with the knowledge of the healing power of stones, the physical, psychic and emotional bodies can be healed and aligned with the source of life energy-spirit. Crystal healing, through the art of laying on stones, is one of the most advanced and effective methods of cleansing the aura, releasing suppressed traumas, and connecting a person with his/her own source of truth and power. . . . Crystals and stones assist in [a] self-empowering process by increasing the amount of light present in the aura which stimulates and activates the more powerful subtle realms of being. In the practice of crystal healing, the stones become crystallised light forms that are placed onto vital nerve centres, chakra areas and plexus points on the body. The stones act as a catalyst to perpetuate and integrate more colour and light into the subtle energies of the human aura. This increased energy frequency serves to dissolve and dissipate the dark shadows of suppressed or un-released pain that cloud the aura, confuse the mind and dis-ease the body. The crystals can neutralise this negative charge and energy is released from the mental-physical blockages. The transforming power of the stones recirculates that energy to its source, to be used for con-scious purpose. It is then the responsibility of the individual receiving the healing to let go of the old and receive the new energy, using it to recreate a positive identity based in self-love and truth. This then be-comes the foundation upon which dreams are built and visions lived.[4]

It may sound convincing to someone whose wisdom is the New Spirituality, but according to biblical wisdom, it's certainly not the foundation upon which dreams are built and visions are lived.

THE GULF OF FOOLISHNESS

Christians who are steeped in biblical wisdom look at all this with amusement, though the meditator is absolutely serious about it be-cause it is a part of her wisdom, just as the Christian is absolutely serious about, for example, prayer. The problem is, Christians are going to have to learn how to overcome the gulf of "foolishness" between the two different wisdoms in order to communicate effectively in the world of the New Spirituality, where the marketplace is teeming with oddities. And this will occur only through increasing our understanding of the different wisdom and through learning how to communicate with its people in a way that makes sense to them. (This is the purpose of Part Two.)

We may find ourselves talking to people who visualize world peace, globe-trot on goddess pilgrimages, access their past lives, cleanse their auras, bond with their zygotes, eat macrobiotically, make friends with their tarot, search for their soul mates, undergo vision quests, achieve shamanistic communications, practice psychic self-defense, endure rolfing, recount visits with UFOs, consult transpersonal psychologists, arrange preconception contracts with their children, meditate on the fixed stars, explain their near-death experiences, and so much more.

In one way or another these activities are either derived from or engulfed by New Age wisdom. More seriously, so many seekers are sincerely searching for so much: answers to life's meaning, life after death, spiritual power, personal/social/global transformation, love, healing, ecological stability, (w)holistic health care—concerns that we all share. These, too, are part of a New Age wisdom. These seekers are trying their best to make sense of life and live in it as effectively as they can, as Christians are—but quite unlike Christians, people of the New Spirituality do it outside the context of the wisdom of God in Christ. Thus the communication problem runs both ways, as the New Age person also shakes his head in disbelief at Christian values, practices, lifestyle.

At the outset of this chapter I posed questions that now have an answer. It is one's wisdom that influences what is thought and the choices that are made, not only about practical matters like voting and schooling but about spiritual beliefs and interests as well. I also mentioned that wisdom brings together theory and practice; yet it also relates inner development to outer behavior, or interior matters to a person's outer realities. You will remember the difficult radio interview that I had with astrologist Marjorie Orr (see Chapter 5). Orr has gone through a process of inner transformation in which an interior dynamic of irrationality now influences her outer behavior.

Irrationality is part of the New Age wisdom, and this played havoc with that interview. We will see in Part Two how to get past such communication barriers.

Christians, therefore, have a certain wisdom for life, and non-Christian spiritual seekers do, too. The former is God's as found in Jesus Christ; the latter is worldly, human. In the two wisdoms, the basic assumptions about God, human beings, and the universe are very different. This difference poses great communication problems. Foolishness is the bridge that must be crossed between the two wisdoms so that effective communication can occur.

1 3

ACQUIRING
WISDOM

—∞—

THE THING TO remember about wisdom is that it is chiefly about people. Wisdom does not sit in a hermetically sealed can next to the tomato sauce. People hold wisdom, and we are mysterious, complex, and different from one another. What makes the wisdom model feasible and convincing for understanding the New Spirituality and its adherents is that it seems to be able to handle all the complexities, diversification, and contradictions that people and their beliefs are.

One of our Christian failings has been the rather simplistic way that some of us have looked at non-Christian spiritual seekers. They represent a highly complex and greatly diversified mosaic. There may be ways to simplify the evaluation, but there is a great difference between the simple and the simplistic. To treat a person and his wisdom simplistically is to invite disaster into the communication process.

Wisdom builds up in people from childhood. People, therefore, are not born with New Age wisdom any more than being born in a hospital gives you surgical skills. Wisdom is not a characteristic of birth; it is absorbed while growing up and throughout adulthood, too. John Peck writes that wisdom is much like a language we pick up as we go along, by hearing, by imitating, through others correcting us:

> Long before we go to school to "learn English" from textbooks we are already using it with considerable fluency. By that time it is so much

101

second nature to us that when we begin to study it from books, the way it comes to us as a subject looks strange, like algebra. We develop in the wisdom of our culture in the same way. . . . We do not formally learn our wisdom. We absorb it as we go along.[1]

By adulthood, our wisdom generally includes an unlikely collage of ideas, beliefs, values, habits, and practices that have been accumulating from many and diverse sources throughout life. That is because we absorb it from a host of diverse and at times inharmonious sources: family, friends, neighbors, associates, books, teachers, ministers, newspapers, television, films, music, videos, cult(ural) heroes, and others. The wisdom model, therefore, gives us a means by which to explain and speak to that diversity and incongruity.

DISSATISFIED SECULARISTS

In the West, absorbing wisdom has generally meant that a child takes on board values and beliefs that are materialistic, rationalistic, and naturalistic. In simple terms, this is what it means to become secular. This, then, has been the wisdom of the West for a long time. What is occurring in our day is that an *incoming, cosmopolitan spirituality that is unbiblical is informing and transforming existing secular wisdom, and this in turn is creating a New Age wisdom,* a wisdom in which nonbiblical kinds of spirituality are informing existing secular ways of looking at life and behaving in it. The seekers to whom we shall be speaking will have a wisdom that includes the cosmopolitan spirituality as well as secular ideas, values, beliefs, assumptions, and practices. This process of the transformation of secular into New Age wisdom is so important, and influences communication in such far-reaching ways, that we need to understand the transformation as best we can. For me, approaching it from a historical perspective has been very helpful.

Slowly in the 1950s and with increased momentum in the 1960s, Westerners rose satiated from the table of secular wisdom and stepped back to consider the feast in a new light. What is that gnawing hunger within us? they asked one another. What appetite is the current banquet unable to satisfy? It was not long before it became clear that they were empty in spirit. There was a spiritual hunger. As a result, many secularists who had once believed that they could reach their fullest potential without spiritual sustenance began to admit that the well-being of the human race could not be produced without it.

But let's go back a bit farther. Under the sway of eighteenth- and nineteenth-century Enlightenment thinking, the unseen, that is, the spiritual, the supernatural, and the religious, became the butt of public jokes everywhere in the West. The unseen became unthinkable, at least in the minds of those professing themselves wise, and by the late nineteenth century, large numbers of influential Westerners belittled religion and spiritual concerns. The unseen became unthinkable largely as a result of philosophical materialism, which was a controlling force of Enlightenment thinking. The dominant principle of philosophical materialism is not, as is frequently thought, an excessive regard, or penchant, for acquiring more and more possessions and wealth. This is but a fruit of it, because it sees physical well-being, worldly possessions, and affluence as a high value. The dominant principle of philosophical materialism is that "all that is seen will explain all that is."

Generations cut their intellectual teeth upon this presupposition, and so removed spirituality, the supernatural, and religion from being much of an influence in public life, in such areas as education, art, science, politics, and economics. The unenlightened could entertain themselves privately with religion—or superstition, as it was usually called—if they liked, but the wise saw it as a security blanket that they could do without.

Physical matter, with its movements and modifications, became the only reality. The entire universe, including thought, feeling, mind, and will, was said to be explainable by physical or natural laws. Science and technology seemed to confirm that this was a comprehensive principle for all of life, and a secular wisdom and the culture it produced arose to the glory of materialism.

Yet after nearly two hundred years of trying to bury a ghost—such is the exercise in futility demanded of human beings by materialism— droves of secular folk today are admitting defeat. Spiritual denial cannot be maintained. People can for only so long deny a God-given aspect of their nature before it turns to taunt them. And so such people are now confessing that "all that is seen *cannot* explain all that is." They feel that there must be more to life than meets the eye, and that materialism is not comprehensive enough to explain all of life. They wonder whether there is a spiritual dimension to life.

The spiritual pioneering began in awkward fits and starts with the rebellion of the Beats in the 1950s against a society whose "mind is pure machinery, whose blood is running money, whose love is endless oil and stone, whose soul is electricity and banks!"[2] The road (the search) was their symbol, and while traveling it, the Beats offered marijuana, meditation, and drugs as vehicles for spiritual enlightenment. Allen Ginsberg, Gary Snyder, and Jack Kerouac were three famous and articulate mouthpieces for the Beats, and they influenced many teenagers and others in the direction of Buddhist enlightenment. Though the media either castigated or made comic relief of them, their energy brought early ecological consciousness into the sixties rebellion, and their trail was followed by countercultural heavies such as Bob Dylan and Jim Morrison as their spirituality trickled into the West.

THE AGE OF AQUARIUS

Then in the 1960s, the beat intensified as the Age of Aquarius dawned. By the end of the decade millions of young people had created a counterculture that was a no-holds-barred search for spiritual food. This spiritual revival would have taken Western culture in the direction of a biblical reformation if the young people who pushed it had done so in the context of Christian spirituality. Yet not being Christian, the revivalists looked for beliefs that would not be morally demanding and yet have the appeal of things spiritual. Because they were raised human-centered rather than God-centered, bending the knee before a holy God was unthinkable to the secular sixties generation. Thus, as the East found its legs in the West, a generation of Aquarians rather than Christians was raised up.

I was one of the burgeoning multitude that embraced this spirituality without morality. I first became acquainted with it in 1963, as a teenager, when researching for a massive term paper on an Eastern religion called Brahmanism. By 1968, I was trading my short hair, oxford cloth shirts, continental trousers, pointed leather shoes, and generally clean-cut look for bell-bottoms, long hair, a Fu Manchu mustache, and the generally disarrayed look of someone on the road. And it is no secret that Buddhism, Hinduism, Taoism, occultism, mysticism, transcendental meditation, LSD, marijuana, hashish, Timothy Leary, Carlos Castaneda, Zen philosopher Alan Watts, Baba Ram Dass (formerly Richard Alpert, a fellow psychedelic drug researcher and Harvard professor with Leary), Paramahansa Yogananda (*Autobiography of a Yogi*), and countless other sources and people formed a kind of cosmopolitan spirituality that people like me enjoyed immensely. It gave us spiritual answers and did not interfere with our permissiveness.

This cosmopolitan spirituality included virtually anything and everything spiritual *except* what was Judeo-Christian, and by 1970, I was well on my way to being one of its spokespersons. I became an astrologer and a meditator. I contacted "spirit guides," was a vegetarian, and trained in psychic healing. But I did not cast away all my secular wisdom; I still clung, for instance, to nice clothes, new cars, money in the bank, and so on as high values.

That was the Aquarian counterculture, and as its spirituality was traveling through Western culture, informing and transforming what it could, it was the genesis for transmuting secular wisdom into New Age wisdom within our young lives. But what about transforming the rest of society? Why remain in cultural backwaters with the greatest thing since electricity and sliced bread? Surely there must be millions of others, in education, health care, politics, science, and business management, who are also dissatisfied with the prevailing materialist philosophy. Why not transform them, and transform society in the process? Good idea! We can have a new culture, a new age.

Leary's mandate, therefore, to "turn on, tune in, and drop out" was reversed: Aquarians cut their hair, shaved, and planned for the future—no mean feat for existentialists! They traded their Indian guru clothes and tie-dye for a more conservative look and reentered universities where they graduated with various degrees and Ph.D.'s. They took respected and influential positions, married, had children, and began amassing finances and networking with the like-minded. And as they did, they were influencing secular culture with the cosmopolitan spirituality. It was not a human conspiracy orchestrated by Aquarians en masse. It was the changing zeitgeist, and the more people there were who had burned out on secularism, the greater the potential for moving the changing zeitgeist along.

By 1980, it was becoming normative to be spiritually attuned. That was not, however, limited to New Age people, for in the 1970s the Jesus movement had won tens of thousands of converts to Christianity. Unfortunately, millions of others became interested in the spirituality now called "New Age." But then, most of it was not really new; it was a revival of ancient wisdom, pre-Christian faiths and pagan traditions, the old occult, Eastern mysticism, meditation, and the like. It was marketed as new because these beliefs and practices had been updated to late-twentieth-century thinking and language. This has been accomplished by changing the nouns of the game in order to present formerly taboo-sounding beliefs and practices in a euphemistic language that won't offend most people. It is also called new because it claims that many of its beliefs and practices have the support and even the ratification of science. This spiritual renaissance is documented in glowing terms by best-selling New Age writer Marilyn Ferguson in her landmark book *The Aquarian Conspiracy*, which was published in 1980.

The past few decades, therefore, have seen secular humanists being transformed into cosmic humanists: cosmic because they are now spiritual in orientation, and humanistic because they are still human-centered. For the first time in a long time nonbiblical spirituality on a massive scale is informing and transforming secular culture. A New Age wisdom is arising.

THE MIXTURE

Yet this is not the whole story, because it is not only ideas but people we are talking about. The effective communicator will seek clues about the degree to which a particular person's wisdom has turned New Age. This will help you in approaching the person and in knowing what topics may be best for conversation.

Let's draw an analogy from the artist's palette. Let the red paint represent secular wisdom, and let the blue paint be the incoming cosmopolitan spirituality. Start mixing a bit of the blue with the red, and it produces purple, a New Age wisdom. Yet it will not be fully purple because many streaks of red and blue will be mixing it up here and there, still on their way to a purple coloration, or perhaps even resisting it. Thus besides discerning what is purple, we want to be wise in knowing that the wisdom of the people we talk to will also comprise hues, tints, and shades of the old and the new. Even the most serious adherent of the New Spirituality, if a Westerner, will have been so thoroughly secularized previously that it is not possible for him or her to have a purely purple wisdom.

If you are having difficulty believing this, take yourself as an illustration. As a Christian, are you thinking and living out of a purely biblical wisdom? If you are tempted to say yes, it means that you are thoroughly consistent with the Father's will in everything you think and do, day in and day out. The New Testament, however, would not speak of the need for the Christian's mind to be renewed if we received the gift of a thoroughly biblical wisdom at conversion. There are still some humanistic or pagan or materialistic or other nonbiblical beliefs and values influencing our thoughts and behavior. These areas need renewal. Only one Person taught and lived a purely biblical wisdom, and He got crucified for it! If you would like to know how biblical your thinking is, ask yourself how close you are to getting crucified.

We shall, then, meet people who have various shades, or intensities, of the new wisdom, and this will affect how we speak to them. Remember the Waverley Market numerologist from Chapter 4? His is a very purple wisdom. Compare him to your friend or neighbor who has for the first time visited a Whole Life Expo or a holistic health-care exhibition. We could think of this as the first dab of blue in the red. Or you may find yourself in conversation with someone who has been practicing wicca for a couple of years. This person may have several dabs of blue mixing with the red, with the purple beginning to influence more areas of her life. The effective communicator will want to become sensitive to the intensity of purple coloration, and in Part Two, we shall discuss appropriate responses.

There is yet a further matter to be taken into consideration. The person may have had an upbringing that included religious beliefs, values, and practices as well as secular ones. The wise communicator will take this into consideration. A Christian only needs to start chatting with spiritual seekers to discover that not a few of them will have had a Christian denominational background, or Jewish, or some other religious influence on them. It may have been in the distant past, merely long-forgotten Sunday school memories, or it may be something that carried a lot of weight until recently, until some final straw . . . , and now the person sees much more hope in the New Spirituality. Or you may engage people in conversation who say they are Christian but who obviously hold to beliefs and values and practices of the New Spirituality, and this can be very confusing.

Immediately after the Nancy Reagan "astrology in the White House" exposé broke in May 1988, I was invited to do a number of

107

media programs. During two of them, one on radio and one on television, I debated with a prominent astrologer who unabashedly claimed to be a Christian. This created a context that was completely different from any of the other programs I did during those months.

Frankly, I would think twice about appearing in this unusual context again, for it meant engaging in two battlefronts concurrently. For the other programs, it was sufficient to have good reasons and a biblical apologetic for the case against astrology. In these two programs, however, I also had to have a case against the idea that someone could be both an astrologer and a Christian, and that case had to be both convincing and sensitive. I found it tiring to wield the sword in both directions. It was difficult to know when the astrologer would change direction and where I would have to pivot to when he did. The double context and short time frames left important areas unresolved for the audiences.

My point in mentioning this incident is to show that spiritual seekers may have religious as well as secular beliefs that are undergoing transformation by the cosmopolitan spirituality. Yet if those religious convictions are Christian, this may be a real boon to us because it may give us something solid to appeal to.

NEW AGE WISDOM IN CULTURE

Just before we move into Part Two, I would like us to see several examples of how philosophical materialism has dissatisfied secular people. This will help us identify areas where the cosmopolitan spirituality has capitalized on that dissatisfaction and so influenced people in the direction of New Age wisdom. (It may also be a motivation to some enterprising Christians to research mouth-watering biblical answers that are better than the cosmopolitan spirituality ever could be, and present them to people at the points of their dissatisfaction.) We will concentrate on only one area of damage done by materialism, that is its reductionist nature. It reduces, or diminishes, all of life to physical matter as the only reality.

Here is an example of a growing secular dissatisfaction in the realm of health care. The domination of philosophical materialism over medical science has reduced health care to a system that treats chiefly physical ailments and symptoms. Materialism has reduced the human being to a composite of minerals valued at the price of a couple of steak dinners. Materialism played upon the minds of many of those who nursed us, and it taught them to view us as flesh, blood, and bones only. Thus most doctors see their patients as living organisms of physical or natural laws that have been collected and understood from centuries of anatomical research.

I do not want to make light of having X rays taken and needles jabbed and scalpels inserted and drugs administered into this living example of physical laws. All that saved my life once. But when little or no treatment can be offered outside this health-care system by its professionals, and when it turns thumbs down to credible areas of chiropractic and osteopathic procedures, and when massive amounts of research have revealed that 60 to 85 percent of the symptoms we take to the doctor may be psychosomatic in nature, and when more and more people are realizing that a spiritual dimension to themselves affects the body, then a hue and cry arises for a health-care system that includes treatment of the whole person.

Today we hear people saying, "Hold on. All that is seen *cannot* explain all that is us. There is more to us than meets the eye, and we need a health-care model that understands our spirituality." The result is holistic health care and alternative or complementary medicine.

It must quickly be said that not everything that goes on under the umbrella of holism is wrong, though much of it is. But I will share with you an observation. In almost every seminar on holism that I conduct, I find myself engaged with two different kinds of Christian health-care professionals. There will be those who see no good in holistic health care and alternative medicine, and there will be those who argue tooth and nail for all of it. The first group seems unaware of the growing body of scientific research that may one day give validity to some areas of holism. The other group, if I may speak frankly, seems overly positive about holism because scientific enterprise, rather than biblical wisdom, acts as a final authority for them in the area of health-care alternatives.

Though the Bible ought to be the final authority over health care, what has tended to happen is that some Christian doctors and nurses have not evaluated holism through the wisdom of the Bible. Therefore, they may not understand the unbiblical spiritual ramifications of much of the holistic and alternative therapies that they are endorsing.

The idea, then, is not to evaluate and critique holism solely by the scientific enterprise; neither is it, as the first group has a tendency to do, to throw out the baby with the bathwater; nor is it to fully embrace holism because we now understand the failings of Western health care. Simply put, the idea is not to critique the East with the West or the West with the East; rather, it is to evaluate what comes to us from *both* camps from the point of view of the Bible. This, I think, must be part of the task, though it is a monumental one, of Christian health-care professionals. The church needs them to do some biblical thinking, speaking, and writing about the spiritual ramifications of holism. Too many people, Christians among them, are in bondage to holism because many of its beliefs, values, and practices are spiritual idolatries.

Another example of reductionism is in the area of nature and the environment. Materialist thought saw no point in treating the earth carefully; the earth was reduced to "simply a stockpile of raw *materials*"[3] that we were free to plunder. Modern-day piracy no longer has to go to sea to satisfy its greed, and as a result, havoc is wreaked upon the ecology—ecosystems are being destroyed, animals are becoming endangered or extinct, chainsaws run amuck in rain forests, chemicals contaminate water supplies, energy sources diminish, the air of the cities grows foul, nuclear waste (deadly for centuries or longer) cannot be disposed of properly, titanic oil slicks float on the oceans and wipe out shoreline marine life, and the threat of widespread skin cancer arises from Chernobyl-type nuclear disasters. Is it any wonder that in the face of these and other environmental nasties, people are looking for a nonmaterialist view by which to respect the planet and find a solution? This is what gave rise to the various attempts to arrive at a spiritual understanding of nature and the environment such as Green ecology and the Gaia hypothesis.

Again, it is not entirely rubbish. Of all people, Christians should be on the leading edge of the earth-stewardship movement. After all, we have been commanded to care for God's good earth (Gen. 1—3). In this respect the "Christian Ecology Link" in England and the "Evangelical Association for the Promotion of Education" in the United States, as well as up-and-coming organizations in other nations are trying to find the connections between ecological beliefs and the Christian faith.[4] Christians like these could become effective communicators to non-Christian spiritual seekers.

The vast and important field of education is another area of great secular dissatisfaction produced by materialist reductionism. In the United States for the past hundred years, nonprivate education has been largely about indoctrinating schoolchildren in what the state deems important. This has been politely called by the euphemism *socialization*. If the state is secular and greatly influenced by philosophical materialism, it becomes necessary to remove any and all references to religion or spirituality from your state schools so that the schools can become secularized themselves. Religious values in general, and Christian values in particular, place limits upon the amount of loyalty one can have toward the state. If you want to raise up citizens loyal to the state, you remove, usually through government legislation, religion and spirituality from your schools and so make education a process of indoctrinating children in what the state deems important for greater loyalty to it.

But in America this process of socialization has contributed to the social disintegration of the state's student bodies. There is great disrespect for teachers; a police presence is needed in some city schools to restrain and discourage theft and violence; an unyielding alcohol and drug abuse problem exists even among preteen schoolchildren; high student absenteeism and dropout rates increase; and much more. "Piecemeal reform of education is hopeless," shout many educators. "The whole basis of education is our problem. It is based on a set of assumptions that is no longer valid. We need a complete redesign of the way we teach our children."[5]

It is not surprising that parents and teachers are listening intently to the incoming cosmopolitan spirituality for advice about transforming education. Here we have room for just one example. When intellectual Jean Houston (adopted daughter of anthropologist Margaret Mead) spoke to five thousand secular curriculum developers at a national education conference in Florida, the gist of her speech, in no uncertain terms, was that the solution to the educational crisis was to establish a world curriculum that would incorporate spiritual motifs from around the world, ancient and modern, into every subject. Houston received several standing ovations during her address.

Here is a case where disgruntled secular educators are getting a few dabs of blue mixed into their old red way of seeing. They have seen that conventional secular education has failed, and they are looking for help from a spiritual direction. It will be difficult, however, to establish spiritual motifs from the world's religions in America's state schools because of the First Amendment appeal to the separation of church and state. It will be interesting to see how these educators proceed with Houston's model. At the least it will entail placing these motifs in an inoffensive nonreligious language to bypass the First Amendment barrier.

Things are very different in Great Britain, where religion and spirituality, especially Christianity, are legally welcome in state schools and sit happily under the protection of national legislation. Yet in Great Britain the cosmopolitan spirituality of the New Age is now up on its own two feet and taking great strides throughout the national curriculum (see Chapter 2). As long as these religious values and spiritual practices, whatever names they are given, further the aims of the state and produce increased loyalty to it, they will probably be allowed to stay.

Either side of the Atlantic, however, it behooves Christians, and especially Christian educators, to meet secular people at the points of their dissatisfaction with reductionist education and offer them biblical answers and alternatives.

To quote the writer to the Hebrews, "What more shall I say? Time would fail me to tell about" scientists, business managers, politicians, economists, filmmakers, writers, celebrities, young people, office workers, postal clerks, salespeople, your neighbors, and all the other secular persons who now realize that there is more to life than meets the eye. Because they are dissatisfied with materialism, it is no longer unthinkable for them to look for answers and alternatives from the cosmopolitan spirituality. Yet in closing this chapter I would like to emphasize that though their wisdom is turning purple, the wise communicator will want to keep in mind that it nevertheless has a lot of red remaining, and this will affect how they are approached and spoken to with a Christian message.

Even those who are thoroughly dissatisfied with materialism will not discard it completely, empty the house, and move in the new cosmopolitan spirituality the next day. Transforming a worldview does not work like that. Too much in the old way of seeing will continue to support them and commend itself to them; after all, they spent perhaps decades deriving meaning, value, purpose, cohesion, and integrity from philosophical materialism, and this is not so easily gotten rid of. It is somewhat like asking the person to give up an arm or a leg. (The tenacity of the old affects Christians after conversion as well. The reason we at times have such difficulty with the renewal of our minds is that there is still much in the old way of seeing and living that commends itself to us. Perhaps our Lord had something like this in mind when He mentioned that no one pours new wine into old wineskins.)

Because of the tenacity of the old, Christians may find themselves engaged with older spiritual seekers, for example, who may still hold to many of the ideas and values of early-twentieth-century secularism, such as Darwinian biological evolutionary theory, Freudianism, or perhaps even socialism. Persons raised in the 1940s and 1950s may still retain ideas and values from Human Potential thinking. Folk raised in the 1960s may still be influenced by the ideas and values of the political Left, humanistic psychology, or illegal drugs. And even younger seekers may cling to "me first" values and the "can do" individualism of the 1970s, or values clarification, self-help endowments, and so on.

This is all about people, and the wisdom model is about people, people who will carry with them many secular, or even religious, values, principles, and ways of doing things. Thus the wise communicator knows that she does not have to speak to the person only about New Age things. There are other ways to win these spiritual seekers to Christ. In speaking a Christian message, the communicator may discern that it is more effective to speak to some of the old red bits within the mix.

And it can be quite a mix. The "me first," "can do" individual may acquire from the cosmopolitan spirituality an even stronger sense of optimism and confidence about demonstrating human capabilities, as a once limited self-potential turns into infinite potential and expression through pantheistic monism. Similarly, ex-Aquarians turned New Age can retain access to altered states of consciousness (ASCs) through a host of available psychospiritual technologies that act as trigger mechanisms for exploring new spiritual territory, and thus be free of the legal ramifications and social stigma of hallucinogenic drug use. Or without fear of too much ridicule, biological evolutionists can cook up theories of spiritual evolution, spiced with centuries-old Hinduism, Buddhism, and Taoism to meet Western tastes. Or those therapists and their clients who are disgruntled with Freudian, behavioral, or humanistic psychologies may now opt for Jungian depth psychology or transpersonal psychology, where one learns how to integrate one's dark side into the personality, or how to lift the veil over human problems to reveal traumas and repressions (bad karma), even from one's supposed past lives.

And the beat goes on. Migration from tradition and materialism toward the new cosmopolitan spirituality is evident throughout the secular landscape. The rational is downplayed. New choices displace initial misgivings. Old limitations are broken through. Inner discoveries feel irrevocably right. Former taboos now line Main Street. Mystical experiences become the way home. Consciousness expansion and exploration provide the fuel. From psychic house parties to cutting-edge physics, impossible dreams become possible.

Whether the mind's true liberation is dawning is doubtful. What is clear is that a New Age wisdom is rising in the ascendant of Western culture to become the most prominent constellation of its night. This is our generation and the people to whom we will be speaking. So let us see how to do it.

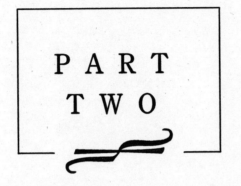

PART TWO

Harmless as a Dove

14

SUBMARINES AND
THEIR DESTROYERS

—⚈—

"EVERYONE SPEAKS WELL of the bridge that carries him over," says an ancient proverb. Non-Christian spiritual enthusiasts may speak favorably of the gospel when we have built communication bridges into their world. Without bridges, there will be no understanding of the gospel story. To paraphrase the teaching of the apostle Paul, "How can they put their faith in Someone whom they misunderstand? And how will they understand without communication?" (Rom. 10:14). Yet even between two old friends, communication is not always easy; a married couple celebrating their fortieth anniversary can still have misunderstandings. Is it surprising, then, to expect poor communication to occur between two persons who may not really know each other or who may feel suspicious, even hostile, toward each other?

Building communication bridges is not about reciting the right texts or applying the appropriate formula. Neither is it about learning a bag of tricks or compromising one's beliefs or engaging in a contest of wills. These and other ploys place strains on any existing bridges and may shatter attempts at building new ones. They can generate bitter feelings or animosity that can last for years. This is particularly true when a contest of wills leaves both parties more deeply entrenched in their positions.

Communication bridges are built as a result of forming relation-

117

ships with people. Some Christians find it difficult to accept this in the context of the alternate spiritualities. Yet relationships, and as a result effective communication, can be established with spiritual seekers without feeling that we have to capitulate to false views or forbidden practices. Such relationships are possible through principled conversation. That is, we will not compromise our convictions, but neither will we force them on someone else. We will not parrot Bible verses, but neither will we downplay the truth.

Most Christians know how irritating it can be when the Jehovah's Witnesses come a-knockin'. It is easy to sense that they do not really want to get to know you. They are usually more interested in reciting certain texts or the party line or whatever strategy they happen to be using in the area that day. Sometimes they want to recite to you whether you want to hear it or not! No one likes to be treated like this.

So we are not talking about gimmicks or formulae or proof texts or even programs per se. We are talking about and to people. Principled conversation will help us to remain morally responsible while developing relationships with people of the New Spirituality. Our Lord was like this, surrounding Himself with sinners without Himself falling into sin. Our principled conversation, too, will help us to be "in" but not "of" the world of the New Spirituality. So, how can we do this?

SUBMARINES AND WARSHIPS

Have you ever watched a World War Two film in which navy warships are searching for enemy submarines? What happens when a submarine spots these warships, either visually or on radar? Panic strikes. Sailors scurry to their posts, Klaxon horns blare ominously, the clamor inside the submarine becomes interminable, and over the intercom the voice of command cries, "Dive, dive!" While this is happening, the battleships turn and race toward their target with their big guns blasting away in an effort to stick a few holes in the submarine before it escapes underwater. Figuratively speaking, we Christians often look like enemy warships with guns a-blazin', and the spiritual seeker cannot move fast enough to get out of the way.

A Christian may lose a listener below the surface of communication. You are talking to the person, and suddenly the horizon is empty! The person has not physically disappeared, but you have lost contact with him intellectually. The person has been listening, conversation has been proceeding smoothly, but then you say or do something, probably unwittingly, that sends the wrong signal to the seeker's radar. Suddenly he sees you as dangerous and dives below the surface of communication. You have now lost the person intellectually. He is now insulated from what you are saying. He is no longer really listening. Soon he may be leagues away from hearing what you are saying. What we need to do, then, is to learn how to keep these "submarines" floating.

As we learn how to do this, I hope it will be entertaining as well as enlightening as we develop the "Submarine Communications Model." Illustration 1 shows how we may appear to non-Christian spiritual seekers, and of course, the question is then one of how to avoid appearing so menacing. If we look more inviting, perhaps we will be able to prevent the radar from urging, "Dive, dive!" The "Submarine Communications Model" offers ideas for creating conditions that will help us not to appear so threatening. It is about building strong and effective communication bridges into the world of the New Spirituality. It draws from the biblical model of wisdom (see chapters 12 and 13) in the context of principled conversation. Its primary aims are to help us change the way we appear and so send better signals in an effort to keep people interested in and listening to our message, that is, floating on the surface of communication.

We will begin by looking at eight characteristics that send the wrong signals and how to avoid them. But let me make three quick points about them. First, you may not find that all of these characteristics subvert your communication, though you will probably find, as I did, several relevant ones. Let these challenge you to transform your thinking. Second, this is not an in-depth look into these areas: it is intended to stir up thinking, in the hope that you will pursue some library or other books on topics you find relevant. Third, the chapter break in the middle of these eight subdivisions is merely a practical device to help us through this section. So, let's now look at these "alarming" signals.

1. Failing to relate to persons

Given certain problems or conditions, it can be tempting to forget that people are people. When you think about it, this is probably at the heart of all failed communication. People need respect and recogni-

I'd get out of the way of this battleship, wouldn't you?
Illustration 1

tion. They need to be able to trust. They probably have different backgrounds and viewpoints from ours, and so they may easily misunderstand and get frustrated, angry, or offended. In other words, as people they are prone to human reactions. They are not merely things or computers or abstract entities from "the other side." Neither are they mere objects upon which we "do" evangelization, as if they are a kind of project we are working on. Nor are they viewpoints, positions, or ideas. They are persons.

This may seem too obvious to need mentioning. But because it is people Christ saves, along the way we cannot forget that our relationships are relationships with people, which places us in the realm of the complex, of the unpredictable, of strong emotions, and of likes and dislikes. It may not be as easy as we think, therefore, to show respect and recognition or for trust to develop. Let's think about these three qualities for a moment.

Concerning trust: if we want spiritual seekers to trust Jesus Christ as Savior, we need to ask what hindrances we may be placing in the way of that. For example, are we making it difficult for them to trust us as the messengers of Christ? Such an incongruity is disgraceful. Why should they trust Christ if they cannot trust us? How will trust develop if in conversations we are continually attacking what gives the person's life meaning, value, integrity, and significance, that is, wisdom, which provides the person with a sense of coherence, purpose, and security in beliefs and actions? I do not mean that beliefs do not need to be discussed, and often critically. We will go on to that. Here we are talking about developing trust, and it is hard to see how that will occur if our guns are continually ablaze against what gives our audience meaning and purpose. When I was a teenager, we had a saying if we wanted to argue to prove who was right: "Jump on my chest. We'll see who's best!" However, this was said with levity between close friends, not in a budding relationship.

There may be some pride in our hearts if we resort to confrontation all the time. We may be building up self by tearing the other person down in our minds. Let us be alert to the possibility. And let us not assume that we Christians have it all together. In our building of communication bridges God will be helping us to grow as Christians, in patience, compassion, caring, insight, and so on. In other words, everyone benefits from a relationship of trust.

Concerning respect: non-Christian spiritual seekers have a value as people so high that Jesus Christ died for them. We think highly of silver and gold—temporal inanimate objects. Surely we ought to treasure those for whom our Lord died. Respect is about courtesy and appreciation. It looks past the spiritual baggage and discovers the person behind it.

Sometimes we fail at respect because we rarely give the other person opportunities to say anything. We may be too busy doing all the talking. If so, we are not listening, and the conversation is strictly one-way. This attitude may betray that we do not think the person has anything important to say. What happens, then, is that we give out too much information at once. Overloading circuits blows fuses, and communication breaks down as a result. Being short and sweet in conversation, however, and using discretion, builds respect.

Concerning recognition: a person's value is worth recognizing. New Age people are not total idiots. Sin aside, they are people with strengths, insight, and normal ways of living. We should recognize and affirm, rather than ignore and downplay, what is of value in them.

Recognition comes when reassurance is given in an area where the person is obviously right. Seekers have some things going for them, and your taking time to affirm these brings recognition. Christians often have difficulty offering recognition to outsiders, so when recognition begins to take place, it can be a powerful means of building a communication bridge.

2. Identifying with a caricature

Our caricature of spiritual seekers may prevent us from relating to them as persons, and vice versa. They may perceive Christians as behind-the-times Bible-thumpers who are narrow-minded, unintelligent, superstitious, or a host of other discrediting adjectives. But let's talk about our caricature of them. Effective communication is not made of the stuff of political cartoons or of flippant wisecracks or stereotypes.

Caricatures are often created by labels, and labels can be handy excuses for remaining intellectually sloppy or lazy. Christians frequently say, "Oh, that's New Age," but they might find it difficult to describe what New Age is. Using it makes them appear informed, but it may be a label without content.

Labels can also be depersonalizing. I once read about a psychologist—he must have been quite honest—who told of how he did a Ph.D. in advanced labeling (clinical psychology). He said that before going to the university he might have categorized someone's thinking as "weird" or "screwy," but after getting his degree, he would have said "neurotic" or "psychotic"! He concluded that such words might sound more scientific but are no less alienating and depersonalizing. It is not that labels are necessarily wrong. It is a matter of usage; tools for thinking or devices for depersonalizing?

Caricatures, too, are often about expectations. We frequently alter our behavior on the basis of our expectations. If we have expectations based upon a caricature, we shall probably be responding to a carica-ture rather than to a person. We may even be acting in Christian caricature ourselves, which will probably heighten the tension of the conversation because it will affect the behavior of the other person toward us.

There is no such thing as caricature-to-caricature communication. Here, then, our task is twofold: to dispel any Christian caricature that may exist in the minds of non-Christian spiritual seekers and to get rid of any caricatures of them that we may have in our minds. So it is a two-way street, but I am afraid the onus is on us to start down the road first.

The words *Christian* and *Christianity* are bad labels these days in much of the media. We must learn how to get around this. In the 1970s and early 1980s, it was different. Then it was fairly trendy to be into Christianity. Charles Colson, for example, had no problems popular-izing his testimony book, even though it was titled *Born Again*. And that was the period when even American presidents, beginning with Jimmy Carter in 1976, publicly professed they were born again. Things are the other way around now, which poses a whole new set of problems.

Christianity is about following Jesus, and He is still calling people to follow Him. But He uses His Christian messengers to do this. The trouble today is that Christianity looks so weird to most non-Christian spiritual seekers that they are saying (to adapt Nathanael's words when he was called by Andrew to follow Jesus), "Christianity! Can any good thing come from there?" (John 1:46).

There is a kind of vague background Christianity in Western culture now; it is a distortion, but that is all people know about it. It is a kind of rumor, and it has changed the true character of Christianity into a caricature. Most people, therefore, haven't a clue as to what true Christianity, with its love and teaching and Savior, really is. No wonder there is little or no interest in what the church stands for. In dispelling the caricatures, you will be perceived as you really are, and Christianity will be perceived as it really is.

Sometimes you will have to be fairly creative to get around the Christian caricatures. During one seminar I was doing on the New Age, a Christian asked me what he could say to his friend who was an astrologer. When I asked if the person would come to the meeting the next day so that I could speak to him, I was told no, because the astrologer always refused to attend Christian gatherings. I then asked if he would mind speaking to me by phone. The next day I was told that he would talk to me by phone, and later I had a long conversation with him that way. That approach was much more profitable than me trying to relate information secondhand. Another time a missionary friend of mine and I met some members of a band in a British pub, to talk to them about Jesus, because they would not come on our turf. So you may have to be creative.

To have communication, both persons must be getting through to each other; they are not engaged in communication if they are speaking to each other's caricature.

3. Sounding like the demanding boss

If you want to get off on the wrong foot with non-Christian spiritual seekers, this is the perfect way, as I have discovered. It took me a long time to stop sinking submarines this way.

The Christian sounding like the demanding boss easily threatens the listener, who then dives below the surface of communication. Here is the judge, the dogmatist, or the professor, looking down his nose from behind the podium, lecturing and so creating distance between himself and his audience. The demanding boss is full of "do not's," "noes," "must not's," "ought not's," and the like. He lays down rules and laws. He is generally hypercritical and negative. He points the finger, often with a horrified look, and says, "You must put a stop to that!" His attitude is that such and such is "nonsense," "stupid," "ridiculous." A person would never know that a Christian is someone with good news when he is being overwhelmed with so much bad news. On the lips of the demanding boss, there is no gracious speech seasoned with salt. The demanding boss often produces a false, heartless submission within the listener and walks away feeling mollified. Or conversely, he may have promoted further defensiveness to Christianity or even rebellion.

To the spiritual seeker, the demanding Christian boss may remind her of a parent who used to criticize, lecture, or talk down to her when she was a child. Such a Christian is stirring up bad memories.

SEEKER: I've been taking yoga classes for three months.
CHRISTIAN: Oh no! That's not a good idea. Don't you know where that stuff comes from? It's . . .

Or:

SEEKER: I'm learning about channeling.
CHRISTIAN: But that's dangerous. It's forbidden by the Bible. You're not supposed to contact demons. That's . . .

The problem here is that the seeker, now an adult, is hearing, "Go and cut the grass," or "Go and tidy up your room," or, "Get back to bed." To this he is thinking, *Now look here. You can't tell me what to do!* Such a person had enough criticism and parental lecturing as a child. We do not want to set ourselves up in that role.

When there are responses like the above, the Christian is mistaken if he thinks the other person is listening. Rather, it appears as if the Christian is blasting away, so the seeker is going to dive a safe distance away from such firepower. A Christian may not even see himself this way. He may in all sincerity be doing his level best. Nevertheless, the net result is the raising of a communication barrier or the shutting down of lines of communication that may already have been established. The other person perceives an attack and is sure to get out of the way. He thinks: *Here it comes again. Another lecture about what I ought not to be doing. He's going to correct me like my father did. He's going to force me into something, like my demanding boss.*

Some people have had so many terrible experiences with demanding Christian bosses that I wonder if they think there is any other kind of living epistle. These people are often well submerged at the start of any conversation with Christians. Having been offended or wounded, they are going to make certain they are well insulated and protected in any Christian context. The thing to do, of course, would be to work to refloat these people, to raise them back onto the surface of communication. Unfortunately, what generally occurs is shown in Illustration 2.

"The submarine has been located underwater. Can't use the big guns now, but man the battle stations and drop the depth charges."

I have yet to discern why some Christians think this is a way to refloat submarines. If you discover a New Age seeker below the surface of communication, or if one is about to dive, work to correct the situation. Even if it means taking a moment to apologize for upsetting the person, conversational equilibrium must be restored, or you may as well pack up and go home.

I was once invited by two friends to speak privately to a medium and the woman to whom he was a mentor. After the five of us had had a fairly reasonable and productive conversation for about an hour, one of my friends accidentally—yet wrongly—called the medium's character into question in a very sensitive area. Though my friend apologized immediately for his faux pas, I am not sure that the medium, or the woman, was ever fully with us afterward on the surface of communication.

Better still, rather than making it necessary to have to restore communication, try to get off on the right foot and remain there. Be harmless as a dove. This means having adult-to-adult communication, which engages both parties in a mature and objective appraisal of whatever subject is being considered.

SEEKER: I've been taking yoga classes for three months.
CHRISTIAN: That's interesting. I know a person who took yoga, but she's not doing it anymore. How much time each week do you spend on it? Do you think it's helping you?
SEEKER: It's much more than just exercising. There's a lot of meaning in the positions, and some of them are pretty strange. I spend a couple of hours a week at it and still find some of the positions difficult to get into. I don't know if it's really helping me or not.
CHRISTIAN: I've never had an interest in it myself. What got you interested?

Depth charges destroying a
submarine underwater: an odd way to try
to refloat it!
Illustration 2

Or:

SEEKER: I'm trying to progress spiritually as much as I can, so I'm getting into channeling.
CHRISTIAN: I recently heard someone talking about that. Doesn't it put you in contact with spirit beings?
SEEKER: That's right.
CHRISTIAN: What does that involve? I've never talked to anyone who was actually doing it.

These are adult-to-adult exchanges, and communication is taking place. And believe me, when it is, the seeker thinks: *This is different. Here is a Christian who is willing to talk to me. He is not lecturing me. He is giving me space to say what I think and feel. I think I will listen to him.* The effect? A communication bridge is being built.

Coercion is not communication. People do not like it, and it can produce undesirable results even if the people know that what they are hearing is right. People may reject what they know is true if they think they are being coerced into following it.

At one time I was in a small group-counseling context once a week for three months. It was led by a wise Christian psychiatrist, and I am thankful that it was. One afternoon a situation arose in which a rather demanding-boss type of person in the group said that he had something important to say to me. Mike, the psychiatrist, being considerate of my thin skin, asked me if I was willing to listen to what this person had to say. I agreed to listen, and I must admit that what came forth, though aggressively given, was accurate. You could have heard a pin drop afterward when Mike said, "Charles, you know that what [he] said is true, don't you?"

I said I did, and then Mike continued, "But what [he] doesn't understand is that you're not going to receive it, are you?"

I replied that I was not.

To which Mike said, "Would you be willing to explain to the group why you won't receive it from him?"

I burst out, "Because I don't like being forced. [He] rubs me the wrong way. [He's] being demanding. I have never liked being forced, and if I think I'm being forced, I will usually refuse to cooperate."

That was quite an eye-opener for the brother, and probably the rest of the group as well! It did not cross his mind that to me he sounded like the demanding boss or the lecturing parent, and he was astounded to discover that he could share a valid insight and have it rejected because of the way it was delivered even when the listener knew it was true. But there you have it.[1]

So try to be conversational. Think about how you talk to your spouse or a friend concerning a film or a restaurant you would like to go to. Think about how you would discuss getting a pay raise from your employer, or the way in which you would agree with a stranger for the price of a house. You won't get very far by dictating your demands to your boss or the home owner!

4. Expressing inappropriate emotions

Emotions and feelings play a big role in communication. Some communication headaches are not relieved merely by understanding a person's thinking. Getting to know a person's beliefs, assumptions, and viewpoints is to become acquainted merely with ideas. But people are emotional as well as thinking beings.

Because both parties bring a mix of emotions to the relationship, emotions that can help or hinder communication, they will need to examine how they feel toward each other. So, how do you feel about non-Christian spiritual seekers? The answer can sometimes be discovered by examining what you think about their world. Thinking often influences feelings, which shows the relevance of our earlier consideration of caricatures and labels. Some Christians exhibit an unhealthy fear of the world of the New Spirituality. Some are nervous, suspicious, upset, worried, or angry. Others are confident and relaxed. The models for thinking about the New Spirituality that we discussed during the Inter-Mission may generate certain of these feelings, and you may want to peruse that section again if you are wondering about yours.

A suspicious or fearful Christian may trigger an angry response from a seeker, who, thinking she is under attack, may become defensive and stop listening. She may even respond with inappropriate emotions of her own. Your tone of voice is important here. If your voice sounds like rifle shots firing at a target, how do you think the listener will react? But if you have control over the tone of your voice, you are probably in control of your emotions. The best tone is perhaps the one in which it is evident that you are teachable, for it sends the signal of a willingness to be corrected if wrong.

Some people do not think that feelings, emotions, and tone of voice matter. A teacher, for example, may say, "I'm interested only in my students learning the subject. I don't care what they feel." I had an Algebra Two teacher who must have had this attitude. After several weeks of trying to tell her that I was really struggling with the subject, she remained unconcerned with what I felt, and I dropped the class.

Emotions can speak even louder than words at times. They can communicate a great deal, especially in forming first impressions. With highly strung people, feelings or the way you communicate may be more important initially than spoken words. Should emotions start to run high, step back. Find ways to defuse. Perhaps it would be best to make your feelings known before emotions run high. Being honest about your feelings with the other person (with yourself, too) can help maintain a conversation's equilibrium. Talking to the other person about your feelings is all right. It does not hurt to say, "You know, I get the feeling that we are misunderstanding each other. Do you feel this way?" Or "I'm sorry for getting upset. I suppose I'm a bit uptight and nervous." It will feel good to the person who hears you say this. Verbal conflicts that seem irredeemable can be cleared up through the sharing of feelings.

You may find that in some situations the other person will feel free to pour out his feelings after you have expressed yours appropriately. If so, let him. Try not to react. It may be the first time that he has ever felt free to vent his frustrations—perhaps about Christianity—to a Christian. Try to hold your emotions in check and really listen. His feelings may be real barriers to the gospel, and if he can get these out of the way, he may then open up to listen to a Christian. His complaints may even be on target. If so, it is foolish to downplay them, which will only make matters worse.

Recognition is the key here. Humbly acknowledge any validity in the person's observations, and if possible, seek to bring redemptive change to the complaints (more on this later). An unwillingness to agree with someone who is obviously right is a surefire way to lose the person below the surface of communication, but recognition helps establish trust and keeps the person floating.

Inappropriate emotions may also prevent us from gaining the grace of empathy. It is difficult to see how we can be empowered by empathy when fear, suspicion, anxiety, or anger has taken possession of us. Empathy feels a sensitivity toward people that helps us tune in to them more fully, rather than the partial focus that comes from zeroing in only on the facts.

We may find ourselves conversing with people whose New Age-ism becomes a peripheral matter because they are hurting deeply. These people will need empathy much more than a discussion about "isms." When we approach our Lord when we are hurting, we know that He has felt what we are feeling and that He will care for us. Will a hurting seeker feel our empathy when she approaches us? If the situation requires empathy more than facts shared coldly and objectively, which of these two kinds of communication will be more valuable for helping the other person feel understood?

The day one of my brothers died unexpectedly, an aunt kept whispering in my ear, "Praise the Lord, Charles. Praise the Lord. He's with Jesus. He's with Jesus." It was not the words but the fact that she had her arms around me and was grieving: *that* communicated.

As the saying goes, empathy walks in the other person's shoes. If the listener thinks, *I'm still not sure what he is trying to say, but I can tell by his feelings that he is trying to understand and help me,* then your emotional sensitivity is building a communication bridge, over which you may get a hearing later for the facts.

Empathy is most likely to be expressed when we have experienced something similar to that of the other person—the death of a loved one, divorce, separation, childlessness, abusive parent, deceased parents, chronic unemployment, disease, car accident, property loss, time spent in prison, rehabilitation, counseling, and so on. Yet empathy can be developed apart from shared experiences through our imitation of God in Christ. In the father heart of God and in His Son, empathy finds its highest expression. God is "the Father of mercies [compassion] and God of all comfort" (2 Cor. 1:3). The writer of Hebrews states that in Jesus Christ we have a High Priest who is sympathetic with our weaknesses (4:15) because He has been made like us in every way (2:16–17). This is the God who, when He became incarnate in Jesus Christ, entered our frame of reference to share in our pitiful condition. The grace of empathy awaits to be gained by those who will be imitators of this.

1 5

SETTING OFF
THE ALARM

—∿—

THIS CHAPTER CONCLUDES the section on eight characteristics of conversation that are likely to drive non-Christian spiritual seekers below the surface of communication. In the previous chapter we considered failing to relate to persons, identifying with a caricature, sounding like the demanding boss, and expressing inappropriate emotions.

5. Corking our ears

Sometimes we are not really listening. This frustrates the person who is speaking. Think of the times you have noticed that someone was not really listening to you. All of us have been exasperated by those conversations in which we are hoping to be understood, but the listener is using her mind elsewhere in the universe rather than in the discussion at hand. Being off in another world is a kind of insult and disrespect. It is a disinterested silence; the person is aloof, perhaps wishing she were somewhere else, or bored, or thinking how she will spend the next paycheck. A form of nonlistening that I find annoying is when it occurs to me that the other person has made up his mind that he already knows what I am going to say (maybe he's right!), and while I am talking, he is arranging his response. Instead of really listening to what I am saying, he can't wait to talk.

Let us be wise so as not to fall into such offensive demeanors. A good listener listens actively. She pays attention. She remembers what she has heard: the other person's name, whether she is working or unemployed, married or single, children, what spiritual interests she has, and so forth. How embarrassing to be arranging another meeting and have to stop to say, "What did you say your name was?" Surely the person must be wondering what else you were not listening to. James 1:19 says, "Let every man be swift to hear, slow to speak." We have two ears but only one mouth. Perhaps this is God's way of indicating that we should listen twice as much as we speak.

Listening will help you get a feel for the other person's emotions and an understanding of his perceptions. What you are hearing might be distorted or muffled by some wrong inner associations (caricatures?) that you have about the New Spirituality, which you may have brought into the conversation. If this is the case, you are not really hearing the person; you are hearing what your inner associations set you up to hear. Try to suspend wrong inner associations and focus on what the person is actually saying. This may be difficult if you are fearful or suspicious. If you are confident and relaxed, you could gently interrupt with, "Is this what you mean . . . ?" Or "I'm not sure I understand. . . ." His answer to responses like these could help reveal if you have any wrong inner associations.

The Christian who is listening is discerning. If he is unsure about what is being said, he asks for clarification. The Christian who is listening is therefore learning. The person will respect your gentle questions. She will realize that you are not trying to score points, respond mechanically, or recite. She will see that you are trying to understand *her*. (For Christians who do not as yet have a knowledge of the New Spirituality, and so shy away from it for fear of getting in over their heads, finding some seekers to listen to may easily make up for that. It could be a great crash course!)

Note, too, that understanding is not agreeing. Once the person has indicated that you have understood her, you are then free to disagree gently. You do not even have to like what you are hearing. What is important is that you hear what is being said, and that you do not let inappropriate emotions hinder any response you may choose to make. Without understanding, how are you going to persuade someone in a direction other than the way she has been going? Without understanding the person's direction, how shall you convince a seeker of another way? Understanding is a prerequisite to persuasion, and listening is a great qualifier.

Listening actively will also help you discern the person's attitude toward Christianity without having to ask. Perhaps there is no problem, but if the seeker has a chip on the shoulder, a bad attitude, a negative experience, a misunderstanding, or bitter feelings, it could easily contribute to failed communication. Listening will help you discern attitudes without having to embarrass the person about them. You can then work redemptively to get these hindrances out of the way and so establish a relationship.

In *Life Together*, Dietrich Bonhoeffer wrote, "One who cannot listen long and patiently will presently be talking beside the point and never really be speaking to others, albeit he is not conscious of it." And you may have to listen for a long time indeed. Even if you are well versed in the subject, your first few times in the presence of non-Christian spiritual seekers does not automatically guarantee that you will have something to contribute. The ministry of listening, then, may be the best service you can render by way of a contribution.

Of course, the ideal is that seekers will also listen to us. I was talking with John Stott once about this, and he called the idea "reciprocal listening," saying that both parties grow from the conversation. I like that. Both persons further their understanding; both gain. Again, we come to this thing as disciples, that is, as learners. We will also gain insight from the Holy Spirit, who will be speaking to us about the person. After all, He is listening!

There are times, however, when no matter how hard you try, you may not be able to listen because the seeker is playing a mind game with you or arguing. This once happened to me when I was doing a public meeting on the New Age in London. After the meeting ended, a woman who was deeply involved in *A Course in Miracles* struck up a conversation with me. She began the conversation by asking me what I thought was wrong with it. I took her question to mean that she would be interested in my answer, but just as I began to reply, she cut me off sharply. I tried again, and she cut me off again. This occurred many times in the space of a few minutes. She never let me get more than a sentence or two into my response. It was plain rudeness, and I broke off the conversation because she did not really want to know what I thought. It was most likely a game to her to see if she could rattle me.

6. Underrating irrationality and passivity

A Christian's inability to work around these two intellectual/spiritual dynamics can easily hinder communication. These dynamics were the topics of chapters 5 and 6 where we saw that people take on board passivity of mind through New Age meditation, and that the irrational offers them a way of transcending the rational in their efforts at spiritual evolution, enlightenment, and mystical experience.

During the communication process, both passivity and irrationality are very touchy radar sensors within people of the New Spirituality. Both dynamics must be kept in mind when we are speaking to these enthusiasts. During a conversation, passivity is touchy to aggressive Christian witnessing, and the irrational is hypersensitive to rational and reasonable spiritual answers. We want to be careful that we do not send wrong signals to either of these dynamics and so lose the person, whose radar may be saying, "Danger, danger! Close the hatches. Guard all entrances. Dive! Dive!"

Because passivity and irrationality act as strong radar against a biblical Christian witness, it is essential that we learn how to outwit them. One thing can be quickly said about this: it does not involve us in becoming passive and irrational! The following chapters offer some solutions to this problem.

7. Ignoring New Age beliefs and practices

By this point in the book, it will be obvious that communication entails some knowledge of a person's beliefs and practices, so I do not want to be repetitive. Several ideas about the necessity of research, however, are worth spending a few minutes on here.

Some Christians find themselves outfoxed in conversation simply because they refuse to admit that they are in over their heads. It is not wrong, necessarily, to find ourselves in this situation; yet because it embarrasses us, we have a tendency to try to save face rather than ask for help.

A spiritual seeker is probably well informed about certain subjects about which a Christian may know little or nothing. Yet the Christian may try to appear as if she is well informed. Worse still, she may think that her scanty knowledge about the subject is enough to justify herself as well informed. The seeker, however, spots such pretense a mile off. (Recall the times you have seen the holes in someone's position.)

Christians who put up false fronts do not earn the right to be heard. They remind me of a gaggle of thirteen-year-olds who traipse out of the school library as if they are the repository of all knowledge and are now set to take on their teachers.

Rather than foolishly putting up a front, a mature response would be, "I'm not too familiar with that. Could you say more about it?" Or "That's a new one to me. What is it?" Sincere vulnerability such as this is often missing from our relationships. We have not been taught how to be honest about our ignorance. Yet for those who desire to be as harmless as doves in communication, it is a characteristic worth cultivating.

I think it would be helpful, by way of example, to cite a specific area (it's a big one, and controversial) in which Christian conversation with New Agers often goes haywire precisely because of the above tendency. And along the way we'll try to take hold of some principles to help us respond more appropriately. I have in mind holistic health care, or alternative and complementary medicine.

We may not like the case put so plainly, but we Christians have a tendency toward pride in the area of holism. We read one or two Christian books on the subject, if that, and suddenly think we are qualified to instruct holistic health-care professionals. I am certainly aware of the specious rationales, the groundless testimonies, the preposterous hyperbolizing, and even the dangerous occult entanglements found in holism. However, I am also aware of Christians who are only superficially informed about holism and yet have decided that they know it all. We must be wise enough to see the whole picture and humble enough to recognize any strengths in holism. For example, it calls our attention to the need to develop a health-care system that includes body, mind, and spirit. And there is also the need to sort out any scientific and medical validity holism has apart from New Age philosophy and spirituality.

Let's get down to some details. Take crystals as a case in point. There are valid and false uses of crystals. A false use of crystals would be what assigns a mystical or spiritual meaning to them in which someone then places his trust. In biblical language, this makes an idol out of a created thing; it exchanges the truth of God for a lie, as one worships and serves the created thing rather than the Creator (Rom.

1:25). The ultimate horror is that if the idolatry is not repented of, at some point demonic bondage can result. (This is something we may want to learn how to communicate to non-Christian spiritual enthusiasts.)

Here is how I have come to understand this, and you may want to be thinking of a way to put it in your own words to be able to express it to spiritual seekers. Throughout its first chapter, Genesis says that the things God created were "good." Whether animal, vegetable, or mineral; whether trees, birds, or fish; whether sun, moon, or stars: it was all good.[1] There is nothing intrinsically evil about leaves or rocks or birds and bees. To this, the Christian will readily agree. Yet let's get more specific. What if the leaves are herbs and the rocks crystals? Is there anything intrinsically evil about them? No, God created them good. It is in giving them mystical meanings that the use of herbs or crystals goes haywire.

Another example is the palm of the hand. I rather like the palm of my hand. It is a good thing. I wash with it, shake hands with it, steer my car with it. It is used in hugging my wife, in holding a knife and fork so that I can eat, and in receiving an honorarium! But when the palm reader comes along and convinces me that there is a spiritual meaning to my palm, that by it I can read my future, the good thing turns sour, and I would be heading for idolatry if I believed it.

So, too, with the moon and the stars. God created them, and they are good. Astronomy is the science in which they can be studied. But when I was an astrologer, I made idolatry of the stars and the planets and offered people their hidden meanings.

Jesus said that when we know the truth, it shall make us free. This truth about created things is very freeing indeed. It means that my wife can hang Swarovski crystals from the kitchen window so that we can see the colorful rainbow designs made by the morning sun shining through them. This is a valid, or natural, use of crystals, and there is nothing wrong with it. Crystals were used in early radio sets, and they are occasionally in use today in chemistry, electronics, photography, and biophysics. Such uses are natural and proper. It is another story entirely when people use or wear crystals because they believe in their supposed mystical meanings.

So, too, with herbs. The herbalist who works strictly within a natural use of herbs in a medically valid way is on the right track. Yet in much of what goes under names like homeopathy, macrobiotics, or

Bach flower remedies, there exist mystical and spiritual meanings, interpretations, and uses of herbs, foods, and the flowers of plants, trees, and bushes. A natural practitioner who believed this would put himself in jeopardy through his idolatrous misuse of the good things of God's good creation.

The rainbow is another case in point. I have met Christians who seem scared to death of rainbow symbols, often after reading Constance Cumbey's best-seller *Hidden Dangers of the Rainbow*. Yet there is nothing wrong with a rainbow; it is a beautiful and good phenomenon that God has created, and it carries with it a covenant promise from God (Gen. 9:8–17). This goes wrong when the world of the New Spirituality appropriates the rainbow and gives it a mystical or occult meaning. Christians ought to be speaking into this unfortunate situation to recover its goodness. As someone aptly said to me, "God holds the copyright on the rainbow." Yes, and on all the other things He created as well.

The previous paragraphs merely highlight areas where we may have put up false fronts. As Christians, we need to do much more thinking and research. Sorting through medical and scientific writings, as well as the Bible and relevant Christian material, will help us to build strong and effective communication bridges. We will not have to try to save face, and it will give us topics for conversation that seekers never thought of. We need to answer questions such as: What else in the Bible is relevant to this? Is there any scientific medical validity and natural use of acupuncture, acupressure, shiatsu, reflexology, iridology, or other complementary medicines? As to the latter, at the time of this writing and after much research (I am not through yet), I have my doubts. And because the jury is still out, at least in my mind, I am not a believer in them. And until, or if, I am ever at peace with any possible validity that may be discovered in any of these practices, I will stay away from their use if they are ever recommended to me as treatments.

The importance of research is therefore unquestionable. It is even commanded in the Bible. Consider these two overlooked passages from Deuteronomy:

> If you hear it said about one of the towns the LORD your God is giving you to live in that wicked men have arisen among you and have led the people of their town astray, saying, "Let us go and worship other

gods" (gods you have not known), then you must inquire, probe and investigate it thoroughly. And if it is true and it has been proved . . . (13:12–14 NIV).

If a man or woman living among you in one of the towns the LORD gives you is found doing evil in the eyes of the LORD your God in violation of his covenant, and contrary to my command has worshiped other gods, bowing down to them or to the sun or the moon or the stars of the sky, and this has been brought to your attention, then you must investigate it thoroughly. If it is true and it has been proved . . . (17:2–4 NIV).

In other words, if we hear that any sort of counterfeit spirituality has appeared in our towns *or* within the covenant community itself (note the slight but significant variation in contexts), we are not to run around spreading rumors, because they may be untrue. Quality research is to be done to sort fact from fiction, and then to refute the rumors and deal with the facts.

There is an idea floating around in some Christian circles that outside research is unnecessary and that the only requirement for an effective witness is a knowledge of the Bible. To support this, the story is told of bank personnel in the United States who attend a two-week course to learn how to spot counterfeit money. These bank personnel do not receive the kind of instruction one might suppose. They never study any counterfeits. They concentrate on the features of real money. There are too many ways to counterfeit, so the theory is that by becoming skilled in the genuine article they will then be able to recognize any counterfeit that passes through their hands.

I like this as an illustration of how we ought to be getting to know our Lord and the Bible so that we become spiritually discerning (1 Cor. 2:14–15; Heb. 5:11–14). But this is only half the picture if what we seek to do is communicate what we know to non-Christian spiritual seekers. Because they do not believe in the authority of the Bible, we will need to use facts from other sources that are authoritative for them as we bolster our points. When they are beginning to trust us, then we can try to move them along to discover the authority of the Bible. So, for instance, we may want to discuss with them the difference between a natural and a spiritual use of herbs or crystals or planets. Or we could honestly admit that wholistic health care is

139

biblical, and enter into a discussion about how the Bible emphasizes the whole person: body, mind, and spirit.

Notice, however, how I spell wholistic when I am talking about the biblical picture. It has been a long-standing contention of mine that we Christians ought to place the letter *w* to the word and try to recover the good from what has become questionable or wrong. Wholistic would give us a label by which to mark off biblical from nonbiblical body, mind, spirit models. It would give us a way to communicate biblical models of health care that emphasize the importance of the whole human being and the interrelationships of its parts. It could give us the freedom to have a wholistic view of health that did not have to be informed by New Age wisdom.

If this could be achieved in the power of the Holy Spirit, it would make holism look rather bland by comparison. Then we would have something to communicate! And I think enthusiasts would listen. As it stands now, we have precious little to offer by way of a wholistic biblical alternative.

Besides ignoring research, some Christian circles tend to overlook research because they feel that everything will get changed through intercession or praise marches for Jesus. We may not be thinking this consciously, but the attitude may lurk in our presuppositions. In saying this, I am not suggesting that we stop such activities. I am asking us to be careful that the activities do not become convenient excuses for not doing research.

If you feel called only to prayer and never to communication, this may be enough for you. But for the vast majority of Christians, research is essential. What tends to happen is that in our excitement about doing spiritual warfare, through intercession and praise marches, research comes to be seen as unnecessary or as a kind of secondary spiritual activity. So we neglect it. It pales in our minds by comparison with the really exciting stuff of spiritual warfare.

And yet, research is not unnecessary or secondary. It is to a certain extent the second rail of track along which the engine of spiritual warfare runs. This may give us an idea as to why Moses was so keen on research, as we saw in the above passages. Research can give our prayers direction, and prayer can make our research effective when we communicate it. Both ought to run side by side to guide the engine of spiritual warfare.

Research is not just about spending long hours in university libraries. Research can be as simple as writing a letter of inquiry, making a phone call, or taking a small portable tape recorder and going to interview someone. You meet some interesting people, and you can get to the heart of matters quickly. Research can be enjoyable, gratifying, and even entertaining at times. It can be as easy as talking to a reference librarian and then digging around in a few books, magazines, or journals for an hour. It never ceases to amaze me what this can produce.

Lack of simple research in Jesus' day kept people ignorant of life-saving facts. In John 7:41–42, people are arguing that Jesus came from Galilee and therefore could not be the Christ, who they knew would come from Bethlehem, Judea. A short conversation with His mother, however, would have cleared this up. So let us be wise as serpents here.

Research, therefore, is essential. It gives a means by which to communicate more effectively. And sometimes during research we discover the falsity of our own assumptions or conclusions.

8. Failing to separate people from their beliefs

This eighth characteristic brings us full circle to the first: failing to relate to persons. It is about that common Christian assertion: Jesus loves the sinner but hates the sin. In this and the previous chapter we have concentrated on people; yet still we may so dramatize and hammer away at New Age beliefs and practices that we pound the person to pieces in the process.

It is chilling to find this spirit and tone even in Christian material and books on occasion. And some of the authors must be feeling their own blows, for they insert the odd sentence or two that says, "We don't have anything against these people personally. We love them. We're just standing up for the truth." Yet truth spoken without true love is like trying to coax someone into open heart surgery without an anesthetic. We cannot slip a fuzzy sentence about love into material that has the effect of shrapnel exploding all over the seeker and think that we have done what love requires.

On the other hand, loving people as distinct from their beliefs is not the same thing as divorcing them from what they believe. As we saw during the Inter-Mission, people are so "mixed up" with their beliefs and assumptions that they are held accountable for them. In other words, people are one with their beliefs. So it gets a bit tricky, but because we have the precedent for it in the gospel itself—Christ dying for the person and not the lie—it is possible.

An idea that has helped me make a proper distinction between people and their beliefs, and so speak right to them, has been to recognize the difference between my roles as an evangelist and as a defender of the faith. Dean Halverson's research brought this to light for me, and it has helped me to be much more at ease in my conversations. The idea is that the defender of the faith, or apologist, will want to make as wide as possible the gulf of dissimilarities between the New Spirituality and Christianity, while the evangelist will wisely seek common ground between the potential convert and God in order to create a dialogue to close the gap between the two. Halverson cites the theologian Chadwick, who aptly states:

> Paul's genius as an [evangelist] is his astonishing ability to reduce to a vanishing point the gulf between himself and his [potential] converts . . . to "gain" them for the Christian gospel. . . . The [evangelist] must minimize the gap between himself and his potential converts. Very different is the defender of orthodoxy; he must make as wide as possible the distance between authentic Christianity and deviationist sects against whose teaching the door must be closed with all firmness.[2]

We know that Paul certainly knew how to defend the faith. Yet he also knew how and when to slip into the other, evangelistic role. Like the writer of Ecclesiastes, Paul understood that there was a time for everything, a season for every activity—a time to plant and build (relationships), a time to uproot and tear down (false teaching). Prophets, too, fill both roles. Jeremiah, for example, was commanded to uproot and tear down and to build and plant (Jer. 1:10). When trying to gain converts for Christ, we must be harmless as doves here.

We see this closing of the gap between Paul and potential converts as he padded around Athens, a beautiful city known as the cradle of democracy. Yet it was also a city of gross idolatries, everywhere entrenched, from the meat markets to the ivory towers (Acts 17:16–34). It seems that Paul's appreciation of the city's aesthetics and democratic uniqueness paled in comparison with his grief over a city "given over to idols" which greatly distressed him. Yet though he was deeply grieved and perhaps offended by what he saw, he refused to "jump on their chests to see who was best." Sorrow over their idolatries fueled his passion for the Athenians as persons, many of whom were spiritual seekers, as implied in Luke's reporting of their time in Athens. Paul saw and met with people who were "very religious." Others were God fearers. There were also some serious-minded philosophers and moralists, as well as the body of men called the Areopagus, who met with Paul on Mars Hill.

When Paul spoke to this human mosaic, he worked diligently to close the gap between his listeners and the gospel. He did this by choosing ideas from sources that would place them on common ground with him. For example, Paul spoke of their shared interest in the creation and in the infinity and all-sufficiency of the Divine Being. He quoted the poets Epimenides and Aratus, not to flaunt his insider knowledge of the Greek poets but because his audience was familiar with them, and the verses gave him some common ground to close the gap between them and God. By mentioning that "in Him we live and move and have our being" (Epimenides) and "we are also His offspring" (Aratus), Paul was in essence saying, "I agree with part of your concept of the Divine Being."

He was not using his heavy guns on them trying to blow their idolatries out of the water. Rather, he set aside his work as an apologist here and worked as an evangelist, which entailed closing the gap between his listeners and the gospel, that they might be saved. He set aside attacking their idolatrous beliefs and spoke about what they had going for themselves as human beings. He concentrated on the people. He wanted to present them with the message of repentance and resurrection, and to accomplish that he took their minds off false beliefs and concentrated on the real thing.

And wonder of wonders, Paul got their attention even more deeply by using one of their very idols as a springboard for closing the gap! It has been said that the Greeks had the idol to "THE UNKNOWN GOD" (v. 23) in case they had overlooked placating a god in their polytheism. When Paul comes along and says, "I'm going to tell you who this is," he is in a sense redeeming the thing, and they're deeply interested because it is something for which they already hold an appreciation.

Paul really knew how to capture the imaginations of his listeners. We, too, will learn how to do this as we continue to move through Part Two. In the meantime, remind yourself of Illustrations 1 and 2 in order to recall how we may look to non-Christian spiritual seekers. Then look at Illustration 3 to see how we could appear less threatening and much more friendly. If we transformed ourselves into a luxury cruise liner, we would be sending better signals to the submarine's radar. The sailors might even wonder about our destination and contact us to find out where we are going. They might even come on board to go with us. Wouldn't that be a change!

Well, we have made a start. Just before we move on, ask yourself a few questions: Do I really have a love for non-Christian spiritual seekers? Why am I speaking to them? Is it because I have a passion to see them gained for Christ, or merely to prove I am right? Do I care for them, or am I building myself up by tearing them down? How do I really sound? When we are speaking, we want to sound like reconcilers not adversaries.

Be honest in answering these questions. If you are unsure, ask a couple of trusted friends to give you some feedback. You see, we like to pride ourselves that we have the fruit of the Spirit. Maybe we do. But I wonder if this fruit is as prominent as it could be in the practical matters of patience, kindness, gentleness, peace, love, and self-control in our relationships and conversations with non-Christian spiritual seekers.

Nonthreatening luxury liner: the transformed look
Illustration 3

16

OUT OF THE
QUESTION

—∽—

THERE IS A national crisis. Journalists, reporters, television, and media people are facing leading politicians with cameras, microphones, and notebooks. The public is poised, listening. What will be said? Well, there is one thing that you will rarely hear from the newspeople at such times. They will not make straightforward statements or assertions about the crisis. They will ask questions because their job is to inquire. And sometimes they ask very loaded and cleverly worded questions.

Questions call for a response; they constrain the one questioned to answer. A newsperson who went around pronouncing his judgments upon politicians, saying for example, "If you hadn't done that, we wouldn't be in this mess," would soon be out of a job. At the very least, he would not have the ear of any more politicians. But the newsperson who asks questions will draw the politician into the conversation and the topic. In other words, he helps the politician, who may be in a tight spot, to remain floating on the surface of communication. This principle holds true in most cases: out of the question comes a communication bridge.

Asking skillful questions is a key element in getting used to the Submarine Communications Model. If we, too, learn to ask appropriate questions of spiritual seekers, we will draw them into conversation. Even if you do not like me, if I ask you a series of questions—such as, Why are you reading this book? Are you getting anything out of it? How did you hear about it?—each question requires you to think with me and so evokes a response from you. Questions, therefore, attract one's attention and keep one participating in conversation. They help the listener to feel that she is on an equal footing with the speaker, and they help the speaker to present himself as an interested listener. They help change subjects, should the conversation become too intense. They also free the speaker from sounding like the demanding boss or lecturing parent.

An appropriate question is an especially effective tool for outwitting the intellectual/spiritual dynamic of passivity (see Chapter 6). We have a lot of truth we want to communicate, but there is a problem. Probably 95 percent of the time when we receive information in Christian contexts (attending Sunday church services, going to seminars, reading books, and so on), truth is delivered to us in declarative form—a take-it-or-leave-it situation—and this has conditioned us to hammer ideas out in the same manner.

We have already discussed the folly of demanding-boss-type messages (Chapter 14). Yet even simple declaratory statements can offend New Age passivity and so shut down listening. This is especially true with meditators, who have been transformed in varying degrees by passivity of mind. Questions will help us outwit passivity so that we will not drive the person below the surface of communication. Facts, truth, and ideas coming in the shape of questions seem less threatening. When in the presence of spiritual seekers, therefore, we may want to deliver truth and ideas not so much in declarative statements as in the form of questions.

DRAWING PEOPLE OUT

The Bible itself uses many questions. In fact, after the fall, God's first approach to Adam was with a question, for a question can help people deal with painful choices. When Job's counselors had exhausted their formal theological statements, by way of trying to help Job see the light, God deluged him with questions, for questions can open people up to new and different possibilities. Our Lord, too, used questioning to lead seekers into the light, for questions can be quite revealing. All of this was done to get at the truth. Blasting away usually generates more heat than light. It might not be a bad idea, therefore, to cultivate questioning as a means of leading people into the truth.

For example, you may be talking to a friend, neighbor, or fellow worker who mentions her growing interest in, let us say, reincarnation. Remember, she is taking a risk by opening up to you. She may be sharing something about which she is embarrassed. A few sensitive questions from you will show respect, establish trust, and draw her into a conversation in which the error of reincarnation can be dealt with.

You could say, "I've heard about reincarnation. Where does that belief come from? I wonder how many people actually believe in it? What do you really think about it? Is there any actual proof for it? Where did you hear about it?"

The idea, of course, is not to string a litany of questions together and ask them all at once. Rather, ask one or two, and then listen attentively to the answers. You may then want to make a comment or ask one or two more questions. After the give-and-take of ideas and the exchange of information, the other person should be floating on the surface of communication. Your use of questions and the fact that you are listening should not have alarmed any possible passivity of mind.

If the person is floating, you now have several options. You may want to end the conversation or set a time to discuss it later. You may want to change the subject. Or if the person is still interested, you could continue the conversation.

Let us consider the latter option. You could try bringing the conversation around to the Bible, still using questions. You could say, "This is all very fascinating. I've never thought about some of these things. But it's interesting what the Bible says about reincarnation." Though you have not asked a specific question, you have created the kind of interest that a question does. By concluding with "it's interesting what the Bible says . . . ," you are probably going to stir enough interest for the person to ask you a question, such as, "What does the Bible say about reincarnation?" If the person asks *you* a question, she is usually ready to listen to you.

Let's go a step farther—again, using questions, but now leading into an opportunity to express a biblical view. For example, concerning reincarnation, the Bible does not overtly state that reincarnation is false. In fact, it never uses the word *reincarnation*. That reincarnation is false, however, is implied by biblical wisdom as a whole and also by the truth of resurrection and individual verses like Ecclesiastes 9:6 and Hebrews 9:27. But it may be inappropriate to haul out your Bible (it may seem like blasting), even if she asks what the Bible says. That's no problem. If the person asks, I usually take the indirect approach to the Bible, which allows the truth to be told without scaring her off with the actual Bible.

For example, I would probably respond to her question by saying that the Bible does not actually use the word *reincarnation*. Then in an unhurried manner, I might go on to say that the Bible does give an overall way of looking at the next life, but that precludes a reincarnational view. Then I would pause to give her time to absorb this new information.

You have worked to keep her buoyant on the surface of communication, and she has now given you the green light to bring the Bible into the conversation. This may be the first time, at least in a long time, that she will be listening to the Bible. So you are beginning to move from the use of questions into the area of persuasion, and you will want to be sensitive here. You are offering food for thought, not preaching. This is why I frequently opt for the indirect approach to the Bible, offering the biblical position in my own words rather than quickly lugging out the Book and pointing to verses. Then I will take a step back (in my mind) and ask myself, *Now what is reincarnation* (or whatever happens to be the subject) *concerned with?* Well, it is about the next life. I will then think about what the Bible has to say about the next life, and carefully try to express that in my own words, keeping it informal. By this means I hope to raise the person's level of interest in what the Bible has to say.

So let's say that she has absorbed what I have said, has taken an interest in it, and asks to hear more. Here is a progression of thought that I find helpful to express at this point:

> It is interesting that there seem to be only three views of what happens after death. One view is that of complete extinction, that after death there is nothing else. You're gone. That's it. You are nothing more than a zero with the rim knocked off. Yet not too many people hold this view. It's a bit too pessimistic for optimistic-minded Westerners.

This leaves them with the two other choices. One is the reincarnational view, which is becoming increasingly popular. As you probably know, if there is any one universal New Age belief, this is it. It gives people the hope of a better future after death, and that many times over.

The third view is the resurrectional view—a person lives but once and at the end of his life, he comes before the God who made him, to be judged by Him. This is the teaching of the Bible, of Jesus, of the apostles, and of the Christian church. It is not a popular view, probably because people realize the moral constraints it places on them, and we live in a time when most people are not much interested in following the moral blueprint of the Bible. I think this may explain why reincarnation is becoming increasingly popular. Since the view of complete extinction is too hopeless and the resurrectional view is too morally challenging for most people, they are left with the reincarnational view of the next life. But this is not what the Bible teaches.

You do not want to parrot this. You will want to put it in your own words and in a way suited to your personality. As you are bringing your comments to a close, you will want to be ready to pause and give the listener the opportunity to respond. Try to be attentive and discerning. Have you lost the person at some point, or is she still with you in the conversation, floating on the surface of communication? Has she received some truthful food for thought? If so, you have gotten there through the use of the question. You have been a successful communicator!

I cannot predict what will be said next. You will have to work with whatever response follows. As you do, try to continue getting at the truth through questions or gentle, respectful comments that create the same kind of interest as questions do.

Let us say that the person says, "I've never thought about it like that. I'll give it some thought." If you have had a background like mine, you could round off the conversation with a bit of personal testimony.

CHRISTIAN: I can relate to what you're saying. Did you know that I once believed in reincarnation for several years?
NEW AGER: I think you told me that.
CHRISTIAN: I even believed in it for the first few months I was a Christian.

NEW AGER: Really?

CHRISTIAN: It's true. Then I came across a couple of verses in the Bible that convinced me reincarnation wasn't the way. We could take a look at them later if you'd like. But it wasn't only that that made sense to me.

NEW AGER: What else happened?

CHRISTIAN: Well, it's curious actually. It's obvious that the reincarnational and resurrectional views cannot both be true. One cancels out the other. So it occurred to me that even if it were possible for both to be true, I would be foolish to choose reincarnation instead of resurrection.

NEW AGER: Why is that?

CHRISTIAN: Well, why mess around with many lifetimes, especially when you can never be sure whether you will be suffering or happy? Why bother with all that when there is a shortcut with guaranteed results in Jesus?

NEW AGER: Hmmm . . . I see what you mean.

I have created an ideal exchange here. Yet as you become adept at communicating the truth through the use of questions, conversations like the above will occur.

Another tip: try not to ask the kind of question that evokes only a "yes" or "no" answer. There is, of course, a time for right-wrong kinds of questions, but here you are trying to ask questions that stimulate fresh thinking and create new windows of perspective for people. "Yes" or "no" questions merely ask people to affirm their foregone conclusions. This is why I suggested questions such as: Are you enjoying yoga? What are you getting out of channeling? What kinds of spiritual things are especially interesting to you these days? How did you get interested in that?

Open-ended questions like these generate fresh thinking in the seeker. Just because someone is interested in the New Spirituality does not mean that he agrees with all of it. By asking open-ended questions and by listening to the answers, you can discover what someone really thinks about it and how deeply involved he is. This, of course, is going to influence how you move the conversation along. For example, if you presume the person is a serious adherent but he is only casually interested, you are going to be miscommunicating.

KNOW YOUR LIMITATIONS

But what if the person becomes argumentative, perhaps when you appeal to the Bible as the authority on reincarnation? She may have objected, saying that the early church fathers removed all references about reincarnation from the Bible. She may have said that John the Baptist was a reincarnation of Elijah. She may have said that Jesus was so enlightened that He did not have to reincarnate. It is all right if you do not know how to respond to such ideas. Remember, you are trying not to save face but to keep the person floating. Be honest. Be vulnerable. Mention that these ideas are unfamiliar to you, and then ask the person some questions: Where did you hear these things? Can I have a look at those books you mentioned? You could also offer to find out what other books have to say, and then ask her if she would like to meet with you to discuss it further. (See the recommended reading list for Christian books on reincarnation.)

Of course, there is the entire galaxy of New Age subjects for topics of conversation. I have just given you some of my reincarnation homework to get you thinking, but I am not going to do all of your homework for you! You must make your own decisions as to what areas to study and discuss. These may be based on the frequency with which you encounter the same subjects or what the most popular beliefs and practices are. And the beauty of it is that by using questions, you do not have to become an expert on a particular subject in order to be an effective communicator. You merely have to know how to ask good questions. In listening to the answers you will learn quickly. As you are asking questions and listening to answers, you will begin to discern pockets of ideas about which you can ask further questions.

In conclusion I want to say that with practice you will get used to recognizing the times when you are losing the person below the surface of communication. It is essential to be alert to the undulations. If the person is diving, try to work to correct the situation. Retract or modify what you said. Apologize. Ask the person what he is feeling. Communicate your feelings. Use humor, especially at your expense. Suggest another talk later. Change the subject. Bring the conversation to a close. Do whatever it honestly takes to keep the person floating. You are building a communication bridge, and you do not want to place any unnecessary strain on it now; it is going to hold enough strain later.

Be especially sensitive if the person is signaling that he has had enough for the time being. He may not want to hear any more, and he may not want to upset you by saying so, in which case he will be sending out hints. Do not coerce. Let the person back off. You are speaking to someone in an unreached people group, which means that even small amounts of new information can be overwhelming to him. The information may seem insufficient, minor, or ordinary to you, for you are conversant with it. But to someone in another world, it may speak volumes. Whenever you sense that the person wants to bring a conversation to a close, let enough be enough. After all, the "Submarine Communications Model," as you can guess, certainly is not about flooding the person with information!

Perhaps the best policy would be for us to discontinue the conversation before the seeker becomes inundated with new information. It is all right to leave people hanging. That was one of our Lord's methods. It almost guarantees that the listener will want to hear more later. It takes a certain discipline and humility of mind not to rush ahead. If you take a moment to turn several pages back to the conversation on reincarnation, you will find that I had the Christian put the brakes on his questions and comments at places where he could have progressed to the next point. These pauses and silences permitted the listener time to think. This is one of the initial goals when building a communication bridge, but it does not take long to develop a feel for this.

Perhaps this chapter has stirred up some questions in you. Good!

17

SIGNS OF
TRUTH

—ᘓ—

WE NOTED IN Chapter 8 that deceptions and lies have a power
to fascinate, to allure, and even to solicit obedience because they are
distortions of truth. Of course, the human heart is already deceitful
(Jer. 17:9), but that only makes it easier for these devilries to lead
people astray.

People get excited about New Age wisdom, therefore, because
some of its beliefs deal with lost truths about life. Thus it is scratching
people where they itch, temporarily at least, but it is not ultimately
satisfying because it deals with the lost truths in a distorted manner.
I have found it quite effective to help spiritual seekers to "undistort"
the truth, so to speak, about various matters.

An obvious example is spirituality. Before the New Spirituality
arose in the West, most Westerners were usually closed to discussion
about God, Jesus, the soul, the supernatural, and similar topics.
"There are two things we don't talk about around here: politics and
religion." How often I heard that as a child! During those years,
Christians had to spend time prying people open to talk about the
spiritual dimension of life.

But we have a head start now. Tens of millions of Westerners are
now open to spiritual matters. We have an excellent opportunity to
build communication bridges because it is true that there is a spiritual
dimension to life. Thus one of the strengths of New Age wisdom is

that it gets people thinking about spirituality. As Christian communicators, we can come alongside seekers and say, "That's right; there is a spiritual dimension to life," and then work to undistort what New Age wisdom teaches about spirituality.

Spirituality, therefore, is what I call a "sign of truth" (perhaps we could call it a "point of light") in New Age wisdom. People see it, and it is one of the drawing cards. The effective communicator will recognize truth wherever it is found. Jesus Himself at times acknowledged truth when He discovered it outside the covenant community. His conversation with the Roman centurion in Matthew 8:5–13 is a case in point. Jesus affirms the centurion's insights about faith. The effective communicator will learn to do the same thing in relationships with spiritual seekers.

For example, in her annotated bibliography *Goddesses and Wise Women*, Anne Carson lists 741 titles published between 1980 and 1992 just on the subject of women's spirituality, in which she includes goddess themes and women's witchcraft. Persons who have read in this area may say, "I'm trying to cultivate the sacred in everyday life," or "I'm discovering new inner resources through Sophia wisdom." In the near background of these statements is the signpost *spirituality*. And the listening Christian then has an opportunity to bring the subject into the discussion.

The purpose of this chapter is to point out several common signs of truth and to offer suggestions for making the crooked straight. We will have our listeners' attention because these signs of truth, or points of light, already interest them. What we want to do is come alongside these submarines and use the "Submarine Communications Model" (it will be expanded here) to communicate the true truth of the matter.

GOD

New Age wisdom posits a wide variety of God concepts, with distortions ranging from pantheism to Gnosticism. If you find that a seeker is willing to talk about God, try to use questions as a way of expressing biblical truth about God: What do you believe about God? Where does your understanding come from? Have you ever thought about what the Bible says about the nature of God? What are the differences between God as impersonal energy and as a personal Being?

You will remember that one of the benefits of the "Submarine Communications Model" is that you do not have to be an expert to be an effective communicator. Asking questions lets you discover where you may be lacking, and it shows how you may want to respond.

If the person remains open, you will want to work carefully to make the crooked straight. If you have been respectfully listening to the person's view of God, there should be no reason why she will not want to listen to your view. You may want to offer the idea that God is personal in nature, trinitarian, or creative, or that He is Truth as well as Love. You could then springboard off these ideas to suggest that we, as human beings, have characteristics such as personality, love, forgiveness, creativity, and a capacity for truth because we are made in the image of this God.

An idea I like to develop is to help the person understand that the word *God* is a most ambiguous word and can mean virtually anything or everything until you define what you mean by it. Never take for granted that you know what someone means by God, that he knows what he means by it, or that he knows what you mean by it. Both of you have to put some clothing on the word and give it an image. Then you can start to make some sense to each other. Otherwise the word *God* in the conversation is ambiguous, and neither of you is really communicating. Helping the person to give some meaning to his view of God can be a great clarifier for him. He may decide that he does not like holding to a thoroughly impersonal view of God, and you may be the first person to bring this to light.

Remember, too, to let yourself be vulnerable. Forget about trying to save face if you find yourself in over your head. You are in the realms of theology and philosophy here, and it is all right to admit your limitations. There are many other signs of truth ready for discussion.

JESUS CHRIST

The historical Jesus is another sign of truth within New Age wisdom. One of the common distortions here is when New Age wisdom makes Jesus a cosmic Christ. This occurs when Eastern religious thinking informs a person's view of Jesus Christ; the historical man Jesus is held to be separate and inconsequential to the enlightened office of Christ that came upon Him and subsequently departed from Him immediately before He died. *The Aquarian Gospel of Jesus Christ, The Unknown Life of Christ,* and *The Lost Years of Jesus* are three popular books that distort the person of Jesus Christ along these lines.

This distortion in particular undermines the gospel story at the fact and meaning of the resurrection. Josh McDowell's *Evidence that Demands a Verdict* is a good book to refer to on this vital point. This topic can get historically technical, and you may want to let some Christian books do your talking for you. You could say, "I know of two books that show that the evidence for Jesus ever having been in India is highly questionable and probably false. I was wondering if you would like to read them?"[1] Even if the person refuses, you have planted a seed of doubt about the New Age view of Jesus, and that may be enough for the time being.

But let us say that the person wants to see the books. If so, I suggest that you purchase one or both of them as a gift. Offer to do that, but try to get a firm commitment from the person that he will actually read the books. This is how I usually go about it. I will spend money to get Christian books into the hands of New Age seekers, but in turn they must be willing to read them. If the person is merely trying to be polite and accept a gift that he has no intention of reading, I do not need to spend my time and money on it. Before you buy the book, one way you can almost guarantee that the person will read it is to arrange a time to discuss it after he has read it.

Another suggestion is to ask the person to think about what she personally believes about Jesus Christ. Many people will respond by saying that He was a great teacher or a prophet.

CHRISTIAN: So, then, you believe what Jesus taught?
SEEKER: Sure.
CHRISTIAN: Why, then, don't you believe that Jesus rose from the dead, that He is the only way to the Father, or that He is God incarnate?
SEEKER: I'm not sure I follow you. Where does that come from?
CHRISTIAN: These are some of the things that Jesus taught about Himself in the Gospels. And there's no point in saying that Jesus was a great teacher if we are not willing to accept what He taught about

Himself, especially His claims to be God and the Savior of the world. Jesus has not left any opening for us to believe that He was just another great human teacher. As C. S. Lewis has said, "He did not intend to."

Another way to provide food for thought here is to offer the three possible explanations for Jesus' claims: Jesus deliberately misrepresented His identity, He was sincere but deluded, or He was sincere and correct. As someone has said, He was liar, lunatic, or Lord. And now with the Aquarian view of Jesus as an avatar, we have a fourth option. One must make a choice, and we can offer the possibilities to the seeker.[2] The idea is to highlight that Jesus Christ is Lord, God in the flesh, Savior, and Redeemer. The person may not yet believe it, but in expressing the truth about Jesus Christ you are helping to undistort the matter. You are giving the person something to think about.

THE FALL

Even though New Age wisdom offers people a supposed godhood status and an unlimited potential to create their own realities, it would not get much of a hearing if it refused to admit that something is preventing this from happening. That is, something is very wrong with life, with the world, and with us. And people know that something is wrong. The issue then becomes: What wisdom are you going to use to explain the wrongness—theft, murder, poverty, injustice, heartache, alienation, suffering, sickness, and all the rest? This brings us to the distorted sign of the fall of humankind within the New Age world.

If you ask seekers what is wrong, they will give any of a number of answers: bad karma from past lives; the failure to integrate the dark half of self into the personality; nothing is really evil or wrong—that is just the way one perceives it. As you are listening to what they think is wrong with life, the goal afterward is to try to coax them to listen to biblical ideas on the subject.

There is an important point to keep in mind here. I am thankful to the late Dr. Francis Schaeffer who pointed this out years ago in his books. There is not much point in talking about what is wrong, that is, the fall of humankind, if people have little or no belief in creation. This will be true for most non-Christian spiritual seekers. Schaeffer's advice was to discuss the creation story first. The fall, sin, its attendant miseries, and death make sense only against the backdrop of the creation story. By talking to the person first about creation you have produced a context in which the fall now makes sense. It may not as yet be believed, but at least the seeker will have to admit that it makes sense against the backdrop of a pristine creation.

When talking about creation, it would be important to say that God desires people to have a loving relationship with Him. Historically, "something" happened to interfere with that, but God had planned the way back should it happen. People can once again have friendship with God just as Adam and Eve did before the fall.

Notice how the previous paragraph is worded. It is put in such a way as to arouse the listener's curiosity so that he will ask us *what* happened to interfere with that relationship and *what* is the way back into it.[3] In the context of creation, a discussion about sin and redemption will not seem so out of place to the listener.

NEW WINDOWS

Some Christians may think, *These suggestions are just so much dillydallying. Let's get straight to the heart of the matter, man!* However, these suggestions are far from a waste of time. We Christians already have an imagination in which the gospel story makes sense. Not so New Age enthusiasts. We Christians often tend to take it for granted that everyone has an imagination in which the gospel makes sense. As a result, we live with a kind of unspoken conclusion that non-Christians understand the gospel, but they just do not care about it and are rejecting it knowing full well what they are doing.

Yet many spiritual seekers are not accepting the gospel's offer simply because they do not understand it. They live with an imagination in which the gospel does not make sense. It cannot make sense in the context of New Age wisdom. Our task as Christian communicators is to help their imaginations through a process of transformation wherein the gospel will begin to make some sense. We can accomplish this by creating new "windows of perspective" in the person's imagination. This is one of the reasons why Jesus used parables, stories, and questions. The ideas that constitute the "Submarine Communications Model" are similar.

New windows of perspective are created in the person's imagination as we carefully express the ideas and truths of biblical wisdom. This is a significant task because slowly but surely it gives the person an imagination in which the gospel will one day make sense to her.

And like all windows, they function two ways. They allow a person to look out, and they permit light to enter in. By sharing biblical insights about God, Jesus Christ, spirituality, and other signs of truth, as well as topics that will be brought up in the following chapters, we are helping seekers to see life through new (biblical) categories of thought.

However, the light of God also shines *into* the person's imagination through these new windows. This is exciting to me because the light of Christ can then enter into the person's shadowy world, and the coat no longer has to look like an intruder! Things can be understood for what they really are. The person may not as yet believe, but as the bits and pieces of biblical wisdom begin to fit together in her mind, you are helping her to make a decision to believe. Then doors will be opened for gaining this spiritual seeker for Christ.

This is the process, and let us not be put off by it, be ashamed, be impatient, or think that it is a waste of time. It is not a subspiritual task. It is vital if we hope to gain people for Jesus. If we work diligently and faithfully here in the power of the Holy Spirit, we will hear our Lord's "Well done." Seekers need a sound basis on which to place their faith in Jesus Christ. Without this there will be false births or poorly conceived births that lead to backsliding because they did not understand what they were doing. Therefore, we want to introduce people to ideas in which the gospel will one day make sense to them.

REDEMPTION

Just as New Age wisdom offers reasons for what is wrong with life, it offers hopes for a solution, for example, enlightenment, higher or expanded consciousness, the round of rebirths, spiritual evolution, asceticism, and others. If these come up for discussion, the sign of redemption is nearby.

When you are identifying the person's hope, remember that the word *redemption* carries with it ideas that the seeker will not understand. Try painting some new windows of perspective by talking about it in terms of being rescued, freed, or ransomed, which will help undistort the matter.[4]

You could also help the person come to some understanding about the nature of the various New Age solutions to what is wrong with life. As a general rule, New Age wisdom offers either a metaphysical or an epistemological hope of a solution. From the metaphysical point of view I am too small, too little, too finite in comparison to God, and the solution is sought in mystical, or spiritual, experiences, by which it is said I can increase my spirit in bigness and so discover my godhoodness. That is why the intuitive, the irrational, and the supernatural play an important part in the New Spirituality. From the epistemological viewpoint, I simply do not know enough, spiritually speaking. I am in ignorance about God and my nature as part of God, and the solution lies in studying the ancient wisdoms, esoteric religious and occult knowledge, or in meditating upon Eastern religious thought. In this way I can accumulate a wealth of hidden knowledge that will save me. The true solution, however, is not found in receiving a long course of metaphysical shots in the spirit or in becoming wiser than Solomon.

Much can be honestly discussed about our littleness before God and our pint-size knowledge of Him. But this is not what separates us from God; therefore, the hope of a solution is not found in knowledge or experience. It is found in a relationship because our problem is a moral one. There is nothing wrong, necessarily, with being spiritually little or lacking in knowledge, but there is something unavoidably wrong when we are moral rebels in the universe. It is not increased spiritual size or enlightenment that we need. We need to regain our personal relationship with God, which was broken off by our moral failure.

Redemption is about a sinner's access to God. Many seekers understand this in terms like "connecting with the sacred" or "access to the divine (or the spirit)," and they believe that this is possible through an almost infinite number of spiritual techniques (doorways). This theme is dominant in the New Spirituality. For example, in *The Feminine Face of God*, Sherry Anderson and Patricia Hopkins write, "We enter our sacred garden through a variety of gates. We go through these entry points in different ways and at different times in our spiritual unfolding. . . . That is just what we need to find and live from: the penetrating alertness that lets us connect with what is sacred."

Christians know that access to God is possible only through the cross of Jesus Christ. So if this topic came up, we might at least be able to narrow the range of options down to one true Hope for the human problem. If we can leave seekers thinking that their deepest problem is moral and relational, in that they need to get in orbit around their Maker, we have accomplished a great deal for the time being.[5]

THE SUPERNATURAL

A discussion with spiritual seekers about the sign of the supernatural can become highly charged. Be as harmless as a dove here. If you think that the person feels threatened, try to restore conversational equilibrium.

In the New Spirituality there are many explanations about the nature of the supernatural realm and its attendant beings. As you are talking to its enthusiasts, you will hear about ascended masters, entities, channeled energies, "spirit guides," UFOs, Higher Self, the Force, and so on. One suggestion is to ask the person why he believes what these spirit beings say. After all, there is no way to give a "spirit guide" a lie detector test. Maybe it is lying when it says that it is a 35,000-year-old warrior spirit from Atlantis (J. Z. Knight's "Ramtha") or a highly evolved being from the seventh dimension (Penny Torres's "Mafu").

It may be helpful if the person could see that ultimately she has only the spirit being's word on the matter. Could it not be lying? If the person does not think that the spirit beings are lying, ask her why not. Suggest that she ought at least to allow for the possibility that the entities are not telling the truth. Maybe the guides are a Trojan horse at the gates?

Related to this is the issue of faith, and this, too, may be something that seekers have never thought about. I do not mean the Christian faith here but the principle of faith in general. There is a tendency among seekers to accept declarations from spirit beings about God, Jesus, karma, reincarnation, spiritual evolution, and so on as if they are statements of scientific fact. Much New Age literature purports to document scientific evidence to back up its metaphysical and epistemological claims. The literature thus capitalizes on the almost unquestionable authority and drawing power that science has today over the minds of Westerners. If something can be made to seem scientific, we are convinced. The problem is that most New Age claims must be taken by faith, faith apart from any real proofs of science.

For example, in states of deep hypnotherapy people have reported events that are interpreted as past-life recall experiences. These anecdotes have piled up over the years and are now considered by many to be proofs that we have lived before. The effective communicator will want to point out that there are other significant interpretations for experiences that are labeled past-life or reincarnational. The experiences themselves, whatever they are, may at times be real enough, but are they necessarily reincarnational? If a person chooses to believe that the experiences indicate reincarnation, he may never have thought that the grounds for this are not scientific but religious faith assumptions.

The British magazine *She* once ran a major article on reincarnation. It began by saying, "Many scientists are finding that children often provide the best reincarnation case histories."[6] (Notice the many hidden assumptions in that statement alone.) The article then trots out three modern incidents of children claiming to have had past lives. It is not that these children have not had some sort of mental or mystical experiences; it is that their betters interpret them as reincarnational.

We can offer seekers two suggestions here. One would be the other ways to interpret such experiences, such as buried memories of events in *this* life suddenly surfacing; people wanting to feel special; adults recalling incidents from historical novels they have read but forgotten until hypnotized; even self-deception or hallucinations. All of which, and more, have been documented as the more reliable interpretations. The other suggestion, which is perhaps valid more often than we care to admit, is that reincarnational experiences in deep hypnosis may be generated by demonic powers.

The author of the article concludes, "A few years ago I was definitely among those who maintained that a serious belief in reincarnation was simply nonsense or superstition. But looking at the latest evidence, it does not seem so likely any more."[7] By her use of the word *evidence*, she assumes it to be what proves the fact of reincarnation, and this is the misunderstanding. What the evidence actually proves is that some people are having strange mental, spiritual, or supernatural experiences. That is the only thing it actually proves.

But then people want to know what these experiences mean. The question becomes, By what wisdom are you going to interpret these experiences? If it is a New Age wisdom, there will probably be a reincarnational meaning assigned to the experience, but this meaning is based on a faith assumption that the Eastern religious view of the afterlife is the correct one. We will want to point out that the experience itself does not prove the reincarnational meaning to be true. All the experience proves is that you had an experience. There are other ways to interpret the experience, and those meanings, if believed, will be based on faith assumptions, in most cases.

This faith principle ought to be brought up in many contexts within the New Spirituality. The Christian communicator will want to help the person to see that much of what she believes is based not so much on scientific evidence as on a leap of faith. Many people have never considered this to be true, or its ramifications.

A final point, if you will allow me the image, is that you could bring the conversation around to the greatest "spirit guide," the Holy Spirit. How about asking the seeker why she wants to fool around with an innumerable multitude of lesser entities when she can have a relationship with the Holy Spirit, who is one of a kind? Why not suggest to the person that she can have the Holy Spirit as her personal Counselor today, and that you will help her discover how that is possible? Of course, this will mean that first she bows the knee before God and receives Jesus Christ as Lord. But that is what you are there for. You never know what might happen.

A NEW AGE

I feel a sense of loss that in the almost twenty years that I have been a Christian, I cannot recall hearing a message preached in the church about the new age to come (though I did hear an indirect message on this topic once). Has this been your experience? Sometimes when I am on the road, I ask audiences for a show of hands here: "How many of you have ever heard Christian preaching or teaching on the new age that the Bible speaks of?" To this, only one or two persons may raise their hands. Nevertheless, the sign of the true new age to come is another muddied point of light that people find in New Age wisdom.

The Bible is not silent about a coming new age; it even speaks of "coming ages" (Eph. 2:7 NIV). It speaks of a time and a place where "there will be no more death or mourning or crying or pain, for the old order of things has passed away" (Rev. 21:4 NIV). Old order? Hmmm! It speaks of a time when "the wolf and the lamb shall feed together, the lion shall eat straw like the ox" (Isa. 65:25), and

> *The leopard shall lie down with the young goat,*
> *The calf and the young lion . . . ,*
> *And a little child shall lead them.*
> *The cow and the bear shall graze;*
> *Their young ones shall lie down together. . . .*
> *The nursing child shall play by the cobra's hole,*
> *And the weaned child shall put his hand in the viper's den.*
> *They shall not hurt nor destroy* (Isa. 11:6–9).

That is a new age indeed! It is about the kingdom of the rock "cut out of a mountain, but not by human hands," the kingdom of "the God of heaven" that He Himself will set up and "that will never be destroyed, nor will it be left to another people" (Dan. 2:44–45 NIV). And the church is a kind of firstfruits of this coming age, wherein are "righteousness, peace and joy in the Holy Spirit" (Rom. 14:17 NIV).

The city of this new age "does not need the sun or the moon to shine on it, for the glory of God gives it light, and the Lamb is its lamp" (Rev. 21:23 NIV). Its river is "the water of life, as clear as crystal, flowing from the throne of God and of the Lamb down the middle of the great street of the city" and on each side stands "the tree of life . . . yielding its fruit every month" and "leaves . . . for the healing of the nations," and "no longer will there be any curse" (Rev. 22:1–3 NIV). New Age? Certainly.

This true new age makes the dawning new Age of Aquarius pale by comparison. In fact, there is no comparison, only contrast. Astrology's mythology about the Age of Aquarius states that the earth is leaving the Age of Pisces (said to be the last two thousand years, the passing Christian era) and entering into two thousand years of peace and harmony, the Age of Aquarius. This Aquarian mythology has been touted in various forms by New Age people since the late 1800s. It is just getting more publicity in the media these days.

You may want to point out in your conversations that the evidence seems to be against any possibility of Aquarian peace and harmony dawning on the earth. Instead there has been an increase in wars, border disputes, starvation, environmental catastrophes, urban suffering, broken homes, crime, poverty, epidemics, and the like. Despite the fall of the Berlin Wall and the collapse of communism, at the time I am writing this the U.S. Army has a list of more than forty trouble spots in the world. If we are looking forward to two thousand years of peace and harmony on the planet, and if the past hundred years are indicative of what is to come, it does not look too hopeful.

You may want to ask the person, "Why are you opting for only two thousand years of peace? Isn't that a bit shortsighted? And besides, what is going to happen afterward?" The question will likely trigger the response, "What do you mean by that?" Then you could carefully mention that you are opting for an *everlasting* life of peace and harmony. If the person shows further interest, you will have created a new window of perspective.

These are just some of the signs of truth or points of light within the world of the New Spirituality. These are its strengths, so to speak, its drawing cards. It will take only a few conversations with seekers before you discover possibilities of Christian witness in these related areas. When you discern a sign of truth in the conversation, you can either ignore or affirm it. By ignoring it, you may well lose the person, but if you affirm it, you have the opportunity to capture the person's imagination and open his mind to what you have to say.

18

AREAS OF
AGREEMENT

——∿——

DESPITE THE EXTENT to which the Christians and people of
the New Spirituality differ, there is nevertheless territory that they
share, common ground. Both groups share mutual concerns and
interests. This will occasionally land both parties on what I call "areas
of agreement." And as with our use of questions and our discussions
about the signs of truth, areas of agreement, or common ground,
provide contexts for building communication bridges. In fact, areas of
agreement are perfect for establishing relationships, which we have
already noted are essential for ongoing effective communication.

Jesus, for example, knew the background of the woman at the well
(John 4), and He had important things to say to her. He found some
common ground between them—water—to say it.

Consider also the prophet Nathan's common-ground language
with David, when God sent him to rebuke David for committing
adultery and murder. Nathan was in the presence of the king of Israel,
who could have had him executed because of what he was about to
say, for showing the king his sin. But Nathan's story about the evil
done to the poor man's little ewe lamb, which was like a daughter to
him, struck a deep chord in the shepherd heart of David (2 Sam. 12).
Nathan's story was a work of art that invited David into the picture.
David really related to it, and it then produced what it was sent to
accomplish: the king's repentance.

167

Areas of agreement are also superb for helping to dispel the notion of Christian irrelevancy, to erase caricatures, to create new windows of perspective, and to establish trustworthiness. Here are several areas of agreement worth reflecting upon.

GLOBAL ISSUES

No one any longer doubts our need to be aware of global problems. Though domestic, regional, and national concerns remain priorities, no one with a radio, television, or newspaper can doubt that global ills demand urgent political and economic action as well. Our Christian thinkers are going to have to become systems thinkers in a biblical sense, using the wisdom of the Bible to help all of us to think and offer solutions for global ills. Global issues give us quite a large area of agreement with many non-Christian spiritual seekers. Because it is such a large area, I am only going to take up one subject here to show how we could close the gap between these people and the gospel.

The media hype surrounding Earth Days, World Healing Days, and harmonic convergences has given many people a global perspective. Since the mid-1980s, principally, large numbers of people have been gathering at selected locations around the world at the same time to think, meditate, and visualize world peace and planetary healing. The figures for the numbers in attendance are generally highly inflated, but on the whole the popularity of these planetary activation events is increasing. Participants are in part motivated by friendliness, goodwill, and the issues by which they hope to ensure that there is a planet here in the future for their children to enjoy.

Unity of thought seems to be their key as they assemble as many like-minded people as possible for a global mind-link, to meditate on understanding and trust internationally and on the healing of all global ills, be they economic, political, environmental, or whatever.

Organizers know it will be a long, arduous task but are not deterred. To contextualize their ideas, they use terms such as *global village, global consciousness, planethood, Gaia, Earthmind,* and *global interfaith peace strategies*. They write books, hold symposiums, and enter politics. They believe the strength of their movement is founded in everyone's desire for world peace and planetary healing. "We are world citizens," they say. "Our thoughts and actions affect each other, so let's all get together and think peace instead of war, think healing instead of disease."

The rallying point seems to be the planetary activation events. As far as I have been able to discover, the first of these to be held on a large scale was the World Peace Meditation Day on December 31, 1986. A very highly publicized harmonic convergence was then held on August 16–17, 1987. Then came Earth Link Day, February 1988, and then a massive Earth Day celebration on April 20, 1990, in memory of the first Earth Day in 1970, which was a sort of turning point, environmentally, for many Westerners. There have been regional events as well, such as Star Link (1988), Crystal Light Link (April 1989), and Time Warp (November 1989). Both the regional and the global mind-links are considered to have *thought* the planet and humanity into varying stages of universal Oneness, planetary healing, brotherhood, love, and so on, or at least to have had a transforming effect that ushered people into new levels of consciousness.

Then on January 11, 1991, came a fairly high-profile planetary activation called Opening the Doorway of the 11:11. It was held at selected locations worldwide, but it was centered at the Great Pyramids of Egypt and on the South Island of New Zealand. And on June 8, 1992, there was Earth Chant Day, which was held to coincide with the United Nations Conference on the Environment and Development that took place in Rio de Janeiro.

So the word is out. If we all assemble to think, meditate, visualize, and chant with one mind, we can tap into the universal Oneness of all things to release peace, healing, and transformation to ourselves and our world. The idea is that the people participating in these mind-links are resonating together with the universal Oneness of all things in an effort to draw the rest of humanity into it. Many participants believe that they are communicating telepathically or psychically with the universal consciousness and its highly evolved spirit beings, who will help us in solving global ills if only we will cooperate.

Global mind-links seem to have taken a cue from transcendental meditation founder Maharishi (Mahesh Yogi) who for years, long before the popularity of harmonic convergences, had been telling his followers that they could lessen poverty and crime and reduce accidents and hospital admissions in their locales by gathering regularly to practice his form of meditation in small groups. The Maharishi is now more scientific about it than ever before. He claims (even running expensive two-page advertisements in major newspapers) that it takes only the square root of 1 percent of the population of a country practicing the Maharishi Technology of the Unified Field (an exponential kind of TM) to transform national consciousness, produce greater health, enliven student awareness, and (note this) give nations victory *before* war by "creating an invincible armour of coherence and radiating an influence of friendliness and harmony that prevents the birth of an enemy"![1]

It may be a different beat, but it is not a different drummer. It's the same old story with a new set of words. The Maharishi's goal for his TMers agrees like soup with water with the purpose of harmonic convergences.

Certainly, we can agree with non-Christian desires for global ills to be resolved. But the Christian knows that harmonic convergences, world healing days, and thinking peace and wholeness will never solve the fundamental problems. You may be able to talk to seekers about the radical difference between a harmonic convergence and united Christian prayer.

I once attended a festival and heard a Jesuit priest speak on the topic of praying about global problems. By the time he had finished speaking to us, I was unsure if he really knew what Christian prayer was. To pray for world peace, he told us to visualize the United Nations building in New York City, then visualize the people inside it changing. To heal the ozone, we were to visualize its holes being healed. And so on. I regret that at the time I did not know what to say. Today I would question him about why he did not tell us to pray that God would bring repentance and grace to the hearts of the people who contribute to the ongoing problems of global ills.

ECOLOGY

Ecological concerns and the environment are high-priority items of the New Spirituality. We may not be able to agree with its analysis or solution for nuclear waste disposal, the ozone layer, the tropical rain forests, industrial pollution, and so on, but certainly, we can agree that these are real and weighty problems in need of attention. These could provide common ground for building relationships.

For example, when speaking to a Green New Ager (not all Greens are New Age), you may find that he has some good points to make, or conversely, you may find that he draws from the viewpoint of Deep Ecology[2] for his analysis and solution. It is not possible for the Christian to say "Amen" to Deep Ecology because its religious and spiritual mantle is pantheistic monism, making it a kind of ecomysticism. Still, you could have agreeable discussions around any good points the person is making, such as the menace of industrial pollution or radioactive waste.

Conversation can begin with questions such as, What do you think about the deforestation of Brazil and the Philippines? What can be done to prevent a nuclear reactor disaster? What do you know about the Green political movement? How can we be better stewards of the planet?

Remember, when you are listening to the replies, you want to be conscious of your limitations and keep your responses to areas that you feel confident with. Remember, too, that you may have to listen a long time to earn the right to be heard. When listening to a reply with which you disagree, the temptation is to jump right in with, "Yes, but. . . ." Yet if this is a new and growing relationship, I would suggest holding off on discussions about areas of disagreement. Of course, if the person is enthusiastically floating on the surface of communication, you may want to try out your disagreements, but not dogmatically, I think, with this particular issue. Who actually has the right answers for our ecological dilemmas anyway?

If you should find yourself becoming dogmatic, turn off your demanding-boss persona and restore conversational equilibrium. There is a lot to be said for the calming word *perhaps*. "Perhaps I ought to take a look at that more thoroughly." "Perhaps I had it wrong." "Perhaps that's a better way to look at it." For the sake of communication bridges, this may be the best approach at times. Later the conversation can be moved to biblical ideas about ecology and earth stewardship. "Perhaps there's a better way to look at it. Could I tell you about it?"

I was weak in this area until I began to understand that the gospel of Jesus Christ and the Bible have a redemptive message for the ecological dimension of life. The Old Testament in particular has much to teach us here. Let us therefore use all available resources in our efforts to have something intelligently biblical to say to environmentalists.

HEALTH CONSCIOUSNESS

An increasing number of people are becoming health conscious. They can no longer ignore the large body of medical evidence that an improper diet, for example, can cause a great deal of ill health, and they are now interested in what constitutes sound nutrition and a diet balanced for their individual needs. Some are changing their eating habits to alleviate allergies, arthritis, or migraines. Others are interested in the role of vitamins and minerals and the balance of fats, carbohydrates, and protein. It is no longer unknown that foods brimming with saturated fats increase the potential for heart and circulation disorders, that caffeine can cause headaches, that excess weight can shorten life expectancy, and that a diet high in refined sugar can produce a host of ills. As a result, freshly cooked foods are more frequently served, low-calorie diets abound, junk foods are eaten less, and people are happier and finding themselves with more stamina and energy.

Certainly, we can agree with much here. Yet what is happening is that many people now let New Age wisdom inform these areas of health consciousness. As a result, well-meaning people are being led out onto dangerously thin ice. People are going on spiritual cleansing diets, extensive spiritual fasts, and relying on unusual substances in the place of basic foods. Others are trusting in mystical-minded herbalists, turning to Zen macrobiotic diets, or becoming vegetarian to pay off their bad karma.

One line of reasoning that we could take would be to help people see the difference between natural and spiritual, or religious, uses of health-care procedures, so creating a new window of perspective for them. Many of these people have moved into a religious meaning for health care without being fully aware of what has happened. Take macrobiotics as an example.

I have talked to several people who were either on or had been on a macrobiotic diet because they thought it was strictly something natural. They were quite surprised to discover that macrobiotics is much more than a diet. In their definitive text *Macrobiotic Diet*, Michio and Aveline Kushi (perhaps the leading Western purveyors of macrobiotics) write, "Macrobiotics is not simply or mainly a diet. Macrobiotics means the universal way of life . . . with which we will maintain our health, freedom and happiness."[3] Strong claims for a few choice carrots and turnips! Yet the Kushis are even more forthright: "Macrobiotics includes a dietary approach but its purpose is to ensure the survival of the human race and its further evolution on this planet."[4]

One senses a kind of "divinity through eating" metaphysic at the back of this. Years ago, Michio Kushi was a political science student in Japan. There he met George Ohsawa who was a teacher of Zen macrobiotics. Ohsawa challenged Kushi with a theory about applying dietary principles to solving the problem of world peace. Kushi says that he then stopped studying political science and took up Zen macrobiotics. Afterward he lopped off the word *Zen* and brought it to the United States.

If someone is going to use macrobiotics, it is not possible to separate the nonbiblical religious philosophy from the way the vegetables are prepared, for instance. The idea is that carrots, turnips, lettuce, tomatoes, potatoes, and suchlike resonate with certain subtle universal life energies, with which they are one. We, too, it is said, are one with the universal life energies. The vegetables must then be cut and prepared in exactly the right way in order to release these life energies into the person, that all might be one. Amusing? Don't forget about the foolishness between two different wisdoms.

It has been argued that we are just talking about vegetables. Yes, but it also involves the mystical energy meaning that has been assigned to them. If a person is going to eat macrobiotically, it is not possible to separate this religious philosophy from the way the food is to be prepared. If the person so eating thinks he has, then why is he still bothering with cutting the vegetables only in a certain way? The religious philosophy teaches that this is done in order to release the universal life energies of the vegetable(s) properly. We may be able to help the person see the difference between a natural and a macrobiotic use of vegetables.

Another case in point is a person's reasons for being a vegetarian. It was for Eastern religious reasons that I became a vegetarian during the latter years when I was a New Ager. That was a logical outcome of trying to live consistently with New Age wisdom. I reached a depth of involvement where I encountered teaching that said eating animals produces bad karma. This belief is found in Hinduism, and it is appealing because one can accrue good karma by not eating meat. Since I have never been much of a compromiser with whatever I choose to believe, I had a long heart-to-heart talk with myself and decided to stop eating meat.

As into a pool of cold water, I eased slowly. For a year I did not eat red meat, and then I encountered teaching that said I would accrue even more good karma if I stopped eating poultry and fish as well. I took that next step up the ladder of spiritual evolution. I was a lactovegetarian. Really on my way!

Several months before my conversion to Christ I had soldiered on to the next phase to become a strict vegetarian, one who eats only nuts, grains, fruits, and vegetables. Funnily enough, you find yourself buying much less variety but spending three to four times longer in the grocery store shopping for food. I vividly recall the scene: a tall, thin young man with a Fu Manchu mustache, tight bell-bottoms, and long brown hair hanging straight down to the middle of his back; he is standing virtually motionless in every grocery aisle scrutinizing the labels of cans and packages to ensure that what he buys is not "contaminated" by any kind of animal products. It takes a long time to shop that way! The Eastern religious motivation for vegetarianism had me in its grip, so much so that I remained a vegetarian for several months after my conversion to Jesus Christ, though I had gone back to eating all foods except red meat.

It was my uncle Louis who helped me sort it out, and he did it during a long-distance phone call to me in which he asked a lot of good questions. "Have you ever thought that you could start eating meat again?" he asked. After we had talked about this for a few minutes, he then asked me if I was familiar with the story in Genesis 9, when God talked to Noah after he left the ark to begin his life again. I said that I was not familiar with it, and then Louis suggested that I might want to read it sometime. "God had changed things around," Louis said. "He permitted Noah and his family to eat meat."

That got my attention because for years it had been drilled into my head that God was severely displeased with meat eaters because He was one with animals. My uncle said that was a common misunderstanding, and Jesus Himself had to clear it up once when He was talking to the Pharisees. That was news to me, too, so Louis suggested that we get out our Bibles and read a couple of passages. I returned to the phone with my Bible, and we read Matthew 15:11: "Not what goes into the mouth defiles a man; but what comes out of the mouth, this defiles a man." We also read 1 Timothy 4:4–5: "For every creature of God is good, and nothing is to be refused if it is received with thanksgiving; for it is sanctified by the word of God and prayer."

I certainly hung up the phone that day with a new window of perspective. Books on vegetarianism had put a fear in me that if I ever ate meat again, I would probably become ill, as well as spiritually inferior. Yet after several days of mulling it over, I decided to put

Jesus' words to the test. I was not up to cooking meat at home, so I drove to a favorite restaurant. With some trepidation I ordered and ate a really great-tasting hamburger and then waited anxiously for some kind of negative physical or spiritual reaction. None came. And at the restaurant I even bumped into an old friend whom I had not seen in years, and when she asked me what I had been doing lately, I talked to her about my recent conversion to Christ. You just never know.

Being able to eat meat again brought much greater freedom into my life. I remember a friend saying to me, "You're so different now. Before, your life was like a bear hibernating in a cave. But now you've come out of the cave." I do not attribute this freedom so much to the actual eating of meat again as I do to no longer being bound to a false religious belief. I had made an idolatry out of vegetarianism; I was now free of that. I do see that people can be vegetarian for strictly natural or medical reasons, and that would be all right. But I have felt such great freedom in this area that I have not had any desire to return to even a natural kind of vegetarianism.

The above are but a few areas where Christians may find common ground with spiritual seekers on health issues. If these are not of interest, you will not have to fish around long to discover other agreeable health-care topics for conversation.

ONENESS

This large patch of territory also has some shared ground with the Christian. Let us review for a moment. In Part One, we noted that irrational mystical experiences may produce altered states of consciousness that the seeker thinks are his discovery of the Oneness of all things. He makes this assumption because New Age wisdom instructs him that this is what such experiences mean. It teaches that the things of creation are not really individual separate entities but part of an undifferentiated whole.

This idea fascinates many people today who are tired of the great influence of Cartesian science—which pulls life apart to analyze it, and then pulls the analyzed bits apart even farther. Life becomes fragmentized. We see ourselves as drops separate from the ocean rather than drops *in* the ocean.

This three-hundred-year-old habit we have of breaking things up into pieces is said to have led to the fragmentation and alienation that are so much a part of our lives today. It is said to have resulted from overemphasis on Cartesian rationalism. According to New Age wisdom, this has blinded us to an intuitive awareness of the Oneness, or wholeness, of all things.

Christians would agree that we have indeed lost the forest for the trees. We would also agree that there is a certain interconnectedness and interdependence within the things of the creation. After all, all things are dependent on God for their existence, and without Him would become nonexistent. Yet it is a little more subtle than that, for the objects of creation, though distinct from each other, share things in common. Take, for example, minerals and leather-bound Bibles. Any interconnectedness there? Let's see.

Minerals are found in soil, which, through the natural building blocks that God has established, the grass takes up into itself so that it may grow. Grass, therefore, is dependent on soil that is dependent on minerals, which means that grass, too, is dependent on minerals for its existence. Then along comes a lumbering four-footed beast munching grass. The cow's existence is therefore dependent on the grass, which is connected to the soil, which is connected to the minerals. Here, then, is a biblical understanding of the interconnectedness and interdependence of all things.

Yet the process goes further. Both the butcher and the leather binder are dependent on the cow, and you could be dependent on both—that is, if you want roast beef on the table on Sunday after you have read your leather-bound Bible in the morning.

There is therefore a real sense of interdependence among the things of creation, of which the above is barely an inkling. One place where New Age wisdom goes wrong is when it takes this to extremes, either to blur or to eliminate the distinctions between things that God has made. The distinctions are not illusory but real. There are therefore both interdependence *and* distinction. But this is not ultimately the case in New Age wisdom.

We can agree that there is a wholeness to life and offer a new window of perspective on it. We must try to help the person get a feeling for the masterly substructure of God's creation. And try to be patient when you come across some of the more eccentric extremes of monism, in which thoughts and actions here on earth are said to influence things even in the farthest reaches of the universe. Personally, I do not believe it. Somehow I find it difficult to believe that I influence the gravity of Alpha Centauri when I tip the dust and fluff off my kitchen floor into the trash can.

SHARED SUFFERINGS

Grief, tragedy, despair—has any one of us not been touched by them? Divorce, a runaway teenager, a suicide in the family, a friend struck down with a terminal illness—these and a host of other misfortunes may provide common ground for relationship building between Christians and people of the New Spirituality. Suffering is universal, and it is not unusual to find that disease, adversity, or an unexpected loss got someone interested in spiritual concerns. The Christian who finds a parallel in her life can speak with empathy here and so build a communication bridge.

This area of agreement is also perfect for Christians who feel they may get in over their heads discussing a person's beliefs. Instead, you could talk about your shared sufferings. For example, in asking a question such as, "What got you interested in astrology?" you may discover that the person had gone through a divorce and afterward turned to astrology to find a compatible mate. You may be divorced and perhaps remarried. The temptation here is to push the conversation quickly into the area of the dangers of astrology. But you could set that aside temporarily, show a bit of vulnerability, and say, "I'm sorry to hear that you went through a divorce. Isn't it awful? When I went through mine, it was as if my whole reality had been torn apart."

> NEW AGER: It was terrible. When did you go through yours?
> CHRISTIAN: Almost nine years ago.
> NEW AGER: I just went through mine last year.
> CHRISTIAN: It took me a couple of years to really feel as if I was whole again.

Here is adult-to-adult conversation, and a relationship is building. All spiritual baggage has been set aside for the time being. With conversation on shared ground, you may find that the person wants to know how you got through your tragedy, for example, the depression that accompanies divorce. You are moving into the realm of personal testimony here, and it can be quite effective because most spiritual enthusiasts are open to personal testimony. They may not believe too much about what you say, but I have never heard a seeker attempt to argue away a Christian's experience. Yet this is not to say that your testimony is noninfluential; it may be very penetrating indeed, though the person may not admit it at first.

If someone is willing to listen, you may want to explain that it was through prayer, grace, and Christian fellowship that you were able to cope with the depression. Remember, the seeker probably does not understand prayer or grace, and you are offering him bits of biblical wisdom in an effort to give him some imagination in which he will one day understand these things.

You may be a Christian who first seriously considered the claims of Christ, or came back to Him after backsliding, because of a personal crisis. If you find a parallel with a seeker, you may want to explain that you found what you most needed in Jesus Christ. Again, your testimony can be influential.

You might discover that the person became interested in channeling after a loved one's death. She may explain that she wanted to find some evidence for the soul's existence after death, so she visited a medium, hoping to contact the deceased. This eventually led her into spirit channeling. Instead of jumping right into the dangers of this, you may want to ask if she has found the assurance and comfort she sought through mediums and spirit channelers. If you have had a loved one die, you may want to express how you received assurance and comfort from God. You may even be able to bring a biblical viewpoint of death and the afterlife into the conversation.

These and other shared sufferings can be instrumental in bringing comfort into a person's life. They help the relationship develop apart from shared interests in spiritual matters. They establish common ground with people who suffer and grapple with what it is like to be human.

A brief summary of the principles behind areas of agreement would look something like this: discover places of common ground and begin there; then try to build upon the commonality. As you are doing that, notice the areas where you deviate. Then try to move the conversation along to explain why you believe differently. (Do not forget the submarine's sensitive radar.) If the person remains interested, offer to share further, and then try to arrange times together again.[5]

ON BEING
HUMAN

—∽—

WE HAVE NOTED several times that in New Age wisdom a human being is not seen in strictly materialistic or naturalistic terms, that is, as a biological machine or closed system without any reference to things spiritual or transcendent. The aging behavioral and deterministic models for being human are seen as old paradigms, and new models that incorporate the spiritual and the transcendent have taken their place in the New Age world. To date, these new models are framed within various attempts to say what it means to be body, mind, and spirit from a non-Christian spiritual perspective.

In an effort to give us another powerful area for building relationships and conversing with people, I would like us to explore this from the point of view of being human. I think that most non-Christian spiritual seekers are realizing their uniqueness or specialness as human beings. Ultimately, they are sensing that they are made in the image of God—for that makes us unique. The problem is that they are coming up with the wrong reasons for what they are sensing.

Certainly, we cannot take issue with the fact that we are unique; as someone has said, we are the "crown of creation." We can agree with seekers about this. But we can take issue with the New Spirituality's explanations for human uniqueness, for when its wisdom addresses this significant question, "all day they twist [distort] my words" (Ps. 56:5). Most often, New Age wisdom answers the question of human uniqueness with some variation of pantheism.[1] And one no longer need be a philosopher to understand pantheistic models for what it means to be human, for they are being made comprehensible and palatable to the person in the street.

Shirley MacLaine's New Age autobiographies are an example. She and her editors have found ways to describe and popularize pantheism. Take just one scene from *Dancing in the Light,* in which MacLaine is in a trance-state, talking, so she says, to the "spirit guide" that she calls "Higher Self":

> "Then what is the difference between you and God?" I asked.
>
> "None," it said. "I am God, because all energy is plugged into the same source. We are each aspects of that source. We are all part of God. We are all individualized reflections of the God source. God is us and we are God."
>
> [Later in the same dialogue, Higher Self says,] "You will each have to deal with your own inner selves . . . in relation to knowing that you are God. However, the discrepancy comes in your not understanding that every other person is God also."
>
> "But down here we believe that people are people, and God is God, as though we are separate from God. I mean, almost everybody believes that."
>
> "Precisely what is causing the problem," said H.S. "You will continue to be separate from each other until you understand that each of you *is* [her emphasis] the God source. Which is another way of saying that you are One. You are having problems with this because your spiritual development is not advanced enough. You each need to become masters of your own souls, which is to say, the realization of yourselves as God."[2]

Here is pantheism in pop language, and we can see that if this were true, it certainly would be the reason why we are unique. Yet even at this point in her spiritual search (the book was first published in 1985), MacLaine is unsure about accepting pantheism. However, by the end of the book, lest any of her readers remain in doubt as to her conversion to pantheism, MacLaine leaves us with these closing words:

> For me to deny the Divine Force now would be tantamount to denying that I exist.

I *know* that I exist, therefore I am.

I *know* that the God source exists. Therefore *IT IS.*

Since I am part of that force, then *I AM that I AM.*[3] (Her emphases and capital letters.)

Though we may find it shocking that MacLaine has used God's words about Himself to Moses—see the burning bush incident (Exod. 3:13–14)—we cannot let the fact that we are greatly distressed at the idolatry prevent us from remaining calm and using "Submarine Communications Model" ideas to speak to this situation. It will probably be fairly easy to bring this topic into a conversation. You could begin by saying that you agree that we are unique, but that there are other ways to account for it.

CREATED BY GOD

To offer the biblical alternative, try using the definitive word *person.* Suggest to the *person* that we are unique not because we are God but because we are persons, created in the image of a personal God (Gen. 1:27). Remember, at this point, that you are trying to create new windows of perspective. Try not to worry if the seeker does not believe what you are saying yet; you are trying to impart information that he can carry with him and think about.

You may want to capitalize on the person's bewilderment by saying, "I know this is different from what many people think, and I had difficulty understanding it for a while. I still don't fully understand it, because it is quite a mystery. But I have picked up a few clues about it from the book of Genesis." If the person remains interested, you may be able to communicate, for example, that it seemed to take three ingredients for God to make a person. One was a physical body formed from the dust into which, two, the breath of life was breathed (Gen. 2:7), and that made man, three, a living soul, a person.

This biblical idea could be brought into the conversation without hauling out a Bible, and it would give you a context in which to discuss the fixed differences between this and pantheistic models of human uniqueness. You should be careful to say that though the creation story accounts for human uniqueness, it does not support the notion that a person is God. There are certain absolute differences between a person and God.

Man [is] a limited physical creature . . . totally dependent upon God not only for the origin of his existence, but also for its continuation. Nevertheless, though unlike God in certain important ways, Man [is] like God because Man [is] a person.[4]

Our being personal, like God, marks us off in certain unalterable ways from other kinds of life. I am so tired of hearing that we are animal, however highly evolved. *We are human.* Being made in God's image distinguishes us from the animal kingdom. Dogs may hear commands and speak by barking, but we hear and speak not just sounds but language. We have not mere instinct but capacities for compassion and understanding. We have minds for thinking and reasoning. We have faculties for memory, aesthetic appreciation, moral decision making, and repentance.

These and other unique features are intrinsic to our being human. They are what it means to be like God (Gen. 1:26), and they make us special—persons—indeed. Pantheism, however, is not content with the uniqueness of being *like* God. It brings its disciples up the mountain by another way, through a secret passage, whereby they think they are God. We can help the seeker make the crooked straight here.

Yet the conversation would be truncated if left at the point of our uniqueness. Our uniqueness is not the whole story, for we live this side of the Garden incident and our uniqueness is now painfully marred. It will be important, therefore, that in our conversations we distinguish between what was sacrificed in the fall of humankind and what was retained of human uniqueness. Again, we are trying to create new windows of perspective. It may be helpful to

distinguish between man as the image of God *before* the Fall and man as the image of God *after* the Fall. Those faculties which are peculiarly human, which designate us as persons—love, morality, rationality, creativity—indicate that we continue to be the image of God after the Fall. . . . Since the Fall . . . these faculties . . . have been defective. . . . We no longer reflect God's perfect moral character. Though perfect at the beginning, humanity is no longer so. As we pollute our physical environment, so we pollute our moral environment. We pollute because we ourselves are polluted: "For from within, out of the heart of man, come evil thoughts, fornication, theft, murder, adultery, coveting, wickedness, deceit, licentiousness, envy, slander, pride, foolishness. All these evil things come from within" (Mk. 7:21–23 RSV). In this respect we are unlike God.[5]

It strikes me as amazing that our being in the image of God was not lost in the fall. Thus, even very idolatrous persons may still sense their uniqueness. Dr. Francis Schaeffer used the apt metaphor "glorious ruin" to describe our current situation. He used the discovery of an old, soiled, and deteriorating painting as a starting point. No one was quite certain just who the artist had been, but all were agreed it was done by a genuine master, someone who knew how to use his superb gifts. The decomposition was taken to the proper expert who lifted the stains, unsullied the canvas, examined distinctive brush strokes, analyzed the style, discovered the time period, and so on. After his careful scrutiny, he was able to declare who the artist was beyond any doubt, even though the work was in ruins. So, too, when we help people see through sin and fallenness, the great Artist of the human being is revealed. Yes, we are in a state of ruin, but our uniqueness can be traced back to the former glory given us by God.

We have not lost what it means to be persons. That is why we can still approach one another as persons and why we can have relationships with anyone, including the person of God.

When I was a child, we used to play a game called "Pretend." You could play a very instructive adult game of Pretend with seekers:

SEEKER: I'm not sure I can believe all this stuff about being in the image of God. It doesn't make sense.
CHRISTIAN: I'm not asking you to believe it until you are convinced. But what if we were to pretend for a moment that it was true? Could you think of any evidence of God's image in yourself or someone else?
SEEKER: What do you mean?
CHRISTIAN: Well, based on some of the things we've been discussing, does any of it make sense? Does it seem to fit our human situation?
SEEKER: I'm still not sure what you mean.
CHRISTIAN: For instance, if God is an impersonal energy, as you say, I have always found that that assumption about God's nature makes it impossible for me to see how I can have personality. I mean, you cannot get personality out of impersonality. You can't squeeze blood out of a rock.

SEEKER: In that case I guess it does make sense that from a personal God you could easily get personality.
CHRISTIAN: That's it. And what else?

Again this is adult-to-adult conversation. You are showing respect and recognition. You are working to keep the *person* floating on the surface of communication, to dispel his Christian caricature, and to create new windows of perspective. This is communication.

BABYLONIAN WISDOM

In closing this chapter, I would like to say something about the Bible's view of pantheistic beliefs. God Himself seems to take them quite seriously. If a seeker is interested in hearing what the Bible says about them, here are my suggestions.

In Isaiah 46:1–2, the prophet disclosed the futility of two Babylonian gods, Bel (sometimes called Bel-Marduk [Jer. 50:2 NIV]) and Nebo. These were important deities, and Nebo was Bel's son, a god of learning and *wisdom*. With stinging wit, Isaiah contrasts the false father-son gods with the true and living God. The former have no life but are heavy loads that must be borne about by beasts of burden. Because of their stone nature, they are wearisome for people who are already tired and burdened and who will be brought even lower by the heavy weight of Bel and Nebo. Later in the same chapter God the Lord is then revealed as Life Giver, Sustainer, Load Bearer, and Savior.

In the next chapter, however, Isaiah becomes specific as to the teaching of Nebo, Babylon's god of wisdom. Isaiah 47 makes a useful study because it describes a virtual Babylonian counterpart that is like the cosmopolitan spirituality of New Age wisdom in many ways. Here we will cite only its pantheistic element.

One of Isaiah's descriptions of Babylonian wisdom is that it is a wanton creature lounging in its security and saying to itself, "I am, and there is no one else besides me" (47:8). (MacLaine appears to be echoing this "I am.") Then after prophesying the great disaster that shall come upon it because of its wickedness, Isaiah says,

> *Your wisdom and knowledge mislead you*
> *when you say to yourself,*

"I am, and there is none besides me"
(47:10 NIV).

Seen in the light of biblical wisdom, the linchpin of Babylonian wisdom seems to have been its pantheistic element, the result of Nebo, its god. But notice it is a wisdom that, like the New Spirituality, misleads. There have been wisdoms like this ever since Eve accepted hers from the serpent: "When the woman saw that the fruit of the tree was . . . desirable for gaining wisdom" (Gen. 3:6 NIV). Wisdom like this is under God's judgment because, among other things, it falsifies the uniqueness of what it means to be human. It drove a man and a woman from the presence of God in the beginning, and it has been the driving force of many cultures ever since. Again, the New Spirituality is not really new. It is "error" (Isa. 47:15 NIV).

Try to recover what it means to be human for the seeker.

20

FLXYBL

—∞—

NEW YORK (AP)—American management has become burdened by imprecise and almost senseless words that disguise sloppy thinking, a professor says, and he blames the academic community for it. He cites such words as mission, vision, empowerment, stress, benchmarking, strategic, consumer confidence, self-esteem, career limiting, bottom line and more, and states that they can mean almost anything or nothing. The erosion of meanings has been under way for several decades.[1]

THUS BEGAN A newspaper article about the confusion of language in the business world. Change the jargon words, and this could have been describing the state of language in the New Age world, which Catherine Bennett of *The Times* aptly described: "The language buckles, meanings bend—and even then there are no words adequate to express concepts."[2] In describing and defining what is, the nomenclature of the New Spirituality takes great liberty with language, and those who have not yet met its obscurity and ambiguity are in for a real eye-opener.

RENAMING THE GAME

Amazing examples of changing the nouns of the game can be found throughout the New Spirituality as it renames the basic elements, ideas, and practices of the old occult, mysticism, and paganism. Renaming the game seems to be intentional and done without qualm. For a New Age activist, Dick Sutphen is exceptionally transparent:

One of the biggest advantages we have as New Agers is, once the occult, metaphysical and New Age terminology is removed, we have concepts and techniques that are very acceptable to the general public. So we change the names and demonstrate the power. In so doing, we open the door to millions who normally would not be receptive.[3]

This presents us with a challenging language barrier, and the advice is being taken by spiritual seekers en masse, from the stars to the starstruck. I have already mentioned the book *Spiritual Parenting in the New Age*, in which, perhaps taking a cue from Sutphen, the author boldly tells New Age parents to say "prayer," not "magic" or "spell," say "ceremony," not "ritual," and so on. And she calls this the language of diplomacy.[4] The language of diplomacy? To trip up those whom you love? It is more like the language of deceit.

When a leading New Age luminary was asked by a journalist why a spirit would choose to be a Jew slaughtered in the Holocaust, she seized this opportunity for an abrupt change in terminology. "Don't call them spirits, call them souls, *souls*—spirits sound oogabooga, occult."[5] In this semantic legerdemain, demons and evil spirits are renamed *spirit guides*, *channeled energies*, *ascended masters*, and suchlike. Spirit mediums become *channelers* who *channel entities*, and when they do this, it is called *channeling*. Witchcraft passes as *wicca*. Astrology is sometimes called *Astrograph*. Ancient alchemical and shamanistic practices become *therapies* within much of Jungian depth psychology and transpersonal psychology. Eastern meditation is rife in classrooms as *centering, stilling, grounding, going within*, and other generic-sounding terms. *Guided imagery* and *visualization* become ersatz terms for occult forms of meditation in which schoolchildren can be taught to contact *imaginary helpers*, *guides*, or *wise persons*, which can be appellations for demonic spirits. (I do not say that visualization and guided imagery are necessarily demonic.)

When the U.S. Navy offered Eastern meditation, it was called *human resource management training*. I have seen Hatha yoga offered as *stress relaxation therapy*. Zen macrobiotics is now merely macrobiotics, losing its Eastern religious connotation but not its connection. A methodology for so-called psychic healing, very much like what I was taught in the occult in the early 1970s, passes as Therapeutic Touch. It was developed by Dolores Krieger, R.N., Ph.D. It is the New Spirituality equivalent to the Christian laying on of hands, and she teaches it widely to Western health-care professionals. I once saw Therapeutic Touch billed as "the actualization of potential for therapeutic field integration." I wonder if Krieger has met the Maharishi somewhere on the occult map. His TM has recently been advertised as the "Maharishi Technology of the Unified Field."

I have already mentioned the precedent that Carl Jung set for this New Age newspeak (Chapter 10), but the precedent dates even farther back. When the nineteenth-century medical community began to take an interest in eighteenth-century mesmerism, they changed the name to hypnotism. And in the late nineteenth and early twentieth centuries, the SPR (Society for Physical Research), snubbed and ridiculed by the materialistic scientific community, hammered out new terms for the old occult in order to bypass the word barrier of terms such as *seance, medium, spirit contact,* and other occult-sounding phenomena. In this way the SPR got offensive language out of the way and so slipped occult phenomena into the scientific community for study under terms such as *ESP, paranormal, parapsychology, telekinesis, PSI phenomenon, clairvoyance,* and more.[6] But as Jung himself freely admitted, changing the name of the game in no way changes the nature of the game. The Christian communicator will want to bring this point home to listeners.

Language is about the words we use to describe and define things. It ought to be a vehicle that conveys coherency and consistency between what we are describing and what it actually is. Because our choice of words ought to convey as closely as possible the nature of a thing, the importance of right language goes without saying. This is why naming in Hebrew implies an understanding of the things being named. In the first two chapters of Genesis, for example, the language used shows accuracy between word and object. We see this, too, in the often overlooked Genesis 2:19, where Adam names the animals. He was ever so accurate.

I have said that language "ought" to reflect the things named because we live in a fallen world in which entropy touches even our ability to name things. If we do not struggle against this downward linguistic spiral, little by little our language reflects less and less accurately what is. If this is not checked redemptively, eventually all reality becomes more and more subjective until it all becomes an illusion (at least in language). Yet long before the finale, the ability to really communicate diminishes greatly. Put a whole world together in which this erosion of language is predominant and you speed up the process. I think this is an accurate picture of what is happening in the world of the New Spirituality.

But there is also this to consider. According to the Bible, a corporate confusion of language is a judgment of God upon communities or nations whose idolatries reach dangerous heights. The Tower of Babel story is an example. A large pagan community had migrated a long way from the mountains to the plains. While in the mountains, they met with their gods in the high places, which is often a prerequisite of pagan worship. They had now settled in the plains, hundreds of miles from the heights. To worship their gods properly—that is, according to their tradition—they had to build a tower that reached to the heavens. The tower was raised, in a sense, by the collective unconscious of a community that needed access to its gods in the heights. This in turn would serve a secondary purpose: keeping order. The priests could maintain the community's security and allegiance to certain established religious principles through tower worship. Therefore, they would not be scattered over the face of the earth. But when the community's idolatry reached a certain pitch, God judged them at the heart of what held them together: language, which broke down and became a divisive rather than a unifying dynamic (Gen. 11:1–9), and they were scattered.

Language therefore is an important area in which we will have to work redemptively when speaking to spiritual seekers. We will want to offer solutions to the problem of changing the nouns of the game.

REDEFINING BIBLICAL LANGUAGE

Another sizable language barrier, besides renaming the game, is the New Spirituality's penchant for redefining biblical terminology, and even doctrine, to conform to New Age wisdom. Never presume that non-Christian spiritual seekers mean what the Bible means by its terms. When New Age wisdom informs biblical terminology, there will be radical redefinitions and subsequent communication headaches. Those who are unaware of this will assume that both parties were in agreement on certain points because biblical terms were used during the conversation. Both parties, however, may have been miles apart in meaning.

Here is a striking example. In *A Course in Miracles*, the language of the Bible is used throughout to convey New Age ideas (wisdom). (*Course* is now one of the most widespread books of spirit-channeling material.) *Course* implies that

> the true author is Jesus Christ speaking in the first person. As the work progresses, however, it radically redefines the person of Christ, the meaning of the atonement and the concept of revelation. None of these redefinitions is in line with the scriptural teachings of Jesus.[7]

Course redefines much more. We will look quickly at one area: forgiveness. Throughout *Course*, forgiveness is said to be a key for the healing of relationships. So far so good. Here is a sign of truth: forgiveness. Yet after the reader's attention has been caught, the distortion begins. According to *Course*, forgiveness is not about pardoning sins or offenses because there really are no such things; they are merely illusions. Forgiveness, therefore, is merely about a change of perception. I only perceived that you sinned against me. *Course* teaches that it was not really sin because sin does not really exist. I only perceived that what you did was sin because of the prevailing Christian ethos in the West. I therefore merely need to change my perception of what you did to me. You really did not do anything to me. This is forgiveness. "What you thought your brother did to you has not occurred. [Forgiveness] does not pardon sins. . . . It sees there was not sin."[8] "Sin is the home of all illusions [and stands] for things imagined."[9]

If this is true, God Himself has been pretty foolish, for we did not really sin against Him. Instead of sending His Son to die for our sins, He merely ought to have changed His perspective on what we did! *Course*, of course, is wrong, and in making such wild claims it has declared open warfare on biblical truth.

We must be alert. We can have a failure of communication even though both people groups are using the same language, English. Remember, two different wisdoms are using English, and there is a failure to communicate because each wisdom uses the language in a radically different sense. British philosopher and theologian John Peck puts it like this:

> [When] we talk the same language but we do not understand each other, this must mean that there is a difference of thought behind the

same words—what St. Paul would call a different wisdom, a different way of making sense of the creation.

We discussed this at some length during the Inter-Mission, where we noted that very real communication barriers are created whenever two different wisdoms use the same language. Paul, in 1 Corinthians 1—2, spoke of the foolishness that exists between different wisdoms. We also noted that foolishness (between two different wisdoms) is the bridge that must be crossed before effective communication occurs. We will discuss this further in a moment, but first a look at a third language barrier.

CHRISTIANESE

In the arena of language, we are not only up against a renaming of the old occult, paganism, and mysticism and a redefining of biblical terminology. Renaming and redefining things are problematic areas within the New Age world itself that we must overcome. Another handicap to communication exists within the Christian community, and that is the mischievousness of Christian jargon, buzzwords, and clichés. When we use them in our conversations with non-Christian spiritual seekers, misunderstandings are commonplace.

There is the story of the concerned mother who came upon her dejected five-year-old late one afternoon:

"What's wrong, David? How come you're not outside playing?"

"My teacher called me names today," little David replied sulkily.

"Oh, I don't think Mrs. Green would really do that, do you?"

"Yes, she did. She called me a scurvy elephant."

"Well, you're certainly not a scurvy elephant are you? Now run along and play and I'll call you when it's time to eat."

This calls for a quick word with Mrs. Green tomorrow morning, thought David's mother, *when I drop him off at school.*

"A scurvy elephant?" said Mrs. Green with surprise. "No, no. David was getting a little out of hand yesterday and I told him not to be such a *disturbing element.*"

I am afraid that this is an apt analogy for us. We may be saying something that is clear to us, but it is picked up differently inside the submarine. In general, most seekers will mishear words such as *born again, saved, gospel, converted, minister, share, fellowship, Lord, God,*

Jesus, and many others. Nor will they understand our frequently used phrases such as "Jesus died for you," "give your life to Jesus," "the blood of the Lamb," "confess your sins and repent," "are you saved?" and so on. Words and phrases that fairly gush out of our mouths are by and large probably not communicating to seekers. This is *our* problem. It is like speaking without thinking. Someone has called it the Christian mouth on automatic pilot.

I have to laugh when I look back to when we long-haired, bell-bottomed hippies spoke the jargon of the Aquarian counterculture in the 1960s and early 1970s. We thought that we were pretty hot stuff and that we had all the right answers. The more zealous among us thought that all we had to do was shoot off our mouths and all the outsiders would see the sense of it and quickly become Aquarians. It was a long time before I realized why we alienated more people than we converted. The longer we remained in the counterculture, the more our vocabulary shrank. I am not joking when I say that some people ended up with a vocabulary of only one or two hundred jargon words, which only the elect understood.

No wonder our parents, neighbors, teachers, employers, fellow employees, the parents of our boyfriends and girlfriends, acquaintances, and others remained outside the Age of Aquarius. They could not understand a thing we said. We understood it; it was in the music we listened to, the books we read, the films we watched, and the people with whom we associated. And we assumed, falsely, that outsiders would understand. What a joke! We thought we had the answer to life, but the only clear signal we sent was that we had no answer at all. Our language disabled our message. It was the dilemma of Scotty Briggs in the extreme.

Non-Christians are tone-deaf, so to speak, to Christianese, and we must take great pains to see to it that we are understood.

WORDS FOR THE WISE AND HARMLESS

So how can we get around these three language barriers? Let us start with renaming the game. Using the ideas of the "Submarine Communications Model," try to call attention to the original language. If the person is into astrology, tarot, spirit mediumship, channeling, and such, you could try to paint a window of perspective that would show the adherent the potential for demonic contact. If you have a history like mine, you could bring personal testimony into the conversation as evidence. You could express how it took Jesus Christ to free you from demonic influences that you once thought were benign.

Probably, the seeker will dismiss this and say that it has nothing to do with the devil. Remember not to sound like the demanding boss. For the moment you are merely trying to create some new windows of perspective and keep the person floating on the surface of communication. You could at least cast doubt upon what he believes. Ask the person if he can prove that demonic supernatural influences cannot ever be associated with astrology or channeling. Or ask how he can be so sure that the Bible is wrong about this. Even if you do not see any immediate fruit for your labors here, you are nevertheless redeeming the language by introducing into the conversation terminology that is more accurate and consistent with the nature of the thing being discussed.

In the second area, the New Age's redefinition of biblical terminology, the best idea is to ask the person what he means by words such as *God, Jesus, spirit, forgiveness, love, transformation, spiritual, prayer, the holy, the sacred,* and so on. Give the person plenty of space to say what he means. You may find that he is not too sure himself. After you have listened, try to offer biblical meanings.

And I'd like to emphasize something here. I mentioned in an earlier chapter that some Christians seem scared to death of rainbow symbols. So, too, there are Christians who are paralyzed when it comes to using words like *transformation, transcendent, paradigm, global village, holistic, green, interdependence, oneness,* and even *psychology,* as well as many others. Some Christian schools of thought imply that such words are strictly taboo, as if they were evil in themselves. As a result, Christians who use these words are often thought by other Christians to be closet New Agers.

However, cursing aside, we are not to be afraid of language; we are to be those (of all people) who redeem language. There is nothing wrong with the terminology. The fault lies in the wisdom that informs the terminology. The terminology, therefore, can be informed by biblical wisdom. This is hardly inconsequential. It gives us a means to redeem language. Therefore, "let your speech always be with grace," that is redemptive, "seasoned with salt," that is tasty, "that you may know how you ought to answer each one" (Col. 4:6), including New Age seekers.

So our battle is on two fronts here: (1) solving the riddle of renaming the nouns of the game, and (2) recovering the meaning of biblical terminology. Each front engages us in the redemption of language.

This still leaves us with the problem of Christianese. Are we speaking so as to be understood or merely setting our mouths on automatic pilot? The least we can do is help our listeners try to understand our biblical terminology when we use it. It is all right to stop and ask the other person if she has understood. She may say that she has. If so, do not take that for granted. Carefully ask if she could paraphrase what you said, so that you can ensure she really has understood a particular term. When you are sure that you have been understood, continue the conversation.

Yet another means would be good for us to adopt. Besides being careful and clear in our use of biblical terminology, we could try to bring fresh ideas about the gospel into our conversations. New ways of expressing the old gospel can be devised using the thought forms of today's New Age imagination. This will take some forethought and reflection, but the effort will be well worth it.

When I say new ways, I am absolutely not talking about a new gospel, a gospel other than that of Jesus Christ. By new I do not mean original in the sense that it has not been around before. *New* here is about what is fresh to one's experience and relevant. Something like this is behind one of Jesus' rather curious statements. It is found in Matthew 13:51–52, in a passage about communication, under-standing, Bible teachers, and the kingdom of heaven:

> Jesus said to them, "Have you understood all these things?" They said to Him, "Yes, Lord." Then He said to them, "Therefore every scribe instructed concerning the kingdom of heaven is like a house-holder who brings out of his treasure things new and old."

The word *new* here is not about what has not existed before. It is close to our English word *freshness*. Those who are instructed in the kingdom of heaven bring out something other than stale bread and stagnant water. They bring out something other than jargon. As the Amplified Bible puts it, they bring forth "the fresh [as well as] the familiar." As communicators, they offer to their listeners what is satisfying and alive with meaning. It may be familiar to us, but it has to be fresh to them.

If you are wondering just how important this is, ask yourself this. You are sitting in church on a Sunday morning when the preacher says, "Turn in your Bibles to John 3:16." Or perhaps it is Romans 12:1–2 or 1 Corinthians 12–14. Insert any passage that you have heard preached on so many times that, well, let us be honest, you are tired of hearing it. And you are tired of hearing it because it has become a cliché to you, passages so overworked that they are consequently without appeal. Wouldn't you like something other than shopworn preaching? Wouldn't you like something fresh, the same glorious truths preached from unfamiliar passages? I think we would all like this. We want something fresh and alive, and so do our listeners.

I tried to do this in chapters 12 to 14 of *What Your Horoscope Doesn't Tell You*. While writing the book, I put myself opposite myself on the other side of my typewriter and said, "What would have made sense to me if I had heard the gospel story during my years in the New Age world?" I then tried to put fresh meaning to biblical truth by using some New Age concepts such as spirituality, life after death, metaphysical power, and wisdom. This approach has really spoken to some quite dedicated followers of the New Spirituality.

There are many precedents for this in the Bible. We need only read our Lord's parables to see that He showed a mastery of the thinking of His day and how to use its images and language to communicate. The early apostles and evangelists also faced this problem of how to catch the imaginations of people of different wisdoms. John and Paul in particular showed great skill in putting the gospel in the language of their day, and they felt quite free to do that.

John's use of the word *logos* is instructive here. If the early Greeks were known for anything, it was for their search for the ultimate reason or meaning for life, what we would call God. They were part of a tradition that looked for a single principle that was comprehensive enough to explain all of life, and they felt that this single principle was operating through the mind. Thus for them, the one explanation for the universe and all of life became reason or, more correctly, reason that found expression. Their word for this was *logos*, which was commonly used in the religious and philosophical discussions of the day; it was made especially popular by the Alexandrian Jewish philosopher Philo, at the time of Christ. *Logos*, therefore, was chiefly used by the Greeks to signify what was behind all of life, also thought of as abstract reason or world of ideas. Thus, surrounded by the great jigsaw puzzle of life, the Greeks hit upon the single principle *logos* to explain it all, to give it meaning and coherence, to rationalize and justify what they did and how they lived.

For this reason, *logos* had a strong association with ideas surrounding the creation and what sustains it. Thus when John used the term to begin his gospel (John 1:1–3), the Greeks were immediately with him. It struck a deep chord within them. "Yes, yes," they might have said, "we have no trouble with you calling the *logos* God." Harmless as a dove, John used the language of the day to capture their imaginations. And they would be pretty much in agreement with John until he disclosed that the true *logos* became flesh and blood (v. 14). To that the Greeks would not agree. It was unthinkable to them that their pure idea, their *logos*, should become contaminated in the "evil" material world by incarnation in a human body.

Greek wisdom precluded that the *logos* could ever take on flesh and bones. They never conceived the *logos* as a person but as a kind of thoroughly pure spiritual idea. But John came along and said, "Look, you're right up to a point. *Logos* is certainly about the creative activity of God, but this creative activity is not a spiritual idea or a principle. It is a person. Jesus Christ. God the Son."

John had found some common ground in the contemporary language of his day, and he built a communication bridge with it to show them the distinctly biblical Christian truth about the *logos*. His statement that "the *logos* became flesh" marks off his use of the term from that of Greek wisdom. This distinction would be crystal clear to John's Greek audience, and it would take a humble Greek to bow the knee and accept it. Yet that was what John was aiming at, and he used the language of his day to do it.

Other examples are found in Paul's use of contemporary language. In Chapter 15, we saw that when the apostle was among educated pagans and philosophers (Acts 17:16–31), he used some of their concepts as a springboard to make the gospel known. Paul clearly understood this secret of communication. When he was among uneducated rural folk (Acts 14:8–18), he used little religious terminology, which they would have found difficult to understand. Yet when in a synagogue, Paul used the overtly religious language of Zion because that was familiar to his Jewish audiences.

That must be part of what Paul meant when he said, "I have become all things to all men, that I might by all means save some"

(1 Cor. 9:22). Even Paul's use of the word *redemption* was redemptive. *Redemption* in Paul's writings, such as Ephesians 1:7 or Colossians 1:14, is a picture taken from the slave market. It was a general practice in the ancient world for a slave to be bought and set free from some evil by being dedicated to a god. The person became free by becoming a slave, at least technically, to Zeus, Ares, Artemis, or whomever. This was *redemption*. The apostle captures the contemporary imagination by his use of the term, but then, like John, Paul shows his audience the distinctly biblical Christian meaning and truth of it. "If you want true freedom, and not just in a technical sense," says Paul, "you want the redemption that has been bought for us by Jesus Christ."

Let us therefore take a cue from these apostles and from our Lord. "Our business is to present that which is timeless (the same yesterday, today, and tomorrow) in the particular language of our culture,"[10] or of the world into which we are sent with the gospel.

> To conclude—you must translate every bit of your Theology into the vernacular. This is very troublesome and it means you can say very little in half an hour, but it is essential. It is also the greatest service to your own thought. . . . Power to translate is the test of having really understood one's own meaning.[11]

21

EFFECTUAL
PRAYER

―∞―

WHAT SOIL IS to seedtime and harvest, so prayer is to effective communication and evangelization. Thus we do not minimize the importance of prayer, but we pray that the lost might hear and believe. In this chapter I do not want to interfere with the way you pray by weighing one school of prayer against another. Neither will I offer new prayer models. What I have in mind is to suggest several contexts for prayer that seem particularly effective in regard to the kind of spiritual seekers we have in mind in this book.

These contexts can then be taken into whatever kinds of prayer models you use. James wrote, "the prayer of a righteous man is powerful and effective" (5:16 NIV). Christian communication is also made possible by effectual prayer. I find this comforting, for it asks the Holy Spirit to be with us in the communication process.

PRAYER CONTEXTS

Pray for spiritual seekers to understand God as Creator and the implications of this. Many, if not most, New Age followers think that God is an impersonal energy, and they have also been steeped since childhood in evolutionary views of the cosmos. The gospel story makes no sense in this milieu. It will take God Himself to help these people understand that He created all things. Once that puzzle piece falls into place, it will help them to understand what has gone wrong with life and why the gospel is the good news.

Pray that God will send the Holy Spirit to convict seekers of their sinfulness. This may seem too obvious to mention; yet it is a particularly good prayer in this spiritual environment because New Agers, in general, do not believe that they are morally guilty before a holy God.

It was an increasingly weighty conviction of sin, which seemed to come from out of nowhere and was quite unlooked for, that started the month-long process that ended in my conversion to Christ. During a long, leisurely drive from Michigan to California (I was alone), I suddenly felt horribly guilty of sin. The weight of this intensified daily and was extremely annoying. Worse still, several days after that had begun, I remembered from my childhood religious training where sinners went! I did not see flames or anything like that, but I was thoroughly convinced that I was a sinner, that hell was real, and that I was on my way there.

Try as I might, I could not shake the conviction of God that I was a sinner. It certainly got my attention, I can tell you. For years I had believed that my problem was my bad karma; sin and its consequent moral guilt were illusions of outdated religious traditions. I could save myself by paying off my bad karma with my good karma, through the round of rebirths. Of course, it was a doctrine of self-salvation, but it made sense to me. Suddenly, I was now under daily anguish and despair over my sinful nature, without any hope of a solution. I knew I could not save myself.

The attack upon my New Age wisdom was even more frustrating because I did not know where it came from. I did not know that there was such a person as the Holy Spirit, whom Jesus had said He would send to convict people of their sins (John 16:8).

It was a very trying month for me. I thought I was possibly cracking up. Yet it was necessary. It freed me of false beliefs and awakened long-forgotten memories about the truth of human nature and the eternal state of one's soul. Pray, therefore, that the Holy Spirit would convict New Age enthusiasts of their sin.

Pray for the power of God to dismantle false intellectual strongholds within the person's wisdom and mind. You may have some clues as to what these are, but God will clearly know what they are and how to discharge them from the person's mind.

This may seem an unusual prayer, yet it was the second phase in the process of my conversion. Some Christians refer to this phenomenon as a "truth encounter," that is, false beliefs coming face to face with the truth of God. And effective it was, too! During the more than seven years that I studied occultism, meditation, and mysticism, these beliefs organized themselves powerfully in my thinking to become dominant features of my wisdom. They greatly influenced my behavior, and part of the process of my conversion had to be to get them out of the way. It happened several days after the conviction of sin had begun, and just as suddenly. My New Age wisdom neatly arranged on the shelves of my mind, somehow disappeared as an authority (power) over me. It was as if God bulldozed the library of my mind, and it left me scratching around in wide open spaces intellectually. I had no recourse to previously held beliefs about the big questions. And I was grappling with the biggest one!

It was not that I had lost my mind (well, maybe I had, in a sense!). I could still think about karma, spiritual evolution, astrology, and meditation, but they had completely lost their power of appeal to me. Previously treasured beliefs became only words; the power that had informed them and had made them fascinating was no longer there. I was convinced that something was terribly wrong with the beliefs. They seemed a fabrication, without substance. In turn, I was forced—I always tried to be honest with myself—to call into question my years as a New Age follower.

That was an important turning point for me for the following reason. I had grown up in the United States, and one of my chief reasons for entering the New Age world had been a thorough disillusionment with the American Dream. The West did not have the answer, so I looked East. Yet now the Aquarian Dream had been blown out of the water. Where else was there to look? Whatever meaning and power New Age wisdom had had over me, it had disappeared. Pray, therefore, for God to disarm spiritual seekers of the power of false beliefs and intellectual strongholds.

Pray that seekers would believe in and accept the reality of a loving and living infinite-personal God who longs to forgive them. An impersonal god force cannot forgive. The best that can be done with it is to manipulate its spiritual laws or principles, like those of karma and reincarnation, in your favor. The problem is that laws and principles cannot forgive you; only a person can forgive. If the forgiving person happens to be the infinite-personal God, the potential for life is indeed endless and can begin immediately. This makes the hope offered by reincarnation look bleak by comparison, bleak in the extreme.

It was the hope of forgiveness that brought to a climax my conversion experience. After weeks of anguish, despair, and hopelessness—my sins before me like the Empire State Building, myself a speck on the pavement about to be crushed—I broke down and wept bitterly one evening over my sins. It then occurred to me to ask God, though I did not really know what I was doing, to forgive me. But I did not have a clue as to how to go about that.

So while kneeling beside a bed in a small hotel room in Costa Mesa, California, in July 1976, sobbing heavily, my face buried in the bedspread, I simply said "God, I'm sorry. God, I'm sorry. God, I'm sorry," over and over. For what seemed like the longest time I soaked that bed with my tears. Then slowly, though surely, the knowledge that God had forgiven me washed over me. As someone once described it, it was like finding a sea of liquid love. I knew that there was a personal God and that He had forgiven me. I had been forgiven, and the heavenly peace that accompanied it was utterly amazing. Pray, therefore, that seekers would begin to imagine the possibilities.

Pray that seekers would have a change of mind about who Jesus is, that they would see Him as Lord, God the Son, and not as merely another avatar in the constellation of Eastern god-men who are dead, buried, and gone. Jesus Christ was dead, buried, and resurrected. People must see this.

I will never forget awakening the next morning after the night I have just described. The first question on my mind before I even got out of bed was, "What in the world happened to me last night?" Immediately a Voice as clear as a bell answered, "You're working for Jesus Christ now and not Satan. Jesus Christ is now your Lord." I will always recall the words. A thousand lights suddenly went on inside me, and I was soon to understand that it was the Holy Spirit, leading me and teaching about Jesus. Just as I had not known that there was a Holy Spirit who would convict people of their sins, neither did I know that He would instruct Christians about Jesus Christ; but God was greater than my ignorance. And after all, He knows how to care for His newborns.

I was later to read in John's gospel where Jesus told His disciples, "When the Helper comes, whom I shall send to you from the

Father, . . . He will testify of Me" (15:26). There was no longer any doubt in my mind about who Jesus was because the Holy Spirit was indeed testifying to me about His presence, power, and person. Pray that spiritual seekers would begin to see the uniqueness of the Lord Jesus Christ.

Pray that the person's objections to God would be transformed into calling on Him. I think the devil must work overtime to keep people from asking for God's help. Something unfair happens, a tragedy strikes, or an injustice is felt, and the victim responds, "Why would a loving God allow that to happen?" Reactions like this are common, and they have a cumulative effect on people over the years. Many seeds of doubt are sown and crop up to undermine the goodness of God. People start to question His character and purpose, and as a result, they eat the fruit of a great revulsion to the gospel. Seekers often hold the gospel at arm's length because of such objections.

The Bible, however, indicates that during times of personal tragedy, injustice, grave doubt, and such, the humble person seeks God out, while the proud inveighs against Him and so meets with resistance, finding little or no comfort. Pray for seekers to open up to God, and to have the humility that brings grace.

Pray that Jesus would deliver the seeker from any possible demonic spirits. I do not want to quibble here over moot questions about demonic possession, oppression, demonization, deliverance ministries, and the like. Rather, because I believe—and rightly so, I think—in the existence of personal devils, demons, and evil spirits, and because I understand at first hand their suprahuman power and the bondage into which they can bring people, I conclude that prayer should be made to God requesting Him to deal with whatever the situation calls for here. He is able.

I experienced deliverance, too, on the evening of my conversion. As an occultist, I had several "spirit guides"—I had asked for them, and through meditation and visualization, I had increasing esprit de corps with them. It was not until the evening of my conversion that their duplicity was revealed to me by Jesus Christ, and I saw clearly that they were demonic and not the helpers and friends the New Spirituality claims them to be.

I cannot take the space here to relate all that occurred surrounding my deliverance that evening. There was some struggle, and it was unpleasant to sense, and even at times to hear, Jesus casting them out. Yet what stands out most in my mind, and this, too, is what seekers need to see and experience, is that the mighty power of Jesus Christ made the demonic power seem inconsequential by comparison. It was perfectly clear to me, during the process, that they knew who their Master was and that their power was no match for His. If you meet a person whom you believe needs to be cleaned up in this important area, start praying.

Pray for discernment to become aware of occasions when a spirit may be sitting in as an unwanted third party, influencing a conversation. This, too, may seem an unusual prayer, especially for those Western Christians whose wisdom is still too rationalistic. Yet we will be talking with people whose wisdom includes a high degree of the irrational, which gives the spirit world ample opportunity to interfere. Whenever this occurs, I have found that effective communication ceases.

Certainly, this is a foggy region, and I do not think that it is even possible to make much of a map, even by way of outlines, before we face these curves in the road. Which is why we should rely deeply upon prayer, discernment, and our Lord's immediate help here. One marker I do see, however, is that this dynamic seems dissimilar to the classic sense of possession in which a demon is deeply controlling someone's behavior. Rather, it is a situation in which, without notice, a spirit imposes itself upon a conversation and hinders the communication process.

No one must make a theology out of the following experience or even think that it is a spiritual law. But because it is not someone else's story, I will risk telling it, trusting that it will shed light on certain curious dynamics that readers may have faced when conversing with spiritual seekers, and who may still be wondering about it.

I met Tom when I was a young Christian and he was slipping steadily deeper into the occult. He was single, in his late twenties, and up to his neck in numerology. As our relationship developed, I became even more concerned by discovering that he had serious interests in meditation and mysticism and that he was under the tutelage of a New Age prophetess, whom I eventually met. When Tom told me that he was leaving his job in Michigan to move into a monastery in California, I thought that maybe he had had a secret interest in Christianity that was now beginning to show. But when I asked what kind of monastery, he told me it was a Hindu ashram (a good illustration of changing the nouns of the game).

During the months in which our relationship had been building, we had established a fair amount of trust and respect for each other. I had worked hard to dispel Tom's caricature of Christians and to keep him floating on the surface of communication. Because of his impending jaunt to the ashram, I felt it was time to have a heart-to-heart talk with him about the dangers of the New Spirituality and the truth of the gospel. I felt that he was floating solidly enough and that I could have this conversation without losing him below the surface. If he was determined to enter an ashram, I was determined he would go there with some new windows of perspective, at least.

We set a day to have lunch at a restaurant near where we worked. The day came, and for the first half hour our luncheon conversation went smoothly, even though we were not talking merely superficially about our beliefs. We were listening intently to each other, commenting, and a clear though weighty exchange of ideas was taking place until . . . subtly (when I look back, though, I see it was an unmistakable shift) it became difficult for me to answer Tom's questions in such a way that he was taking them on board. I didn't think I had lost him below the surface, so I did not know what to do. Yet that was only part of the sudden new dynamic.

Tom began saying things in a manner that made it extremely difficult for me to make my points. Then when I knew that a point had gotten through, instead of his usual habit of mulling it over, he would immediately respond in such a way as to oppose it. The give-and-take became very disconcerting because whatever I said next was being answered with powerful (ir)rationalizations that left me befuddled. Soon it was hard to get a word in edgeways, and that was out of character for Tom.

I wondered what was happening, though I do have a confession to make. When the atmosphere had begun to change, I got the impression that I ought to halt the conversation in order to pray. However, I let the opportunity pass. Rationalizations for not praying controlled my actions: *It's ridiculous to start praying in a crowded restaurant, too embarrassing.* After I failed to act on the inner urge, I watched our conversation deteriorate until it was evident to us both that there was nothing else to do except pay the bill and return to work. The thing was, I had not lost Tom below the surface of communication; something else had happened. Some dynamic that I was unfamiliar with had ruined our conversation.

Several months later I happened to be talking to a Christian couple who provided a clue. "Your conversation with Tom," they said, "reached a point where a spirit surfaced and you were no longer engaged in conversation with Tom alone. The spirit's presence scrambled the conversation and probably fed Tom all kinds of unusual input to disrupt communication. It was as if you were no longer talking with Tom." I said that sounded a bit extreme to me, but they suggested that I think it over and pray about it. They concluded, "Perhaps now you can see why the Lord wanted you to stop and pray."

I now think that there is sense in what they said. Tom had indulged in occult beliefs and practices for a long time, to the point that he had become, to some extent, demonically influenced. When the spirit surfaced to become part of the conversational dynamic, communication became confused, argumentative, and at times irrational. I now believe that had I had the nerve to stop and pray, I might have received discernment about this, and then in the power of God prayed to bind this spirit from interfering.

Before we move on, please do not leave this chapter thinking that Strohmer believes or says that every conversation with a follower of the New Spirituality is a talk with a demon. Conversation is often ineffective or breaks down simply due to human denseness, that is to say, either party may lack basic communication skills or be ignorant of the other's wisdom. For others, however, a little bell will have rung, as the story illustrates some outside interference they may at times have faced.[1] Through prayer, we can become aware of yet another device of our common enemy to frustrate effective Christian communication (see pages 42–43).

Pray about any wounds, bitterness, or similar obstacles that the person may have toward Christianity. Seekers may have had injuries that make them resistant to the gospel, and these may have come from Christian sources. If you discover this, it may be best, for the time being, to make it a matter for prayer rather than trying to help the person sort it out. Or if the person is ill, or perhaps suffering from an inner wound that is unrelated to being hurt by a Christian, you may want to ask if you could pray for her. You never know. Your offer may demonstrate for the person the reality of a personal God who hears and answers our prayers. It could reveal God much more effectively than words ever could. And if healing occurs, you would have a context to discuss the differences between answered prayer and the New Spirituality's explanations for healing.

Pray that God will give you the grace to work around the intellectual/spiritual dynamics of irrationality and passivity. We have much more than human resources available to us during our conversations. We have not only God's power but also His wit and wisdom to help us keep the person floating on the surface of communication, even in the face of the irrational and of passivity of mind. Pray for God's grace to help you remain level-headed here.

Pray that God would prepare specific groups of people within the New Age world to be saved. Our tendency is to pray for individuals; yet if certain groups of seekers became Christians, it would boost the gospel's impact in that world considerably.

Consider the following. In the nineteenth century, when there was a great disparity between Western Christians and Eastern cultures, Christians often went into these cultures to preach by setting up exploratory mission stations. These missionaries

> acquired a piece of land, often with great difficulty. They built residences suitable for white men. Then they added churches, schools, quarters to house helpers, hospitals, leprosy homes, orphanages and printing establishments. The mission station was usually at the centre of the village or tribe. From it, extensive tours were made into the surrounding countryside. It was the home of the missionary staff and all the activities of the mission took place around the station.[2]

These mission stations remind me of attempts to set up Christian booths at New Age festivals, or of sallying forth from our suburban churches to go witnessing during the psychic fair at the local mall. I am certainly not opposed to this, and it does pluck the odd brand from the fire. But why should we have to settle for that? The Christians who worked in the mission stations described above will tell you that that kind of missionary approach was never very successful at winning large numbers of people for Christ. It was successful, however, at identifying what peoples were ready to become Christians, and therefore in what directions missionary efforts could usefully be made on a large scale.

At the time I am writing this, it is my opinion that New Agers as a people group are uninterested in becoming Christians, but how about if we could begin identifying groups within the New Age world that show some deepening interest? If we knew which groups, we could go to them. More than one missionary leader has theorized that this was how the apostle Paul went into various gentile populations to win converts. We know that he had the leading of the Holy Spirit, but he also had his common sense. He probably identified gentile families who had some interest in the gospel, and then he went to them. How did he identify them? He could easily have had conversations with his Jewish converts who knew Gentiles. Or once he gained certain Gentiles for Christ, he could easily have asked them who he might go to next. Such information would have been especially useful if the Gentiles were respected in the community, which might have opened more doors for the apostle.

If we could begin to identify particular groups of non-Christian spiritual seekers who show some interest, we could at least begin praying for them. This is how the Billy Graham team goes about it. Once they target a certain city for a crusade, they raise up prayer vigils in as many churches as possible in that city a year before the actual crusade. I worked in this context once, and it was amazing how powerful the effect was on certain groups when the crusade finally came to town.

Perhaps you already have one or two lines of communication open with some seekers. What interests do they have? Is there a particular spiritual group that they usually associate with? Is this group at all open to your influence as a Christian? If the group is open, pray that God will help you to influence it in the direction of Christianity. If you cannot identify any groups that are open, perhaps you could start a prayer group just to pray for those groups.

No doubt you will be able to think of other prayer contexts. Pray in faith, believing. And remember that effective communication is helped along by effectual prayer.

22

GETTING
PERIPHERAL VISION

AN EARLIER SUGGESTION was that we should transform ourselves from battleships into luxury cruise liners in an effort to appear less threatening and more inviting (see Illustration 3, Chapter 15). I trust that we have made at least some alterations in our appearance by now! The ultimate goal is not merely to keep the submarine floating but to get seekers to come on board with us and head in our direction. Illustration 4 would be the ideal. Yet even if we take the material of the previous chapters to heart and are transformed, there may be some mischievous presuppositions hidden within our wisdom that, after all is said and done, still hold us back from building relationships with spiritual seekers. I want us to challenge these presuppositions here.

Have you heard the story about the Christian leader and the butterfly? One sunny afternoon, a Christian leader (I have forgotten his name; let us call him Don) went fishing. With his legs dangling in the cool water as he sat on the dock, his fishing pole resting at his side, Don spied a new butterfly struggling to get out of a cocoon. He watched for some time, never having seen anything like it. Soon he felt sorry for the poor butterfly because it was having such a hard time getting out of the cocoon. Don took out his penknife to help the little guy out. He made a narrow slit in the cocoon and out fell the butterfly—grotesquely deformed, especially its wings. It could not

Former New Age seekers come on board with us

Illustration 4

fly and now would never be able to fly. "That's just like you, Don," the Lord said to him suddenly. "You cut My people out of their struggles and think you are doing them a favor, but they are walking around half transformed instead."

We, too, must finish our God-ordained struggles in order to be thoroughly transformed by His grace. I say this because you may find some of the following sections quite personal and challenging, and so may not want to struggle with them. These sections may indicate areas where your presuppositions are holding you back from interaction with seekers. If so, you will want to struggle with them, by God's grace.

THE FORTRESS MENTALITY

Jerram Barrs calls it the "castle mentality," and aptly so, I think.[1] When we get saved, the drawbridge is lowered to us, and we are received into the Christian subculture and religious scene as into a castle. Then the drawbridge is raised, and we are left to roam around inside this massive religious fortress. Here we learn lifestyles that make it possible to go for long periods of time without having to be around non-Christians. I realize that this is changing, slowly. Some churches are recognizing the problem, that they have been isolationist, and they are overhauling their structures to allow themselves to be more involved with non-Christians. Nevertheless, many of us still must admit that we find it puzzling to communicate with non-Christians simply because, in our disassociation from them, we do not know how they think or what their interests are. We have superficial associations with fellow employees, the habitual "Thank you" to salesclerks, the occasional "Hello" when passing a neighbor. But do we have any significant relationships with outsiders? If not, is it any wonder that our attempts at outreach—personal or group— often fail miserably?

Life in the fortress has left us unable to relate to outsiders. As I travel, I find that some churches like to hold public meetings in non-churchy-looking buildings to create contexts for inviting and reaching non-Christians. So far, so good. Yet with rare exceptions—so far, we are working on it!—as I look around during these so-called public meetings, it is obvious that the audiences are almost entirely Christians. What happened to the point of the meeting? Where are the non-Christian spiritual seekers? The problem lies in what was done to get them into the building. Posters were tacked up around town, an advertisement was run in a local newspaper, perhaps several radio spots were aired, or maybe leaflets were handed out around town. That is to say, the process of inviting persons was largely impersonal.

Life within the fortress has made it difficult to know what else to do. Going forth with advertising becomes our chief activity, and it is nearly pointless for drawing a crowd of non-Christians unless your guest speaker is well known. The solution would be for everyone in a congregation to extend personal invitations. Pleasant and appealing invitations are rare, however, because we do not know non-Christians well enough, or if we do, we are still inept at extending invitations. I have seen entire congregations look at me with a blank stare when I have tried to fire them up to invite seekers to these public meetings. I know that they would like to know how to be able to do it, but they just do not know how. For too long they have been taught their Christianity from presuppositions that may forbid them even to have an imagination for being involved with non-Christians. They have been indoctrinated to believe that spare time ought to be devoted to more religious meetings and activities inside the fortress, where isolationism, and its fruit irrelevancy, become the normal Christian life.

We may agree with the problem, but some of us will still have difficulty lowering the drawbridge and getting out to build relationships. For one thing, the fortress mentality has created in us an "us versus them" mentality, that is to say, "an embattled feeling; we feel like a beleaguered minority surrounded by an aggressive culture which is attacking and destroying us."[2] This has produced in us an unhealthy attitude and fear of non-Christians, and it is hard for those who perceive people as enemies to feel free to associate with them. For another thing, for many of us, lowering the drawbridge will mean disentangling ourselves from far too many weekly or monthly religious meetings and activities and then using that free time to initiate relationships with non-Christians. Perhaps I could suggest that we could get involved in so-called secular activities and community programs, such as parent-teacher groups, school boards, volunteer work, local election work, or social action projects, where we will meet secular people who are being transformed by the cosmopolitan spirituality of the New Age.

If you think I am being tough on you here, you are right; I am. Contemporary Christianity is seen as irrelevant by and to the New Age world because largely it is. We are seen as being out of touch with reality because to a great extent we are. We have been made into a people, many of whom have a private religion with no public applicability. I have been tough on myself about this. And it is going to take some time before the world of the New Spirituality sees us differently, even if we all lowered the drawbridge tomorrow. I do not know about you, but it has occurred to me that in my efforts to protect myself inside the walls of the fortress I will inevitably get trampled under foot anyway, for that is the place where salt that has lost its flavor ends up.

THAT UNINVITING LOOK

Besides being a *Church Without Walls,*[3] we are going to have to become approachable to followers of the New Spirituality. Our churches (I do not mean the buildings only) often have fronts that not only fail to attract these people but also seem designed to keep them out. Even an interested seeker may see no way into a congregation. The solution to this, I think, is that we are going to have to be more relaxed and appear slightly frayed at the edges. I have been in several churches where this is being tried, and the results are amazing. One particularly striking illustration comes to mind.

The occasion was the Sunday morning when I preached at Fairlight Christian Centre in Tooting, London, on the differences between New Age and Christian spirituality. The meeting hall, which was not churchy-looking, was full of people. I am glad it was because the satanists in the back were hidden from me, and if I had known they were listening, I might have become tolerably reticent! As it was, I finished the message and was soon introduced to them, a married couple who were fully open about being satanists. Hiding it would have been impossible anyway. They were completely dressed in black, decorated with several satanic-looking tattoos, and ornamented with the idiosyncratic jewelry of their beliefs. What was even more instructive for me was that they had their three children in tow, and the wife was pregnant with a fourth.

Fairlight was having a community lunch following the service, and we asked the family to join us. They said that they should probably get going, but when we continued to extend the invitation, they gladly accepted. We ended up talking to them for several hours, and here is a part of their story that really impresses itself on my mind.

Though they lived just down the road, that was their first visit to Fairlight, and they almost stayed away. When we asked why, they said that there was a church across the street from their apartment and that its minister had made it impossible for them even to get into the church building. When we asked what had happened, we were told that the minister could not understand them.

"We've been into satanism for a long time," they told us. "And now we have some doubts about it. We decided to check out a Christian church and went across the street. But the minister couldn't handle us. He told us that if we wanted to be in his church we could not wear black or our jewelry. He threatened us with judgment and told us that we were under God's curse. We tried talking to him, but it was useless. We got upset and left."

This heavy-handed approach is not uncommon and certainly puts up an uninviting front to Christianity. Frankly, I was surprised that they then took the risk of approaching Fairlight, and so I asked about this. Earlier that week they had seen a leaflet advertising my Saturday seminar on the New Age. They had called the church on Friday to find out if I was the kind of speaker who would ridicule them. The church secretary told them that she did not know me, but because of my background she felt that I would be understanding and would welcome them to the seminar. The secretary sensitively extended an invitation, but as it turned out, they were unable to attend on Saturday. Yet it was on the strength of that phone call (the personal touch) that the family turned up on Sunday morning. They stayed through the message, through the meal, through, in fact, the entire afternoon. They talked openly and seriously with several of us. I eventually had to leave, but I found out afterward that the family stayed around to give the minister a lift home. It seems that the minister needed some work done on his car, and the husband was a mechanic.

The Lord does move in mysterious ways. As far as I know, this couple have not yet become Christians, but what I do know is that by making themselves approachable, Fairlight built a communication bridge into their needy lives. Certainly, it meant taking a risk and being frayed enough at the edges to put up with some unpleasantness. But, then, the Christian life is not about comfortableness.

BRAND NAMES

An important question needs to be asked when we are moving away from the fortress mentality and into approachable church settings: Are we offering people religion or relationship? Christianity hit the world running with a person. It turned the world upside down by attracting people to a life. *Life*, not dogma, philosophy, or ritual, was the good news. People were dead, and life was being offered to them as a gift from God through a relationship with His Son, Jesus Christ.

It happens all too often that Christians stop ministering life and start serving up brands of religion. Maybe we ought to push the clock back to what it was that made us Christians and start offering that life. One problem today is that many seekers look at Christianity and all they see are its religious trappings and paraphernalia. And no wonder; they are so paramount to the outsider, who observes institution rather than a life.

Some Christians are thrilled because Jesus has come to destroy the works of darkness. Yet are we big enough to admit that when He comes with such destruction, He may also destroy half of what passes for Christian religion? (Several Christian scandals in recent times are cases in point.) We want to be careful about what we are ministering. Is it religion or relationship? Is it the power of an indestructible life or a form of godliness (2 Tim. 3:5)?

This is not to say that God does not work through denominations and churches, or to say that we are to sacrifice Christian theology on the altar of mystical existentialism. That is far from the case: we will drift from the faith if we are not anchored to a knowledge of what that faith is. Thus we are admonished, "Examine [ourselves] to see whether [we] are in the faith" (2 Cor. 13:5 NIV). This is not a verse about whether or not we have faith in general. It is about whether or not we are in the Christian faith in particular. How will we answer the question without knowing what the Christian faith teaches about itself? And this we learn from our denominations and churches.

Nevertheless, it is the power of an eternal life, not religiosity, that will capture the New Age imagination. A demonstrated life in the Spirit will make the appeal of the New Age world look like a parlor trick. Seekers may be willing to accept the life of the Spirit, but not religious trappings. Christ's life can penetrate their hearts; a crystallized religious system, never.

THE AIDs TEST

Before we offer people the supreme relationship, we may need Attitude Inspection Day (AID). Some of us have derisive attitudes toward followers of the New Spirituality. The mocking, scoffing tone of some of our writers, and even pastors, who snicker at people such as Shirley MacLaine is disgraceful. "Ha, ha! That scatterbrained redhead with her New Age ideas. She's crazy. What a laugh!" This completely misses the point of people like MacLaine who have a sharp native intelligence and are on a spiritual search.

The Christian publishing industry has allowed books to be written on the New Age that are unchristian in spirit and tone. They demean people, and this communicable disease has infected Christian readers. Such books are generally written from the embattled and defensive position of the fortress and are antagonistic and disrespectful. Rather than offer crackerjack arguments in a spirit of humility, they lambaste seekers, mete out sensationalistic conclusions, and generally misunderstand the paradigm shift occurring today in the West (see Inter-Mission). The problem is that most seekers would not recognize themselves on the pages of such books. We would not like it if New Age writers demeaned us like this. And if we carry this lack of recognition into our personal conversations, why should a seeker listen?

What will our AIDs test reveal? The apostle Peter tells us in what spirit and tone we are to express our findings: give an answer with gentleness and respect (1 Pet. 3:15). If we used this as our criterion, we would have to withdraw some Christian books from the stores. The apostle Paul has this way of saying it: "Let your speech always be with grace, seasoned with salt, that you may know how you ought to answer each one" (Col. 4:6). "Always," he says, "always."

We have indeed created some uproar in the secular community, but that has been largely a result of our mocking and scoffing. Uproars will come, but must they result from our derisive attitudes? Why not create the kind of uproar that comes from persuasive arguments that cannot be gainsaid and are delivered in the spirit of humility? Impossible? It happened in the book of Acts (19:35–40), and when it did, God saw to it that even the secular town clerks were on the side of the Christians. They even commanded the crowd to be silent in favor of the Christians. When we have incisive arguments in the right attitude,

I look for the town clerks to be on our side, too, by God's grace. We shall then get a hearing for the life we are offering.

Our AIDs test may also reveal intolerance toward seekers. This may be the result of being offended at people whose values and beliefs are non-Christian. And yet Jesus calls us into contact with these people, which means that we will need some tolerance. Dick Keyes writes,

> Tolerance is living side by side with others who have real and deep differences with us. [It is] living with respect and civility in our personal attitudes as much as possible. Tolerance is not relativism and has no necessary relationship to relativism. A common confusion today is to think that if you question relativism, you must be intolerant. There are some sad chapters in our own Christian history at this point (as there are in all other world religions and secular ideologies). Christians have sometimes been cruel and arrogant to those who did not agree with them. [Yet] followers of Christ are called to live with faith and patience, love their enemies, seek the welfare of those who would do them evil, and be salt and light in the world. Jesus and the whole New Testament encourages [this]. Tolerance does not demand that we never try to persuade someone of the truth. It does demand that we hold that person in respect in spite of areas of disagreement.[4]

THE COMPLAINTS DEPARTMENT

The insufficiencies, failures, and even the evils done at times by Christians are lamentable, and any number of these might come up as a seeker's remonstrance against becoming a Christian. It is foolish to whitewash obvious Christian delinquencies. The offenses must be squarely faced, honestly admitted, and humbly discussed. Few things can ruin a Christian's attitude quicker than receiving complaints about Christianity from non-Christians. However, when we learn how to work in the Complaints Department with humility and grace, we will be able to keep building communication bridges.

A litany of legitimate complaints can come up—immorality, hypocrisy, our high divorce rate, greed, irrelevancy, and more. Others will complain of seeing no life in the church, or of painful experiences with Christians and ministers. The point is, we do create offenses. The problem is, these may keep seekers from Christian inquiry. If we discover that they are wounded, the wounds have to be treated with balm. Some people who now follow the New Spirituality have back-slidden from the Christian fold into the New Age world because of being hurt by Christians. Healing balm is needed.

Perhaps the best way to work in the Complaints Department with humility and grace is to concede whatever legitimate complaints come our way. As representatives of the church, we can accept rather than whitewash complaints on behalf of the Christians who injured people. It is a kind of intercession. As representatives of Christianity, we can apologize to the seeker on behalf of the system. And if you have been hurt similarly by a believer, and if you have been healed, so much the better. It is very powerful to be able to say, "I've been hurt like that, too." The other person is probably expecting your denial or a cover-up, but when he hears you owning up to these offenses, that is an effective witness.

The power of this kind of intercession came washing over me one evening when I was having fellowship with a Franciscan whose name is Father Duane. This story has deep roots and is fairly complex, but here is the gist of it. I was born into the Roman Catholic tradition, and for various reasons, some legitimate and some not, I rejected it in my mid-teens. By my late teens I had become rebellious and was getting interested in New Ageism via the 1960s counterculture. During those years, I only darkened the door of any church when it was absolutely necessary, such as for the odd wedding or funeral. Also during those years, my feelings toward the Catholic church hardened.

After my conversion to Christ, with the redemptive grace of God motivating me, I went at intervals to talk to various priests in an effort to get rid of the chip on my shoulder against the Catholic church. Every one of the attempts failed, and it was difficult not to feel more justified in my negative feelings. I finally gave up the attempt and forgot about it.

Several years passed and I met Father Duane, who lived in a Franciscan seminary in a suburb north of Detroit, Michigan. I attended a course he was teaching called the "School of Evangelization," the object of which was to lead Catholics into a personal relationship with Jesus Christ and then to train them to lead other Catholics to Christ.

Father Duane and I struck up a relationship during those weeks, and one evening after sharing an evening meal together at the seminary, we went back to his rooms to talk and pray. Later that evening the conversation turned to my grudges against the Catholic church. How this became a topic, I do not recall; it was not planned. I opened up my feelings to Father Duane. When I realized that I could trust him to listen at a deeper level, I talked more freely about the hurts I had sustained as a sensitive boy in Catholic schools. Unleashing the anger and bitterness took some time, but Father Duane was a good listener. When I had finished, I was thoroughly surprised, and pleasantly so, at his response. It certainly was in the opposite spirit from what I had been used to hearing.

"Charles," he said, "you certainly do have some legitimate complaints about how we brought you up in our schools."

"I thought that I did," I said, "but I was beginning to wonder if maybe it was all my fault. I have tried several times to discuss this with a number of priests, but they have never understood me."

"No," he said. "I can see that we have hurt you. We haven't done a very good job for you."

I could hardly believe my ears.

"More and more," he continued, "we are discovering how we went wrong with so many of you young people, how we could have done so much better. As a representative of the Catholic church, I ask if you will forgive us."

Tears had been filling my eyes, and the dam burst. Father Duane had been what I had needed all along, a powerful witness of Christ's compassion and love. I had been deeply wounded. Someone within Catholicism had finally understood. In the profound and long silence that followed, Jesus was with us, pouring the balm of healing grace into me.

Many seekers are waiting for Christians to understand their complaints, too. When we do this in humility and grace, we are clearing a lot of hurt out of their lives and so helping them to open up to the redemptive message of the gospel.

The appeal of this was evident during a radio program in which I was "debating" a New Age author who was a clairvoyant and a medium. Partway through the program it became evident that the woman had been badly hurt by Christians who deny supernatural experience today. I realized that her wound had to be healed before she would open up to biblical wisdom. So I took a risk, right there on the air, and changed the subject completely and apologized to her because the church had done so poorly in communicating to her about her subject. She was pleasantly shocked. After being shut down by so many Christians, she was now hearing a Christian who was sensitive to her complaint. You could feel her icy attitude melt. There had been hostility, and now there was openness. "Thank you for saying that," she said. "I now see that not all Christians are the same." Afterward, she was quite open to looking through some new windows of perspective, and some of her views changed.

Be wise, however, when working in the Complaints Department. You may be able to agree with the person that such and such has hurt you, too, but if you have not been healed, if you still walk around with a chip on your shoulder, I would not suggest trying to offer healing balm. If you still have some unfinished business in that area, you will probably send the wrong signal to the other person.

PERSONAL INREACH

This book attempts to equip Christians for outreach in the world of the New Spirituality in order to bring non-Christian spiritual seekers into a relationship with the Truth Himself. I have had a long time to think about the implications of this and in particular how it relates to us. This book on outreach, therefore, would be incomplete without answering the question: How much are we cooperating with the inreach of the Truth into our own lives? How fully are we allowing Christ to transform us?

Let us not be too quick in answering. I have known times when I thought that I was fully submitted to Jesus Christ, times when, if asked (and I was asked), I would have said (and did say) that every area of my life was deeply submitted in discipleship to the Lord. Later, when important relationships self-destructed or ungodly habits were not transformed, I would have to admit that I had been holding areas back from the Truth and so from renewal. What I had done was to convince myself through rationalizations that I was fully submitted, which allowed me to keep indulging the flesh. I wanted so much for outsiders to know the Truth Himself, but my relationship with the Truth ran a distant second. The messenger of Christ was not as radiant with life as he could have been.

I thank God that we do not have to become perfect before we can be His witnesses, but how are we doing in our relationship with our Lord? It is not enough to say, "All right," just because we are not consciously backslidden. The transforming grace of God is also at work upon Christians who think everything is all right. It is a bit more subtle, however, because it may be dealing with hidden deceits, sins, or even idolatries. These can often be identified by asking who or what motivates the decisions we make every day, every week. Is the Truth Himself really the ultimate influence for all of our decisions, or is it possible that other agents hold mastery over what we choose to do? How about ambition, appearance, affluence, freedom, happiness, sexuality, money, irresponsibility, individualism? Certainly, it is not wrong to have ambition and to be happy, but how about when they begin to dominate our decision-making processes? We could be holding back such areas from a deeper relationship with the Truth.

Related to the relationship with the Truth are relationships with others. Because I am a seminar speaker, it has been pointed out to me that more than a few Christians spend far too much time seminar hopping rather than, for instance, using that time to work on deteriorating relationships. They are hoping to become miniexperts in every conceivable contemporary issue that comes along, while all along their important relationships may need urgent attention, and their time should be spent attending to them. This issue is close to my heart because it has made me wonder about what is motivating some of the people who attend the seminars.

If our relationships with others are suffering, it is a sign that our relationship with the Truth Himself is not what it should be. To compensate, we may make a subtle though profound shift that allows us to heap up masses of head knowledge without really knowing the truth.

There is a common misunderstanding about what it means to know the truth. We often speak about hearing the truth, preaching the truth, teaching the truth, speaking the truth, believing the truth, and understanding the truth—all of which is about our minds, our mouths, and our heads. This idea about the nature of truth is not entirely wrong; it is just not entirely right, either.

It is much more a product of a Western understanding of knowledge than it is of biblical wisdom. The Western idea is about access to facts, figures, data, statistics, measurements, the opinions of experts, research, and so on. As translated in Western Christendom, knowing the truth becomes the serious business of accumulating facts and information about the Bible and Christian doctrine, pursuing word studies, memorizing verses, and so on. The thing to do, then, is to acquire several translations of the Bible, a *Strong's Concordance*, a good Bible dictionary, one or two commentaries, and possibly an interlinear Greek-English New Testament or analytical Greek lexicon. In this system for knowing the truth we occupy our time studying these resources, reading Christian books, seminar hopping, and listening to as many tapes and videos as possible.

Again, this is not uncalled for, but it is only a part of, only makes a contribution to, what the Bible means by knowing the truth. It is not the whole story, as we will discover precisely by doing a couple of word studies.

In the Bible, knowledge and knowing entail having a personal relationship with what you know, a personal relationship that carries with it moral implications. Therefore, Adam *knew* Eve (and she conceived). According to the Bible, knowing a woman is not merely a matter of having her biography or information about her looks and character. It means a relationship that carries with it moral implications. Beginning with that invaluable gem of Scripture, this principle regarding the nature of knowledge and knowing builds line upon line, precept upon precept, to include even our knowledge of impersonal things. (If this sounds foreign to us, it is because here is a place where our wisdom diverges from biblical wisdom and needs transformation.)

Thus the Bible presents us with some rather strange-sounding (to Western ears) statements about truth. One of these is from Jesus when He said, "I am the truth" (John 14:6). Think about this. A person, not a stockpile of facts and figures, is the Truth. This is quite different from what we normally think the truth is (see above). If this person is the Truth and if we are created in His image, the implication is that people are in some real sense lowercase truth themselves, so to speak. In the wisdom of the Bible, therefore, truth is about people and one person in particular.

And so we have a very peculiar statement to that effect in Ephesians 4:15, "speaking the truth in love." But wait a moment. That does not sound so odd. No, because the English translation of the Greek is a bit too Westernized here. A closer rendition would have it *"being* truth," or *"living* truth," in love. But I am told that even that does not do justice to what Paul meant here.[5] It is literally "'truthing it' in love." And that sounds odd! This is also the thought behind passages such as 1 John 1:6, where the King James Version, which

221

becomes more literal by default with each passing year, states that when we lie we "do not the truth."

This, then, greatly alters the complexion of what it means to know the truth. It is no longer just an intellectual pursuit. Factual and scientific knowledge, Bible study, and the like make a contribution to the picture, but they are not the whole story. Knowing the truth is about people, their characters, their relationships to one another and to one Person in particular.

When we think, then, of the question of our relationship with the truth, the moral implications are quite profound indeed, because we have that inclination toward being lowercase falsehoods. This is why the apostle Paul urges us to be truthing it, and why the apostle John says that even believers may not "do" the truth.

The apostle Paul is that fellow who, when writing to the church in Rome, said that truth is held a priori by people; thus they either express it or suppress it (Rom. 1–2). Evidently, it is possible to be truthing it (in righteousness) or falsing it (in unrighteousness). This gets so personal that to give even a false impression of one's character can be a lie. So how is your relationship with the Truth? Seminar hopping is not enough.

Yes, we need to move out of the fortress and become approachable, offering relationship—life—not religion; and when we are doing this, we are to watch our attitudes and handle complaints with compassion. But throughout all this we must remain mindful of our own relationship with the Truth.

It is not that God will wait until we are perfect before He will use us to speak to people. Rather, it is a matter of being judged by God for using a double standard. When we are working to bring non-Christians into a relationship with the Truth, do we have a stricter set of principles for them than we do for ourselves? Without becoming morbidly self-introspective, take a little time out for self-examination. It has been said that the largest room in the world is the room for improvement.

23

PRESENTING THE
WHOLE GOSPEL

—ᗯᗯ—

ONE QUESTION REMAINS to be answered: When followers of the New Spirituality convert and come aboard, in what direction are we taking them? Since it is life we are offering them, what kind of life are we leading them into?

Yes, the life of Christ. But what do we mean by that? Well, it's an everlasting, an eternal, life. Yes, but what does this life influence? What does it affect? Well, it influences us. It changes us. Yes, but is that all? For many Christians, that is all.

In the final analysis, we live a life that extends only so far as we believe the gospel of Jesus Christ reaches, or how much of life it touches. And this depends on how far we think the process of salvation and redemption reaches. Answer that, and you will know what kind of life you are offering new or potential converts. We will lead people in the direction of a life only so far as we ourselves have understood its meaning and reach, and have ourselves gone. No more, no less.

How far, then, does the gospel reach? Some people think it is primarily about selling people their fire insurance. I hope that by now most Christians would argue that that is a terribly truncated view of the gospel; that getting the soul saved for the Day of the Lord is merely the beginning of life. It reaches farther than that, they would say. We have to get the new convert up and running. You know, the four points of follow-up. We have to stress the importance of getting the person praying, reading the Bible, attending church, and witnessing. Certainly, these are the next steps but are there no others? Is this the extent of the process of salvation and redemption? Is the life of Christ only about the religious dimension of life?

Of course not, others would say. We have to do good works, behave ethically in our jobs, be more loving to our families, renew our minds, and be sanctified. Others would add that we should do a few acts of charity, perhaps become part of the worship team, get on the evangelism committee, become a deacon or elder, maybe even go to Bible school.

In such a view the gospel seems to be stretching far and wide, but when you really look at it, it is still primarily influencing only the religious dimension. It is the kind of redemption that has little or nothing to say to industry, economics, art, education, politics, ecology, health care, and so on, that is, the rest of life. I am afraid that this is not the gospel we are called to preach, though it has become the gospel for much of Christendom. This contemporary gospel is shaped by the unbiblical idea that life is divided up into two separate realities: the religious (or spiritual) vis-à-vis the secular (or natural, or material), the latter being what God is not really interested in.

DIMINISHING THE GOSPEL

We must travel quite some distance back in time to find the source of this. Greek thought from the time of Socrates, Plato, and Aristotle still carries a lot of weight in the West and in Christendom today. It was characteristic of early Greek thought to hold a low opinion of the material world and the body, which was often felt to be the greatest handicap to the attainment of true knowledge, wisdom, goodness, and spirituality. The body held people back, it was said.

In his dialogues with Socrates, Plato discusses salvation with his mentor, who suggested that salvation equates with separating soul from body. To these early Greeks, the soul was considered immortal and imperishable, the body mortal, perishable. When death attacked, the immortal soul was liberated and released from the perishable body, and that meant salvation.

Not too long after these three philosophers had died, this kind of thinking took a turn for the worse within Neoplatonism and especially within the pagan Gnosticism of the early centuries A.D. Soul and spirit were identified as *good* in these metaphysical systems, and matter, including bodies and the material world entirely, was identified as *evil*. The Gnostic, especially, was to have as little to do with the material world as possible, because matter was considered utterly corrupt and bad, a lower world, indeed, the lowest. Spiritual (nonmaterial) things were the highest, the purest. The Gnostic believed that he had a divine spark within that had been corrupted by his life in the material world. Salvation for him therefore meant raising himself up through the lower worlds to the higher spiritual levels where he would be eventually transformed into a purely spiritual being, uncontaminated by the material world.

The end of this kind of thinking is a thoroughgoing dualism of soul or spirit over matter, nature, or material things. It is seen as essential to get free and clear of the world, for there is nothing good about it. As Christianity spread throughout the Greek and pagan worlds, it certainly took issue with dualistic views of salvation but was itself somewhat influenced by them. And their influence is felt even today in Christianity, often restricting the reach of the gospel to the religious or spiritual dimensions of life. Within the milieu of dualism, the gospel is not understood as what reaches into all of life, especially secular life, and we end up preaching a two-dimensional gospel to a three-dimensional world.

Though this is foreign to the Bible, much of Western Christianity today tends to read the Bible through the dualistic lens of secular/religious, or natural/spiritual, and as a result has evacuated the secular areas of life. We just do not think the gospel has anything redemptive to say—at least more than superficially—to economics, politics, art, industry, and the like.

Hard dualism and soft dualism are afoot within Christendom. In the former, saving souls is the most spiritual thing we can do. Missionaries, pastors, and evangelists are seen as the most spiritual believers, and down the hierarchy slightly come elders then deacons, and then other church-oriented workers. But everything about the world, its art, its industry, its politics, and such is irredeemable. It is in the hands of the devil. So forget it. We should not be concerned about such things because Christians are to save souls.

In the softer Christian dualism, it is all right to be engaged in some worldly activities and careers, but you have to be careful. It is probably not good to be a biologist or a scientist because of evolutionary thinking. Political work and law are looked down upon because of gross corruption. Artist? Forget it. You mass-produce Christian knickknacks and trinkets instead, and fill the stores with them. It may not be art, but nobody will notice. Besides, it is making us money; after all, it is hard to get into the right kind of work. The caring professions are all right if you can get around evolution and holism. But there is no way you should be a psychologist or a psychiatrist because that is the devil's playground. Music? Maybe. But only as long as it is a vehicle for saving souls or includes Christian jargon. You might try the teaching profession if you can find a way to get past the humanism. And within this softer dualism, you would be quite free to start up a neutral business, such as accounting or farming, without fear of wrath.

Dualism in the church puts a lot of false guilt upon those poor mortals who are in a line of work that is so far down the spiritual ladder as to be considered carnal by the more spiritual. And our speech is filled with the language of dualism. We talk about our ministries as opposed to our secular jobs: "I'm looking forward to the day when I can serve the Lord full time." This language about spiritual callings and natural vocations betrays the spiritual/secular split in our minds, of which the Bible is ignorant because the gospel reaches into all of life, the whole of life. And it is that kind of Life we need to be offering seekers.

We have this adage: if Jesus is not Lord of all, He's not Lord at all. Dualistic thinking tends to make this read: if Jesus is not Lord of all of my life. As a result, we live with a private faith in a public life. Thus many Christian businesspeople, politicians, captains of industry, office managers, teachers, salespeople, small business owners, lawyers, and so on are unaware that the gospel can give distinctively biblical ethics and aesthetics to their lines of work. As a result, there may be markedly little difference between the way they go about their jobs and the way non-Christians do theirs. Often, the only difference is that the Christians are in church on Sunday—hearing messages that are presuppositionally dualistic. They hear messages that touch their religious lives only. So they may no longer cheat on their taxes, they may be more easygoing with their employees, and you may even hear them pray or tell someone at work about Jesus. But let them ask their pastors to preach about how the gospel can influence employee-management relations, the design of their new office buildings, how it can shape running a political campaign, the nature of lawmaking, or the use and effect of advertising, and their ministers will either look at them with a blank stare or think that they are joking or being foolish.

A GOOD CREATION

What kind of life are we offering? Examine the kind of life you are living and you will have your answer. Is it a religious life or a whole life? A dualistic or a wholistic gospel? Soul salvation or whole salvation? Whereas dualistic thinking closes Christians up and limits the reach of the gospel, the gospel opens us to a biblical wisdom for all of life and culture. This is the gospel of Jesus Christ. This is the gospel we preach.

Throughout church history, a reacquaintance with the doctrine of creation has always served as a good counterblast to dualistic views of life. Dualism errs chiefly in three directions: wrong ideas about God, the creation, and salvation. For example, the Gnostics could not see how the creation of the material world could have been done by the supreme God, who is altogether good. Since their assumption was that matter was evil, they asked how a good God could have created it. To solve their metaphysical dilemma, they believed that matter had been created by a lesser, evil god, who was utterly hostile to the good supreme God. This belief was widespread in New Testament times, and it left the Christians who imbibed it shut up in an evil body in an evil world, neither of which could be transformed or renewed. People could not wait to leave both.

In no uncertain terms, however, the Bible teaches that God made a "good" creation (Gen. 1). Yes, the human family has fallen into sin and the creation has not been left untouched by it, but this is a far cry from saying it is all worthless, which is to despise the handiwork of God, who made a good creation. It is precisely because the creation is not intrinsically evil that it, like ourselves, can be redeemed, renewed, and transformed. And this is not about starting over from nothing, either. Revelation 21:5 does not read, "Behold, I make all new things." It reads, "Behold, I make all things new." A world of difference exists between the two, the latter implying that there is something around to work redemption on.

Therefore, when the Bible speaks of a new heaven and a new earth (Isa. 65:17; 66:22; 2 Pet. 3:13; Rev. 21:1), they are portrayed in terms of the old renewed, in that they will one day be without sin's influence, and not in an original kind of newness. The apostle Paul goes into this important point in some depth in Romans 8:19–23:

> For the earnest expectation of the creation eagerly waits for the revealing of the sons of God. For the creation was subjected to futility, not willingly, but because of Him who subjected it in hope; because the creation itself also will be delivered from the bondage of corruption into the glorious liberty of the children of God. For we know that the whole creation groans and labors with birth pangs together until now. Not only that, but we also who have the firstfruits of the Spirit, even we ourselves groan within ourselves, eagerly waiting for the adoption, the redemption of our body.

It is not just that we wait eagerly for the redemption of our bodies, but that the creation waits in "earnest expectation," too. Nature/creation shares in what puts us right: redemption. Whereas by human sin, nature/creation suffered (was placed in bondage to decay), so by God's grace it shares in what puts us right: the gospel. This is why the gospel we preach must be the one with a life that reaches all of life with its message of redemption. Thus we preach not merely soul but whole salvation, the provision of grace for the whole of creation. This is the life we want to be offering to followers of the New Spirituality. This is the direction we want to lead them because it will give them grace to be Christians in every area of life.

This is not to say, however, that we do not preach repentance from sin and offer the grace of Jesus Christ for personal salvation. The Christian communicator will always want to be ready to tell the seeker how to become a Christian. This may seem too obvious to need mentioning, but if we are not used to communicating the way of personal salvation to people, we could find it somewhat difficult when the need arises.

During the first seven or eight years that I was a Christian, every year I led one or two people to the Lord. Then there were a few years in which, for whatever reasons, that did not occur. As a result I became inexperienced at knowing how to lead someone to Jesus. The funny thing is, I did not realize that I had lost touch with how to lead someone to the Lord until a Philippian jailer situation actually happened to me. It really caught me off guard.

I had just finished preaching a message at a church in Southampton, England. It was not a message on the New Age; it was not even an evangelistic message. We did not even have an altar call. I had preached on the grace of God, the meeting had ended, and the crowd was filing out. After a few people had finished talking to me, and there was hardly a person left in the church, I was walking around looking for my wife so that we could find our ride. Suddenly, I was approached by a shy young French girl of about nineteen.

"May I speak to you, please?" she said. "You are probably wanting to leave, but could you spare me a few minutes?"

"Yes, what can I do for you?" I said. "What's your name?"

"My name's Patricia, and I was really listening to what you were saying tonight. My life does not seem right. It seems very dirty. I want to know Jesus, but I don't know what to do about it. Can you help me?"

You could have bowled me over! At first I was not sure if I was hearing right, if she was faking this, or if perhaps it was not some distraction sent by our common enemy.

"Sure I can help you," I blurted, wondering what on earth I was going to do and say next. "Perhaps we could take a seat over here, and you could tell me more about it."

We sat down and had a heart-to-heart talk. The first thing I discovered was that she was absolutely serious about her sinfulness, though she did not know it was called that. It was evident that the conviction of the Holy Spirit had been upon her for some time. But as I was gently trying to sort this out with her, it hit me that I was not sure how to proceed. It had been so long since I had led someone to the Lord. I had lost touch with how to do it. I was appalled at myself. Of course, I could have mouthed some formula prayer *for* her, but she wanted to meet the Savior.

After a few more minutes of talking with her, I was able to gather my thoughts together, and I felt confident enough to proceed. I was helped by the fact that out of the corner of my eye I saw my wife and a minister approaching. We waited until they came up to us, and then I mentioned what Patricia was about to do. The four of us then prayed together. Patricia became a Christian and entered into the care of the church.

So you just never know. I suggest that you work out a short one- or two-minute presentation of the gospel and loosely memorize it. In reading through the book of Acts, I have come to the conclusion that was what the apostles had done. Then whenever they were in situations in which people were morally ready to make a decision for Jesus Christ, they could state the message clearly. And this is what to look for: the person's sincere acknowledgment of his moral problem. Into this we can speak about personal salvation in Christ with great confidence.

But there is another reason for having a one-minute gospel presentation ready. Many seekers have never really heard the good news, or if they have, it has sounded more like bad news because it came to them in a distorted form through some branch of the media. In your preevangelistic conversations with a seeker, when all is said and done, and conversation for the time being is coming to a close, and if the person is still floating on the surface of communication, you could ask if he has actually ever heard the gospel. He may say that he has, but you would not want to take that for granted; it may be a distorted version that he has heard. Or he may say that he has not heard it. In either case, you could ask for just one more minute of his time, that day, to share the gospel: redemption from sin.

Try to work out a short presentation of the gospel that you could express at such a time. Put it in your own words, pointing out significant characteristics about the creation, then the fall into sin, and how that has affected all of life, and then tell about God's provision for a restored relationship with Him through His Son Jesus Christ. And remember you are not trying to force belief upon the person; you are painting for him a new window of perspective, the gospel window of perspective. This would be something that, at the end of your conversation, you could leave with the person, simply saying, "Think about it."

I believe it was the Billy Graham Evangelistic Association whose research concluded that it takes six or seven times for a typical non-Christian to hear the gospel message before the person can make an intelligent decision about it. Is there a greater parting idea that we could leave with our listeners? It could be that in subsequent conversations with them they will make that decision for Christ.

And once they are up and running in a whole life, the potential for them is indeed endless. When we present the whole gospel, as applicable to all of life, it will attract seekers who are already aware that society desperately needs spiritual answers, not just for themselves but for all of life. Think about it.

EPILOGUE

We have come a long way toward learning what it takes to be as wise as serpents and as harmless as doves in communicating with followers of the New Spirituality. The New Age world has its own combination lock of communication problems that we have worked to decode in this book. But our mission impossible has just begun, the ultimate aim being to persuade seekers to change their minds about God and themselves, and so to receive saving grace.

The purpose of this book has not been for you to learn about airtight techniques and strategies by which to reach the lost. Rather, you have learned about a life to be lived in the presence of the lost.

We have discussed at some length what kind of a life it will take to build relationships; not relationships in which we end up involved in questionable spiritual activities, but relationships in which people are beginning to take a favorable interest in Christianity and the gospel. We are not going to surrender biblical absolutes, become moral relativists, or take part in ungodly compromise. As Christians, we have a radical identity with Jesus Christ so that we can make a radical difference. Our lives will witness to both qualities, as Christ's living epistles.

It was not clever New Age apologists, demolishing biblical wisdom, that drew me into the New Age world. It was, to a large degree, that its teachers and witnesses were warm, sensitive, gentle, and considerate of my feelings. They had a certain way with me that was appealing. In this book we have studied ways of making that happen.

Jesus enjoyed people, and they were sinners. He liked going to where people were. He established rapport. He built relationships. He spent time with people—in the marketplaces, in homes, on street corners—in order to get to know them, and so that they would get to know Him. None of that displeased the Father. Jesus listened. He was perceptive. He answered. He was the great communicator, and He is our model for that.

If we apply what we have studied (you may want to refer to some chapters or ideas on a regular basis), and now cry out in prayer to God with a desire to reach spiritual seekers, He will respond to us. We do not need to be smart. We do not need to be experts. We just need to be loyal. The Master chose twelve common laborers to be with Him. What they would learn when they were with Him would make them His first witnesses. They had little or no formal training. Eleven were loyal, and they were the ones who later turned the world upside down. Still today Jesus looks for loyal disciples, Christians who will be with Him, whom He will transform into effective communicators.

If you are wondering how to begin, start simply, humbly, and in the power of the Holy Spirit. You may want to start by confessing any unhealthy fears you may have about speaking to non-Christian spiritual seekers. Sometimes we have a kind of cringing, cowering withdrawal from New Age people because of their possible occult lifestyles. Yet it is not part of our inheritance in Christ to carry around an unhealthy fear of things demonic.

Colossians 1:13 states that through Jesus Christ, God has "delivered us from the power of darkness" and "conveyed us into the kingdom of the Son of His love." This is a powerful image, one with deep theological and practical significance. It testifies to the reality of demonic powers; but more than that, it reveals that Christians are set free (delivered) from them. Christians live within the confines of God's kingdom, a kingdom in which demonic power has no authority. This is part of our inheritance in Christ, and it means that we are no longer afraid of the power of darkness. Many Christian lives have been transformed by understanding this.

If you already know this, you may want to proceed by gathering some Christian friends to pray for a plan of action. Perhaps the group could start getting their feet wet by visiting a psychic fair, setting up a small booth with Christian literature at a Body, Mind, Spirit Festival, or going to a New Age bookstore to talk with the manager or owner. Trust in God and begin something. Do not be afraid to make mistakes; otherwise you may never begin. And do not be embarrassed when you make mistakes, for that is how to learn to do better next time.

Ideally, though, try to capitalize on whatever is happening around you, at any given time, to create conditions for Christian sharing that otherwise would never have existed. Jesus did that continually. He was very spontaneous. In reading the Gospels, we do not get the impression that Jesus was program oriented. He did not spend His days wondering or worrying about who His divine appointments were going to be. His was an impromptu ministry. He made use of whatever happened to come His way. Without rehearsal, He taught, healed, and made His points within the context of whatever people were saying or doing.

Followers of the New Spirituality live in a world with a wisdom in which the only ultimate relationship they have is with Self, and their only hope, therefore, is like trying to chase down a desert mirage. As Christians, we are called to build communication bridges that will offer these people the ultimate true relationship as it is known in Jesus Christ, the only true Hope.

NOTES

2. Communication Breakdown

1. Bob McCullough, "The New Spin Is Spirituality," *Publishers Weekly*, 16 May 1994.
2. Author's emphases; see British Government *Department of Education and Science Circular*, January 20, 1989. Several of the more influential RE syllabuses and textbooks that carry New Age motifs are *Global Teacher, Global Learner* (Pike and Selby); *New Methods in RE* (Hammond, Hay, et al.); *Better Schools: A Values Perspective* (Beck); *The New Social Curriculum* (ed. by DuFour); *Stilling: A Pathway for Learning in the National Curriculum* (Beasley).

3. Meet Success and Failure

1. The Christian L'Abri Fellowship Centers were founded by the late Dr. Francis Schaeffer and his wife, Edith. The centers are live-in study and work environments where people can stay for periods of several days up to an entire term. A large percentage of those who come to L'Abri, especially university-age people, are seeking to acquire a more relevant Christianity to take back into their cultures. There are centers in Europe, England, and America, the latter two addresses being listed here for those desiring further information. L'Abri Fellowship, the Manor House, Greatham, Liss, Hants, GU33 6HF, England. L'Abri Fellowship, 1465 12th Avenue N.E., Rochester, MN 55906.
2. This myth is exposed as the piece of fiction that it is by two established Christian authors. See Douglas Groothuis, *Revealing the New Age Jesus: Challenges to Orthodox Views of Christ* (Downers Grove, Ill.: InterVarsity Press, 1990); Ron Rhodes, *The Counterfeit Christ of the New Age Movement* (Grand Rapids, Mich.: Baker Book House, 1990).

4. Entering the Inter-World

1. Don Richardson, *Peace Child* (Ventura, Calif.: Regal Books, 1976), pp. 177–78.
2. Ibid., pp. 179–80.
3. Ibid., p. 180.

5. The Storm of the Irrational

1. Shirley MacLaine, *Dancing in the Light* (New York: Bantam, 1987), chapters 14 and 15.
2. Russell Chandler, *Understanding the New Age* (Milton Keynes, England: Nelson Word, 1988), p. 33.
3. Douglas Groothuis, *Confronting the New Age* (Downers Grove, Ill.: InterVarsity Press, 1988), p. 111.
4. André Kole, The Christian Tape Library Inc., 330 N. Range Road, Carmel, IN 46032.
5. Edwin Kiester and Sally Valente Kiester, "How to Teach Your Child to Think," *Reader's Digest*, 11 June 1991, p. 141.
6. John Naisbitt and Patricia Aburdene, *Megatrends 2000* (New York: Morrow, 1990), p. 295.
7. Keith Thompson, "Helen Palmer: Setting Standards of the Psychic Frontier," *Common Boundary*, January/February 1989, p. 20.

6. The Calm of Passivity

1. Some forms of Hebrew or Christian meditation would be exceptions to this. They would not engage the person in emptying the mind of all thoughts but in filling it with a meditation, for example, on God's works (Pss. 77:12; 143:5), God's law (Pss. 1:2; 119), or God Himself (Pss. 63:6; 104:34). Christian meditation would also engage a person's mind upon the matters of Scripture, preaching, teaching, one's gifts, life, or even doctrine, as the apostle Paul exhorts (1 Tim. 4:13–16). What must be stressed is that the common denominator in these nonmystical kinds of meditation is a *filling* of the mind, and it is a filling with what is true, noble, just, pure, lovely, admirable, excellent, and praiseworthy. As Paul taught (Phil. 4:8–9), when we think about these things and put them into practice, the God of peace will be with us.

   In regard to Christianized versions of guided imagery and visualization, I would say that much of what I have so far encountered is pretty dodgy. I do not practice any kinds of guided imagery and visualization now. Yet I am strongly in support of the redemption of our imaginations. I am not convinced, however, that this is as easy to accomplish as some Christians seem to think. Of the many times the term for *imagination* is used in the Bible, only once, I believe, is it used in a positive light, and nearly half the time it is used in the context of idolatry. The biblical concept of image gets equally lopsided treatment (see Brooks Alexander, "Visualization: Mind Power and the Mind's Eye," *Spiritual Counterfeits Project Journal* 9, no. 3 [1990]).

2. Robert E. Ornstein, *The Psychology of Consciousness* (New York: Penguin, 1972), p. 136.

7. The Genesis of Deception

1. MacLaine, *Dancing in the Light*, pp. 254–55.
2. Monism is a metaphysical system in which all reality, both the material and the spiritual, is conceived as a unified whole. There are various kinds of monistic systems, and the popular buzz phrase "All is one, one is All" sums them up. In the New Spirituality there is a strong antipathy toward the strict dualisms of mind over against matter and spirit over against body that are still common in the West today. Monistic oneness gives the New Age follower a way out of these strict dualisms.

   Now there is some food for thought here, for the Bible itself does not see life in terms of harsh dualisms. The early Greek philosophers gave the West a taste for metaphysical systems framed by strict dualisms, chiefly that of the spiritual over against the material. Yet it was from the time of the philosopher and scientist Descartes (1596–1650) and later Western scientific thought that harsh dualisms were imposed upon Western thought in general. Descartes formulated an almost complete dualism between the physical world and the mind, and later Western scientific thought saw matter as total reality and excluded anything otherworldly from the equation.

   It is the task of Christian philosophy to respond with the biblical view. There is indeed a unity of some kind with the universe and all of its phenomena. This unity, however, is found not in the principle of monism but in the person of Jesus Christ.

8. Identifying Distortions

1. Biblical critiques of pantheistic monism are presented in several good Christian books. See David K. Clark and Norman L. Geisler, *Apologetics in the New Age: A Christian Critique of Pantheism* (Grand Rapids, Mich.: Baker Book House, 1990); Douglas Groothuis, *Unmasking the New Age* (Downers Grove, Ill.: Inter-Varsity Press, 1986); Vishal Mangalwadi, *In Search of Self: Beyond the New Age* (London, England: Hodder & Stoughten, 1992); Elliot Miller, *A Crash Course on the New Age Movement* (Grand Rapids, Mich.: Baker Book House, 1989). Also see glossary.
2. Tim Cooper, *Green Christianity* (London, England: Spire, 1990).
3. John Peck, "Creation and Purpose," Worldview Series, cassette tape No. 11 (Trinity Arts Group, 14800 Middlebelt Road, Livonia, MI 48154), 1985.

4. Lesslie Newbigin, *Foolishness to the Greeks* (London, England: SPCK, 1986), p. 89.

9. Predicting Problems

1. Miguel de Cervantes Saavedra, *Don Quixote*, trans. J. M. Cohen (London, England: Penguin Books, 1950), pp. 636–637.
2. Charles Strohmer, *What Your Horoscope Doesn't Tell You* (American edition—Wheaton, Ill.: Tyndale, 1988; British edition—Milton Keynes, England: Nelson Word, 1991). See chapters 7 to 9 for a deeper look at how "self-disclosures" from the spirit world infiltrate the thinking process of an occult spokesperson's mind to feed information to a client.

10. Darkness as Light

1. Quoted in Ellen Creager, "New Age Parents Sprinkle Their Spiritualism with Diplomacy," *The Detroit Free Press*, April 23, 1987.
2. Carl Jung, *Memories, Dreams, Reflections*, rev. ed. (New York: Vintage Books, 1965), recorded and edited by Aniela Jaffe, translated from the German by Richard and Clara Winston. Jung wrote this autobiography at the end of his long life, and in it he admits to his earlier encounters with spirit beings called Ka, Salome, Philemon, and Elijah. "Philemon and other figures," he wrote, "brought home to me the crucial insight that there are things in the psyche which I do not produce, but which . . . have a life of their own. Philemon represented a force that was not myself. . . . I held conversations with him. . . . I observed clearly that it was he who taught me."

    I know of two evangelical critiques of Jung. One I wrote for the *Spiritual Counterfeits Project Journal* 9, no. 2, 1990. The article is called "Jung: Man of Mystic Proportions." It is available by writing to SCP, P.O. Box 4308, Berkeley, CA 94704. The other critique is found in chapter 14 of Leanne Payne's *The Healing Presence* (Westchester, Ill.: Crossway, 1989).
3. Jung, *Memories, Dreams, Reflections*, pp. 189–91.
4. Ibid., p. 192.
5. Ibid.
6. Ibid., p. 199.
7. Ibid., pp. 194–95.
8. Ibid., p. 349.
9. Ibid., p. 347.
10. Not everything Jung named "archetype" is demonic. For instance, some were merely universal religious symbols. The reason for

introducing the reader to Jung's *demonic* archetypes is to suggest that more may be going on behind the "seens" of New Spirituality's imagery than first meets the eye.

11. Models or Muddles?

1. By way of personal testimony, I would like to say something in defense of the more sensational Christian books on the New Age. After I became a Christian in July 1976, I looked for Christian books on the subject to help me. I found none. (Some years later I did discover that Gary North's *None Dare Call It Witchcraft*, now revised and retitled as *Unholy Spirits*—a helpful book—was around in 1976.)

   Since I could get no help from books, I sought out ministers to help me. They did the best they could. But because of the dearth of Christian material on the New Spirituality, they were at as much of a loss as I was. I am grateful, however, that God was present to make up for all our deficiencies.

   Anyway, I began to pray earnestly that Christian books on the subject would get published. I prayed about this for several years, a period during which I also talked from my heart to pastors, Christian media-people, and others about the growing New Age problem. But there was a general disinterest and lack of concern. Most Christian leaders at the time, in fact, thought that folk like myself (we were few and far between back then) were as weird as the spirituality we talked about. We were to be coddled, humored, and tolerated until the New Age, if ever there was one, and our zeal had run its course. It was a rare Christian leader who noticed the rising temperature of the New Spirituality in Western culture in the mid- to late 1970s.

   My opinion (hindsight being the best sight here) is that Christians were asleep to the problem. Because of that, it took some sensationalism to "stab us awake" to the problem. In my mind, this accounts for the hue and cry that some Christian books on the New Age made during the early to mid-1980s. Several others have been similar in spirit and tone since then as well. I believe God permitted the sensationalism to wake us up. Now that we are awake, it is time to move on.

2. Jerry Bridges, *The Practice of Godliness* (Colorado Springs: NavPress, 1983), pp. 93–94.

3. A good summary of these and other historical spiritual trends can be found in the *Spiritual Counterfeits Project Journal*, "Empowering the Self: A Look at the Human Potential Movement," 5, no. 1,

Winter 1981–82, and also the *SCP Newsletter*, "Mind Power," 11, no. 1, Spring 1985

12. Wisdom in the Marketplace

1. John Peck, *Wisdom in the Marketplace* (London, England: Greenbelt, 1989), p. 22. I highly recommend this book. It is about more than building up ideas and making them work. It aims to assist Christians in the personal development of biblical wisdom, which will become instinctive and govern actions in a spontaneous, godly way. The book is a great help to Christians who find themselves ill-prepared for thinking and acting biblically in so-called secular life.
2. Ibid.
3. Roy Irving and David McCasland, "Old Truth for a New Age," interview with Ron Enroth, *Power for Living*, July 19, 1992.
4. Katrina Raphaell, *Crystal Enlightenment*, vol. 1 (Santa Fe, N.M.: Aurora Press, 1985), pp. 32–33.

13. Acquiring Wisdom

1. Peck, *Wisdom in the Marketplace*, p. 23.
2. From the poem "Howl," by Allen Ginsberg, quoted in Todd Gitlin's *The Sixties: Years of Hope, Days of Rage* (New York: Bantam, 1987), p. 45. Ginsberg read the poem in 1955 to a San Francisco audience, in answer to the question "What are you rebelling against?"
3. Cooper, *Green Christianity*.
4. The address of the E.A.P.E. is Box 7238, St. David's, PA 19087-7238.
5. This is a composite statement drawn from several leading New Age educators to depict their general feeling.

14. Submarines and Their Destroyers

1. This subdivision can be misunderstood. I want to emphasize that in calling for a give-and-take in conversation, I do not mean that we compromise the truth or become soft about moral absolutes. I am not advocating relativism; I am pleading for relationships to be established, in the hope that people will then want to listen to the Bible. Of course people ought not to practice channeling. Certainly it is wrong to be into astrology. There will be times to say so, to mention the dangers, but not, perhaps, in the early stages of a budding relationship. In the early stages you may want to let your negative feelings about the occult be known gently in a manner that does not alienate you from the person. You do not want to be

guilty of dissimulation. But this gentleness is a far cry from the hammering away that some of us do in the early stages, wondering then why we cannot build relationships.

I am not saying you always must take this tack. There are times for plain old confrontation, even in the early stages of a relationship. But if you so proceed, you will have to go cautiously even then. You see, it is unlikely that a non-Christian spiritual seeker will be gained for Christ during the first conversation. I would think, therefore, that you would want to pave the way, whenever possible, for later conversations, which may occur with Christians other than you. You will probably find that it defeats the purpose to play the spiritual heavy early on. An initial conversation is most often an opportunity for attracting the New Age enthusiast to spend further time with you. Principled conversation can facilitate this. If you are having difficulty with this idea of being softer without being a compromiser, stay tuned. More help is on the way in later chapters.

15. Setting Off the Alarm

1. Here I am leaving aside the entire area of the creation's subjection to frustration and its bondage to decay, from which it awaits liberation (Rom. 8:20–21). As I understand this, it is not about an intrinsically evil creation that deserves annihilation. Thus it does not militate against what I am saying about God's good creation.
2. Karen Hoyt and the Spiritual Counterfeits Project, *The New Age Rage* (Old Tappan, N.J.: Revell, 1987). See chapter 10, "Spiritual Autism: Breaking Barriers by Building Bridges," by Dean Halverson, p. 211.

17. Signs of Truth

1. See chapter 3, note 2; chapter 8, the section "Jesus Christ."
2. Because space does not exist in this book to discuss more thoroughly many such matters that are coming up, readers who are interested further should look at the recommended reading list, in which a wealth of information exists. For readers interested in further information about the discussion in question here, see Jon A. Buell and Quentin O. Hyder, *Jesus: God, Ghost or Guru?* (Grand Rapids, Mich.: Zondervan/Probe, 1978); C. S. Lewis, *Mere Christianity* (New York: Macmillan, 1952), book 2, chapter 3; C. S. Lewis, *God in the Dock* (Grand Rapids, Mich.: Eerdmans, 1970), part 1, chapter 19.
3. Strohmer, *What Your Horoscope*, chapters 12–14, for suggestions about why the spiritual power of the New Spirituality is impotent

vis-à-vis our moral problem, and why only God's power in Jesus Christ returns us to a relationship with God.

4. Ibid., chapter 13, for ideas about presenting redemption to seekers in a way that may be more manageable to their imaginations.

5. Ibid.

6. Liz Hodgkinson, "You Only Live (at least) Twice," *She*, May 1989, (United Kingdom), pp. 84–87.

7. Ibid.

18. Areas of Agreement

1. This and other incredible claims appeared in a large and wordy two-page advertisement that the Maharishi ran in the *International Herald Tribune*, April 5, 1990, under the headline "Unified Field Science and Technology: Offers the Balance of Power in the World to Any Government."

2. Cooper, *Green Christianity*, chapter 4. Also see "Gaia: A Religion of the Earth," *Spiritual Counterfeits Project Journal* 16, no. 1 (1991).

3. Michio and Aveline Kushi, *Macrobiotic Diet*, ed. Alex Jack (Briarcliff Manor, N.Y.: Japan Publications, 1985).

4. Ibid.

5. The two concepts developed in this and the preceding chapter may be new to some readers, who may still wonder, "How on earth could we ever agree with followers of the New Spirituality about anything? How could they possibly have anything to say to us?" I can understand this because it has been a struggle for me, also. But how about this? In Chapters 14 and 15 we looked at a number of problems that can crop up in the way we relate to people. We discussed caricatures, the demanding boss, listening, and so on. Was that material helpful to you? If so, you may be surprised to know that some of it came from secular authors on the subjects of psychology and communication. I certainly do not endorse all, or even a lot, of their material, but when I saw several strengths in it, I recast it in a Christian context to help us here. So, in a sense, we learned from several persons who were not Christians. They helped us with truths they had discovered.

I mention this as an example of how Christians can gain from other people, even New Agers. Interested to know what those secular books were? Okay, I won't keep you guessing any longer! See Eric Berne, *Games People Play* (Secaucus, N.J.: Castle Books, 1964); Roger Fisher, et al., *Getting to Yes*, 2nd ed. (New York: Penguin 1991); Thomas Harris, *I'm O.K.—You're O.K.* (New York: Harper & Row, 1963); Marshall B. Rosenberg, *From Now On* (St. Louis, Mo.: Community Psychological Consultants Inc., 1977).

19. On Being Human

1. For an in-depth look at several pantheistic views that are the soil for much of the New Spirituality, see Clark and Geisler, *Apologetics in the New Age*.
2. MacLaine, *Dancing in the Light*, pp. 339–41.
3. Ibid., p. 404.
4. Ranald Macaulay and Jerram Barrs, *Being Human: The Nature of Spiritual Experience* (Downers Grove, Ill.: InterVarsity Press, 1978), p. 13.
5. Ibid., pp. 17–18.

20. Flxybl

1. "Imprecise Words, Sloppy Thinking, Poor Management," *The Mountain Press* (Sevierville, Tenn.), September 25, 1991.
2. Catherine Bennett, "Shirley Finds Her Spirit Level," *The Times*, October 21, 1987.
3. "Infiltrating the New Age into Society," *What Is*, Summer 1986, p. 14; quoted in Groothuis, *Confronting the New Age*, p. 142.
4. See Chapter 10, note 1.
5. An increasing number of seekers believe that through so-called past life recall they now know what bad karma they have accrued to themselves from supposed previous lifetimes. This, they think, helps them understand why they are suffering in their present existences. See Bennett, "Shirley Finds Her Spirit Level."
6. Robert Morey, *Death and the Afterlife* (Minneapolis, Minn.: Bethany, 1984). In chapter 6, Morey helpfully documents many instances of occult terminology being changed and the effect of this on Western culture's understanding of the paranormal.
7. Frances Adeney, "Revisioning Reality," *Spiritual Counterfeits Project Newsletter* 7, no. 2.
8. *A Course in Miracles*, vol. 2, Workbook for Students (The Foundation for Inner Peace, 1975), p. 391.
9. Ibid., p. 409.
10. C. S. Lewis, *God in the Dock*, p. 93.
11. Ibid., p. 98.

21. Effectual Prayer

1. See chapter 9, note 2.
2. Donald A. McGavan, *The Bridges of God: A Study in the Strategy of Missions* (New York: Friendship Press, 1961), p. 45.

22. Getting Peripheral Vision

1. Jerram Barrs helped to found the L'Abri Fellowship Centre in Greatham, England, where he was a worker for twenty years. He is now a professor at Covenant Seminary, St. Louis, Missouri.

2. Jerram Barrs, "Problems and Pathways in Communicating the Gospel in the 90s," L'Abri Cassette No. 2461 (L'Abri Cassettes, P.O. Box 2035, Michigan City, IN 46360).

3. Jim Peterson, *Church Without Walls* (Colorado Springs, Colo.: NavPress, 1992).

4. Dick Keyes, "Pluralism, Relativism and Tolerance," L'Abri Lecture Paper No. 2, L'Abri Fellowship.

5. I am deeply thankful to the Reverend John Peck for sacrificing a year of his time to come to the States to teach us at the Trinity House Theatre and Art Group about Christian worldview, and for his ongoing personal correspondence that helps me to know the Truth better.

GLOSSARY

Note: Words in *italics* are also defined elsewhere in the glossary.

A Course in Miracles: A popular textbook and course of the New Spirituality that seeks "to train your mind in a systematic way to a different perception of everyone and everything in the world." The material is sourced in *spirit mediumship*, or *channeling*. It uses and redefines most cardinal biblical words and doctrines in an antibiblical way.

Age of Aquarius: Astrological lore teaches that the earth's axis slowly revolves through the twelve signs of the zodiac every twenty-five thousand years. The approximately two thousand years that the axis spends traveling through each sign are said to determine at least the general trends on the planet while it is in that sign. These general trends are based on the characteristics of whatever sign the axis is pointing to. Briefly, the earth is now finishing its time in Pisces, which, it is said, gave the earth Christianity. Now we are moving into the sign Aquarius, which promises to bring peace and harmony on the earth for the next two thousand years.

All Is One, One Is All: A contemporary buzz phrase for any of several schools of *monism.*

Altered States of Consciousness (ASCs): States other than normal waking *consciousness* in which the person becomes open to mystical experience, the *spirit* realm, or *cosmic consciousness*. ASCs can be entered through consciousness-manipulating, or consciousness-expanding, techniques such as *TM, meditation, visualization,* and hypnosis. Within the New Age world, ASCs are thought to be a great link with various kinds of healing and *spiritual evolution.*

Alternative Medicine: A term used almost interchangeably with *complementary medicine, holistic health care,* holistic medicine, and *holism* to describe therapies and healing practices that fall outside traditional Western, allopathic, or orthodox, medicine and health care. The list is long and would include ancient, folk, and pagan practices, such as shamanism and voodoo, as well as the less offensive acupuncture and homeopathy. The driving force of alternative therapies seems to be their ability to articulate the human being as a single entity of mind, body, and spirit, not only in relation to the person but to the world. The fuel for this driving force is various nonbiblical beliefs about an invisible *universal life energy* that pervades everything and unites us to one another and the universe. When this *energy* is unbalanced or blocked within the individual, disease, disharmony, or distress is said to result. Rebalancing or unblocking the flow of the energy is thought to aid restoration of health. *Spirit* contact is not uncommon in some alternative therapies.

Aquarian Dream: See *Age of Aquarius*.

Arcane: What is known or understood only by a few. Often used of esoteric *occult* knowledge.

Ascended Masters: A term made popular by Madame Blavatsky and her nineteenth-century Theosophical Society to describe the *spirit* beings with whom she was in contact and to whom she unabashedly credits in her many *occult* writings as the source of her knowledge.

Asceticism: In its broadest sense, the practice of self-denial or self-mortification for religious or spiritual reasons. Its aim is usually some form of *spiritual* purification, such as to pay off one's bad *karma*, to please the gods, or to attain *enlightenment*.

Astrology: An idolatrous use of the stars and the planets whereby people think to gain information about their lives and futures. Uses a *horoscope* to disclose such information.

Aura: A colorful, invisible light said to envelop the body or *spirit* from which it radiates. This light may be seen, it is said, only by *clairvoyants* and *psychics* so attuned and who may diagnose the person's energy body thereby. Various aura hypotheses of a *spiritual* nature are used by New Age healers in their efforts to cure bodily illness.

Avatar: The appearance of "the divine" in human form, often to reveal necessary truths to certain ages. Rooted in *Hinduism* and *Buddhism*, in the persons of *Rama, Krishna,* and *Buddha*. In some New Age schools of thought, Jesus Christ is considered an avatar for the Christian millennia.

Bhagavad Gita: One of Hinduism's most widely read sacred books and perhaps the most important for understanding Eastern *mysticism*. Contains much commentary, explanation, instruction, and doctrine from *Krishna* to his bosom friend Arjuna. Topics include the fundamental Hindu beliefs about *Self*, renunciation, *karma, yoga,* castes, the soul, nirvana, and so on.

Biocentrism: A prevailing view in so-called *Deep Ecology* in which all living organisms—plant, animal, human—have equal intrinsic worth. This reduces the value of being human to that of a Georgia peanut.

Brahma(n): In *Hinduism*, the all-pervading god or essential divine reality of the universe that is manifest in all that exists. It provides a seedbed of thought for *pantheism*.

Buddha: Born sometime in the sixth century B.C. He practiced severe *asceticism* and austerity. Considered an *avatar*.

Buddhism: A religion of eastern and central Asia built on the teaching of *Buddha*. Several of its basic tenets include the avoidance of extremes, nonviolence, friendliness to all, continence, reaching nirvana (bliss), and escape from the round of rebirths (*reincarnation*).

Centering: Broadly speaking, this is a term used particularly in classrooms as a substitute for the term *meditation*. *Grounding, stilling,* and *going within* are other terms being substituted for meditation. These terms are regularly used in the context of the New Spirituality body-work therapies, breathing exercises, relaxation techniques, creativity workshops, *visualization, yoga,* and so on. They are all basically generic-sounding, nonreligious labels for Eastern and mystical meditative techniques.

Channeler: Though some enthusiasts would argue that there are a few significant differences, this is fundamentally the New Spirituality's euphemism for *spirit medium*.

Channeling: The New Age euphemism for *spirit mediumship*.

Chi: In the mystical Chinese religion of *Taoism*, Chi is the invisible *spiritual energy* that is said to flow through all things and organisms as well as the universe. This spiritual *vital force* is said to be divided into two complementary opposites called *yin and yang*, and it forms the basic tenet of acupuncture-type therapies.

Christ (the): In the New Age world, this name must be distinguished from the Jesus Christ of the Gospels. The Christ of the New Age is an *avatar*. The Christ of the Gospels is God the Son, Lord, Savior, and Redeemer.

246

Christ-Consciousness: An *intuitive* awareness of one's godhood status.

Christian Science: A cult founded in the late nineteenth century by Mary Baker Eddy. It stresses divine healing through the mind by manipulation of *spiritual* laws.

Clairvoyant: A person claiming the power to perceive things outside the range of normal sight. The term "clairvoyance" is frequently used in association with *ESP*, telepathy, *psychics, paranormal* research, spiritism, and so on.

Complementary Medicine: See *alternative medicine.*

Consciousness: Often used in the New Spirituality to describe self-awareness and preceded by the adjectives "altered," "expanded," or *Christ.*

Cosmic Christ: The impersonal divine force of the New Spirituality that guides *spiritual evolution.*

Cosmic Consciousness: A state of awareness in which one perceives that *"All is one, one is all."*

Cosmic Humanist: Whereas the secular humanist is thoroughly human-centered without any point of *spiritual* or *transcendent* reference, the cosmic humanist remains self-centered and has a point of spiritual or transcendent reference, but this is outside a biblical context.

Cosmopolitan Spirituality: A name I have coined to encompass all forms of nonbiblical *spiritual* or religious beliefs, practices, rituals, and so on that are prevalent in the West today, regardless of their extent of influence.

Counterculture: The 1960s movement of young people whose values and lifestyles ran counter to the status quo. It was a seedbed for much that is called "New Age" today.

Crystals: Colorful stones of various sizes, shapes, and weights, which are used by seekers during *meditation* and healing therapies to enhance their access to the *universal life energies.*

Deep Ecology: An attempt to develop a religious philosophy about ecological concerns in which the chief tenets are *biocentrism* and *Self-realization* as articulated by Norwegian philosopher Arne Naess.

Dualism: As used in this book, the term applies to the dichotomy people often make between *secular/spiritual*, or body/spirit, or matter/mind, or two equally powerful antagonistic forces of good and evil.

Eastern Religions: Used in this book chiefly to designate *Buddhism*, Confucianism, *Hinduism*, and *Taoism*.

Energy: A term for the animating life force of the universe. May be called animal magnetism, astral body, astrum, auras, bioplasma, *Chi* (Qi), ethers, *the Force*, the Innate, life energy, mana, Odic Force, orgone, para-electricity, prana, *universal life energy*, vital energy, *vital force*, voodoo, *yin and yang*.

Enlightenment: A noncommunicable mystical experience in which the recipient receives inner, intuitive illumination about his or her divinity or Oneness with all things.

Entities: A euphemism for *spirits*.

Entropy: The irreversible degradation of matter and energy.

Epistemology: A branch of philosophy that investigates the origin, nature, and theory of knowledge, including how we come to know things. Several schools of thought that have made a contribution to this area are empiricism, *rationalism*, idealism, and realism.

Esoteric: Whereas "exoteric" is what is not confined to an inner circle of disciples but is known to the larger public, esoteric is knowledge (most likely) that is confined to a select group of initiates. *Arcane.*

ESP: Extrasensory perception. The supposed ability to perceive or sense an object or event by means other than the physical senses. Made popular in the early twentieth century by the work of the *Society for Physical Research* and *paranormal* research. All of the largest bodies of credible evidence and studies that have been conducted in the past one hundred years in this area still show no convincing proof of the existence of ESP. ESP has been shown to account for some instances of mediumistically transmitted information. *Clairvoyant.*

Existentialism: This is not easily defined because of the broad range of emphases and characteristics placed upon it by philosophers. It is a kind of metaphysics in that it tackles the natural order; it is a kind of anthropology in that it explains human nature. It is frequently associated with philosophical or cultural rebellion against established ideas and institutions, such as *ratio-*

248

nalism, materialism, naturalism. Though diverse in how it is propounded, several common threads are: high regard for individual human existence; affirmation of freedom; strong emphasis on choice and its effect on the future; refusal to subordinate decisions to outside authority, such as existing social structures; stresses living in the here and now with little or no regard for the past; history and the universe often seen as meaningless, irrelevant, absurd. Existentialism was a prevailing philosophical motivation for the 1960s *counterculture.*

The Force: Term popularized by George Lucas in his *Star Wars* movies to describe "an energy field generated by all living organisms. It surrounds us and penetrates us. The Force is where the Jedi gets his power"—so says Obi-wan Kenobi to Luke Skywalker. But the Force is also where Darth Vader, or the Dark Side, gets his power. Thus the Force is but another attempt to invent monistic energies for any sorcerers, white or black, who wish to wield it. *Energy.*

Gaia (hypothesis): The personification of the earth after the ancient Greek goddess Gaia. In the hands of British atmospheric scientist James Lovelock and American microbiologist Lynn Margulis, the planet earth is reinvented as the living goddess (creature) Gaia, who must be treated accordingly. The implications for ecology, politics, and religion are considerable.

Gnosticism: A religious and philosophical system of the early Christian era whose central concept was that salvation comes through knowledge ("gnosis") rather than faith in Jesus Christ. It usually contained elements of Jewish, Christian, Greek, and pagan thought. Christ is considered noncorporeal, and matter is believed to be evil. Salvation results from transcending matter. Carl Jung did much to popularize Gnosticism in the West, as did the discovery in the 1940s of the Nag Hammadi Gnostic documents, which were found buried in a large earthenware jar that dates from the fourth century.

Going Within: See *centering, meditation, stilling.*

Greens: A pseudonym often used of people who are ecologically minded from a spiritual point of view.

Grounding: See *centering.*

Guided Imagery: A type of *meditation* in which the person closes his eyes and is mentally walked in his imagination through a scene usually created by another person. It is frequently used by students, instructed by teachers, as a means for visualizing a helper or wise person who will act as a guide for problem solving or motivation. Very easily becomes a mediumistic point of contact with *spirits*.

Guru: An Eastern religious teacher or holy man who has a following of disciples to whom he hands down his teaching. In the New Spirituality often a *spiritual teacher* who shows the way to *enlightenment* or *spiritual evolution*.

Higher Self: Traceable back to Madame Blavatsky's theosophical teachings. Popularized by Shirley MacLaine as a *spirit guide* who can be *channeled* for great wisdom and infinite knowledge. Many spiritual seekers see it not as a separate *entity* but as an unresourced potential of their own personal unconscious and so worth getting in touch with.

Hinduism: A complex body of religious and cultural practices that forms the predominant religion of India. Central beliefs include *reincarnation, karma,* and a supreme being who takes many forms and shapes.

Holism (Holistic): From the Greek word "holos," which means "whole" in the sense of entire or unified. When informed by New Age wisdom, holism is an attempt to explain the integration of body, mind, and spirit and develop and practice healing therapies in such a context. Also used ecologically. See *alternative medicine*.

Holistic Health Care: See *alternative medicine*.

Horoscope: A diagram, or map, of the stars and planets at the time of one's birth, and the interpretation thereof by an astrologer.

Humanism: As used in this book, a secular belief system whose central tenets are: people are totally autonomous from God; opposition to historic Christianity; rejection of the Bible. A person is her own authority and therefore answerable to no higher power than herself. This has led to the various kinds of moral and ethical *relativism*, which has been thrust into education, science, politics, the arts, and so on in the twentieth century.

Hypnotherapy: A complexity of various kinds of hypnosis in which the person is placed in a trance state and coaxed to recall past experiences (traumas, repressions, hurts, and so on), which the hypnotist then uses to create the conditions to bring the person through to healing, sometimes called catharsis. It may be used in medical practice to treat a myriad of habits and diseases such as smoking, overeating, bulimia, improving memory, and so on. In the New Age world, hypnotherapy is very dangerously allied to so-called *past-life recall therapy*.

I Ching: The Chinese practice of divination associated with *Taoism* and using sticks or coins and a book of sayings for telling the future.

Inner Healing: A complexity of various kinds of procedures, Christian and otherwise, for healing and transforming hidden hurts and wounds of the past and their deleterious influences upon present behavior. The purpose is to produce increasing degrees of inner renewal so that the person may live more wholly and fully in the future. Has been a highly controversial area.

Intuitive (the): Often used in the New Age world as a term to describe the act or faculty of sharp insight or knowing something without the use of rational processes.

Karma: The good and bad deeds, actions, and works of one's present and supposed past lives and the total accumulation thereof. Every deed, good or bad, has an inevitable consequence, and the laws of karma are sometimes known as the laws of sowing and reaping. This provides an explanation for one's present condition, and it also offers a solution to suffering, for one can improve one's lot in this or a next life by doing good now. Ultimately, it is a doctrine of self-salvation through *reincarnation*.

Koan: Used chiefly in Zen Buddhism, koans are paradoxical riddles or questions to be used in *meditation*, and they have no logical answer. Their purpose is to aid concentration and gain *intuitive* knowledge. Koans become meditation objects, day and night, and their lack of logical, rational solutions forces the meditator to experience altered modes of *consciousness*. Examples: show me your face before your mother and father met; and what is the sound of one hand clapping?

Krishna: An *avatar*-manifestation of the Hindu god Vishnu.

Left Brain: It is still controversial, but theories now describe the left hemisphere of the brain as predominantly involved in analytical, logical, rational thinking, especially verbal and mathematical functions. See *right brain*.

Life Force: See *energy*.

Macrobiotics: It may seem like a diet to outsiders, but it is a spiritual discipline and way of life to initiates. The term was coined by George Ohsawa, a Westernized Japanese, who had studied ancient Eastern religious philosophies and reinterpreted some of their central ideas, especially that of *yin and yang*, into macrobiotics.

Mandala: Usually a four-sided symbol, sometimes surrounded by a circle, used as a visual aid to restrict awareness during *meditation* and so focus attention and concentration on one object.

Mantra: In *Hinduism*, a vocal sound that is a secret formula believed to embody the divinity invoked by it; also thought to possess magical or supernatural powers. Used in *TM* and other meditative techniques as a word or sound repeated countlessly over and over and over again to focus attention, outwit the rational mind, and enter meditative states. Becomes a ritualistic kind of prayer or incantation.

Materialism: A philosophical theory that physical matter in its movements and modifications is the only reality and that everything in the universe, including thought, feeling, mind, and will, can be explained by physical laws.

Meditation: Chiefly used in this book to describe a deeply relaxed state and an emptying of the mind of rational thought in an effort to attain an *intuitive* kind of knowing and insight or even to contact *spirits*. There is a rapidly increasing number of New Age schools of meditation, each with overlapping or unique techniques, ranging from *TM* to breathing exercises to chanting a *mantra* to practicing *visualization*, and much more.

Medium: See *spirit medium*.

Mesmerism: The forerunner to hypnotic induction involving the phenomenon called animal magnetism, coined by Austrian physician Franz Mesmer (1734–1815).

Metaphysics: A branch of philosophy concerned with the systematic study of first principles and the nature of existence, including the study of being (ontology) and often the study of the structure of the universe (cosmology).

Monism: A system of *metaphysics* in which all reality, both the material and the *spiritual*, is conceived as a unified whole. There are various kinds of monistic systems. The popular buzz phrase *"All is one, one is all"* sums up the New Age version. See note 2, Chapter 7.

Monotheism: The doctrine of belief that there is only one God.

Mysticism: A *spiritual* discipline through which a practitioner hopes to attain contact or union with "God" or "Ultimate Reality" through deep or trance *meditation*. Christianity teaches that access to God is through the cross of Jesus Christ.

Naturalism: The theory that all phenomena can be explained in terms of natural causes and laws without attributing moral, *spiritual*, and supernatural significance to them.

New Age Movement: A now imprecise term to describe the New Spirituality.

Numerology: The study of the *occult* meaning of numbers and their supposed influence in human life and affairs.

Occult: Of or pertaining to demonic supernatural influences, *spirits*, or phenomena and the practices by which one accesses such power.

Oneness: See *monism*.

Pantheism: The doctrine or belief that everything is God or a part of God. See *pantheistic monism*.

Pantheistic Monism: The word "pantheism" comes from the Greek words "pan," meaning "all," and "theos," meaning "God." The word "monism" comes from the Greek word for single or one. The term "pantheistic monism" is being used more frequently to describe what is perhaps the dominant metaphysical presupposition of the New Spirituality. It can be summed up in the saying, *"All is one, one is all,* all is God." This gives New Age wisdom both a God concept and a theory of unity-in-diversity.

Paradigm: A large framework of thought, or conceptual model, for understanding and explaining various aspects of reality, natural occurrences, or phenomena. For example, there was Newton's paradigm for describing the predictability of mechanical forces and how this would explain everything in terms of trajectories, gravity, and force. As science evolved, the framework of Newtonian mechanics became increasingly unable to handle new discoveries and data, which placed stress and strain on this now old paradigm so that a new framework of thought was necessary to contain and explain later discoveries and data. Enter Einstein's special theory of relativity, which became a new paradigm in the sciences to supersede Newton's physics. Paradigm shifts also occur in education, economics, health care, politics, and so on.

Paranormal: Various kinds of phenomena, usually known as *psychic*, which lie outside the range of normal sensory experience and of the scientifically explainable. *Psychic phenomena*.

Past-Life Recall: This generally occurs within the domains of deep hypnosis or trance states in which the person remembers incidents from supposed past lives.

Past-Life Recall Therapy: Identifying the traumas, hurts, and bad experiences of one's supposed past lives in an effort to understand one's lot in this life and bring greater freedom and healing. Usually connected with the laws of *karma*.

Presupposition: An assumption about life that people do not think about and take for granted but that influences their actions in varying degrees. For example, a Christian prays because he assumes in advance that God is personal in nature and therefore able to hear his prayers. But he does not come to every time of prayer thinking, *I'm going to pray because God is personal in nature and so will hear me*. This is simply taken for granted. A person's presuppositions, however, may not necessarily be true.

Psychic: From the Greek word "psyche," meaning "soul." Used in this book chiefly to describe the wide range of *paranormal* phenomena, such as *ESP*, telepathy, *clairvoyance*, automatic writing, spoon bending, poltergeist activities, and other supernormal occurrences that lie outside the range of normal sensory or scientific explanation. Also used as a term to describe a person who is responsive to such forces. Psychic activities may be breeding grounds for mediumistic activities with *spirits*.

Psychic Healing: The practice of healing (usually painless) by someone claiming to be able to manipulate universal healing energies. Some attribute their healing powers to God. Most psychic surgeons, however, practice sleight-of-hand tricks on the bodies of their patients, which makes it seem as if the evil tissue or negative energy of a disease has been removed. There are much fraud and charlatanry in this area, as well as the potential danger of *spirit* contact through the trance state of the surgeon.

Psychic Phenomena: See *psychic*.

Psychic Therapy: Usually done by a *spirit medium, channeler*, crystal healer, or other persons claiming to have supernormal powers. May easily lead to spirit contact.

Psychospiritual Technologies: A name for New Age transformative remedies, therapies, practices, and procedures that may not be *occult* sounding but have Eastern religious, mystical, or pagan *presuppositions*. These would include much that is called *alternative medicine* as well as disciplines like *A Course in Miracles*, *TM*, *visualization*, and others that incorporate the *cosmopolitan spirituality* into their transformative technologies.

Rama: Like *Krishna*, another beloved and adored divine manifestation in human form in *Hinduism*. *Avatar*.

Rationalism: From the Latin word "rationalis," meaning "belonging to reason." As used in this book, it represents a complex *secular* belief system whose march through the West has been chiefly to combat the claims of religion, faith, and spirituality by declaring that reason alone is the only valid source for knowledge, belief, and action. God and the Bible have no place in informing human affairs and decisions.

Reductionism: Theories that reduce complex phenomena to separate simple parts in order to try to explain the whole. When applied to psychology, for instance, reductionism may reduce the whole wealth of human behavior to biological events and reflexes. Or when informing the universe, it may reduce all of life to only what is seen. Or when applied to human beings, it may reduce a person to a collection of atoms and physical laws, or thoughts to a mere combination of sense impressions. Reductionist principles are frequently the presuppositions of the natural sciences and psychology, which is why they are futile for explaining the whole.

Reincarnation: The doctrine or belief based on the laws of *karma* that people live many hundreds or thousands of lifetimes.

Relativism: Used in this book for the theory that there are no longer any moral absolutes; truth, therefore, becomes relative to the individual or group who holds it. This appears in the New Age world as the popular saying, "You've got your truth; I've got mine."

Right Brain: A still controversial theory that the brain's right hemisphere is predominantly involved with the creative, artistic, and *intuitive* aspects. It is highly emphasized in the New Age world as what needs great development and expression in Western people. *Left Brain*.

Rolfing: Developed by biochemist Ida Rolf, this particularly aggressive type of massage is thought to help the body rebalance its energies by softening muscles and so freeing the body from poor postures. Someone has called it massage with a vengeance.

Samsara: In *Hinduism* and *Buddhism*, the eternal cycle of birth, suffering, death, and rebirth.

Secular: Pertaining to what is worldly or temporal rather than religious or *spiritual*.

Secular Humanism: See *humanism*.

Secularism: The view that the present well-being of humankind excludes any religious or *spiritual* considerations, especially in civil affairs and public education.

Secularization: The process of drawing away from a religious or *spiritual* orientation as a chief influence in a culture's activities and beliefs.

Self: In simplest terms, when the word appears capitalized in the New Spirituality it is generally to describe a God concept. See *Self-Realization*.

Self-Realization: In *Hinduism* "Atman" means "Self" and is identified with *Brahma* (the Supreme). The object of human life becomes to discover one's unity with this supreme source. When one becomes enlightened to this, it is Self-realization.

Shaman: In ancient times, a medicine man, principally of northern Asia but also found in Mexico and among Native Americans who worshiped *spirits* and practiced healing through magic and power received from the spirits. A shaman claims the power to compel spirits by various rituals and incantations and to be able to protect clients from harmful influences of spirits. There is a revival of shamanism in the New Age world, especially among women.

Siva (Shiva): The Hindu god of destruction and reproduction; a member of the Hindu trinity along with *Brahma* and *Vishnu*.

Society for Psychical Research: Founded in 1882 by a number of scientists and philosophers to investigate *occult* phenomena. Lost some of its notoriety in the 1930s with the rise of so-called *paranormal* research activities and parapsychology.

Spirit(s): Used in this book to describe demonic supernatural beings with

256

a power greater than that of humans, who can at times interfere in human affairs and who may be communicated with through *occult* means. Often labeled an *entity* or *spirit guide* by the New Spirituality and contacted through *spirit mediumship* or *channeling*.

Spirit Channeling: See *spirit mediumship*.

Spirit Guide: See *spirit*. In the New Age world, often thought to be a highly evolved deceased person who is between incarnations or who no longer has to reincarnate.

Spirit Medium(ship): A person thought to be able to contact the spirits of the dead and the process through which this is accomplished. Seances, Ouija boards, tarot cards, and *channeling* are popular means for this occultism. Channeling is a popular practice in which a person enters a deep trance state and permits a *spirit* to completely take over the personality and so speak to a client about matters mundane or metaphysical. After a session the spirit leaves the *channeler*, who returns to normal *consciousness* often without knowing what the spirit has said through him. Women who are channelers frequently speak in male voices when channeling a spirit.

Spiritual: The areas of life that relate to things that are not tangible or material but are concerned with the soul, God, religion, or the sacred.

Spiritual Evolution: A way of describing the gradual process of *spiritual* development in this life and through *reincarnation*. This is thought to be accomplished by practicing any of the numerous spiritual disciplines such as *meditation, yoga, asceticism*, doing good works, and so on. Spiritual evolution asks the rhetorical question, "Is a human being the best the 'system' can produce?" Of course not, comes the answer. If we have pulled ourselves up this far from the biotic slime by our own bootstraps, maybe we can throw up a whole new order of being someday. And the next stage toward that ultimate goal, it is generally agreed, is to pay off all of our bad *karma* so that we will not have to reincarnate any longer in our earth suits and thus we can be highly evolved sheer *spirits*. After that, who knows? The potential is limitless because we are "God."

Spiritualism: Sometimes referred to as spiritism, and in this book includes spiritualist churches within its context. In its broadest meaning, includes communication with the dead or with *spirits* through a *medium* or *psychic* and a wide range of *occult* or *psychic phenomena*. Spiritualist churches are often confused with Christianity even though they stand opposed to cardinal Christian doctrine and belief.

Spiritualist: One who practices *spiritualism*.

Stilling: Often used in classrooms as a generic, nonreligious label for Eastern religious forms of *meditation*.

Synchronicity: A term largely popularized by Carl Jung to describe meaningful coincidences of events or actions that may otherwise seem unrelated to each other but now have perhaps a special or *spiritual* meaning.

Syncretism: The tendency to blend or reconcile differing beliefs, often religious or spiritual. In the New Age world, these attempts are usually made by trying to take cardinal Christian beliefs and make them compatible with *occult* or Eastern mystical or pagan beliefs. For example, using the name Jesus to mean an *avatar*, or redefining forgiveness as a change of perception, or saying that the *spirit guides* are angels or highly evolved human beings.

Systems Theory: A view of looking at the world as a whole system of interrelated smaller systems. It is a reaction against *reductionism* and the prevailing analytical way of examining things and the world by breaking them up into an unrelated multiplicity of objects. In systems thinking, which is often characterized by words like "organic" and "holistic," the universe is seen as one indivisible dynamic whole whose parts are interrelated. Within this whole are innumerable systems in their own right, for example, an anthill, a beehive, the human family, and these form a complex web of interrelationships between them that make up the bigger system comprising all the interrelationships. In a systems view, things are not remaining static but are part of a continual dynamic process of evolution, as frequently depicted by the saying, "The whole is greater than the sum of its parts." (This description has been distilled from Elliot Miller's book *A Crash Course on the New Age Movement*.)

Taoism: "Tao" is an ancient Chinese word meaning "the way" or "the one," and it describes the ultimate essence, or universal principle or *energy*, by and through which all things have their existence. It manifests itself in all things in the process of antithetic but complementary rhythms, such as *yin and yang* or macrocosm and microcosm, and these correspond with and counterbalance each other. Taoism, which can be traced back to the teaching of Lao-tzu in sixth-century B.C. China, is "The Way" of recapturing and preserving the harmony of this supposed spiritual rhythm that animates all things.

Tarot: A deck of twenty-two playing cards depicting vices, virtues, and *spiritual* powers. These are used in *occult* forms of character analysis and fortune-telling.

Teleology: In its broadest sense, the philosophical study of design or purpose in the universe, as opposed to the view that the universe can be understood by purely mechanical or natural causes or explanations.

TM: Transcendental meditation. It was introduced to the United States in 1959 by the Hindu monk Maharishi Mahesh Yogi and became widely popularized in the West when promoted by the Beatles in the late 1960s. When this Eastern mystical form of *meditation* was redefined in a thoroughgoing scientific language (complete with research graphs and documentation), it moved from the countercultural fringe to mainstream culture, hailed as it was as a great key to physical and mental relaxation, stress management, blood pressure reduction, anxiety relief, job performance improvement, and increased sexual enjoyment. There is much ritual initiation, which includes the giving of a *mantra*.

Transcendent: Often used of deity to describe what is above and independent of the material universe.

Transformation: Used in very broad contexts to describe one's passage from old traditional ways (paradigms) of thinking to an awareness of or awakening to New Age ways of thinking and acting. Marilyn Ferguson has written that transformation is a journey without a final destination, and she analyzes it (Ha!) in four stages. First comes the entry point, in which something catastrophic shakes up one's old understanding. LSD, for example, did this for the hippies. Then comes exploration, in which the seeker searches and practices the *psychospiritual technologies* designed to free the tight hold one has on the old and so expand consciousness to an acceptance of New Age thinking. Then comes integration, in which New Age thinking and its practices are more thoroughly influencing the person's life. The fourth stage she calls conspiracy, in which the *paradigm* shift is so strong that the person seeks to communicate the ideas of the transformation to others and incorporate them into work and family because its social implications have been seen and understood.

Transmigration: Used of souls in *Eastern religions* to describe *reincarnation* from body to body as determined by one's *karma*. Past and future bodies may include animals as well, which is why cows and rats, for example, are treated specially in India and not killed or eaten.

Transpersonal: A term describing levels of *consciousness* above and beyond the strictly personal. Often associated with New Age *spiritual* disciplines and practices and the *intuitive*, or when describing contact with *spirit guides*.

Transpersonal Psychology: A vast and bewildering constellation of psychological practices and therapies that incorporate spirituality into counseling. They would include their own blends of *syncretism* from influences such as Zen Buddhism, contemporary Sufism, *TM*, alchemy, hypnotism, *Gnosticism, Taoism, mysticism,* the Cabalistic tradition, Carl Jung, and much more. *Spirit* contact roams through transpersonal psychologies like a particularly bad Los Angeles smog.

Unity: Officially, the Unity School of Christianity. Called by Dr. Walter Martin "the largest Gnostic cult in Christendom." Highly syncretistic and rejects the cardinal tenets of Christianity. Accepts *reincarnation.* It is easy to find many books promoting *astrology* and the *occult* in Unity church libraries.

Universal Consciousness: A term for God consciousness, which is impersonal. See *energy.*

Universal Life Energy: See *energy.*

Vishnu: Whereas *Brahma* represents the creator and *Siva* the destroyer, Vishnu represents the third aspect of this Hindu triad of the Supreme as the sustainer.

Visualization: Often called "creative visualization" and not necessarily New Age in practice; but when it is, it is a kind of *spiritual* discipline using mental energies to manipulate or create one's own goals, realize dreams, greatly improve or transform health, relationships, and beauty. It is practiced in the context of setting goals, developing *paranormal* senses, relaxation exercises, deep *meditation,* affirmations, and other mystical techniques. It promises that as you control and shape your thoughts, dreams, and desires, you can create your own reality. After entry-level stages, it usually involves one in contact with *spirit guides* and occultism.

Vital Force: Used loosely throughout the New Spirituality to describe *energy,* but it was chiefly popularized by the founder of homeopathy, Samuel Hahnemann, who wrote that "the spiritual vital force [is] the dynamism that animates the material body." According to Hahnemann, "when a person falls ill, it is only this spiritual . . . vital force . . . that is primarily deranged," and so responsible for outer bodily symptoms, which are secondary.

Wicca: A new label for white *witchcraft.* Very popular among New Age pagans and some feminists.

Witchcraft: The practice of sorcery or ritual magic, either black or white, to manipulate supernatural powers thought to exist in nature, animals, and humans. Often associated with a revival of pagan religions and animism.

Worldview: James Sire has written that a worldview is a set of *presuppositions* one holds about the basic makeup of the world. That is about as simple and clear a definition as you are likely to find. Such assumptions about the basic makeup of life and the world include what one thinks about the nature of personal and societal concerns and dimensions, such as education, politics, religion, the family, and so on. In this book I have used the term "wisdom" in its biblical sense in place of "worldview."

Yin and Yang: The two fundamental rhythms or *spiritual* forces in *Taoism* that make up *Chi*. They are said to be complementary opposites forming a harmonious whole when balanced. They are an essential part of *macrobiotics* and most acupuncture theories, methodologies, and treatments and their derivatives, such as acupressure and shiatsu. In the Western New Age world, yin and yang have taken on a wealth of opposite though complementary characteristics. For example, yin: dark, cold, feminine, below; yang: light, heat, masculine, above. Yin and yang have no basis in material reality.

Yoga: From a Sanskrit word meaning "yoking" or "union," usually with "God." The aim of the Indian yogi is the self's liberation from matter and union with the supreme *Self*. This is attained gradually through stages by means of scrupulous practice of self-control, prescribed bodily postures, strict regulation of breathing, *meditation*, and focusing of the gaze. Miraculous powers are promised to the one who attains absorption into the Supreme. In the West, attempts have been made to demystify yoga by marketing it as merely a physical discipline, for training and expanding *consciousness*, experiencing tranquillity, receiving *spiritual* insight, or doing exercise. Various aims of yoga are represented by its different schools, such as hatha, gnana, karma, bhakti, tantra, and kundalini. The hatha, kundalini, and tantra schools, probably in that order, are the most popular in the West.

Zeitgeist: The outlook or spiritual characteristics of a certain period of time. From the German "zeit," meaning "time," and "geist," meaning "spirit."

Zen Koans: See *koans*.

Zen Macrobiotics: See *macrobiotics*.

Zygote: The organism that develops from a mature sperm and egg participating in fertilization.

RECOMMENDED
READING

Also listed are cassette tapes and useful organizations.

New Age and Related Topics

Abell, George O., and Barry Singer, eds. *Science and the Paranormal: Probing the Existence of the Supernatural.* New York: Charles Scribner's Sons, 1981. From a secular viewpoint, many eminent scientists evaluate topics such as the Bermuda triangle, Big Foot, UFOs, ESP, Uri Geller, TM, pyramids, and more.

Albrecht, Mark. *Reincarnation: A Christian Appraisal.* Downers Grove, Ill.: InterVarsity Press, 1982. A short, clear, and informative critique of this cardinal New Age belief. Topics: history of, past-life recall, arguments against, theological objections to.

Amano, J. Yutaka, and Norman L. Geisler. *The Infiltration of the New Age.* Wheaton, Ill.: Tyndale, 1989. Examines central New Age beliefs. Chapters on Self and inner healing. Five helpful appendices.

Ankerberg, John, and John Weldon. *Astrology: Do the Heavens Rule Our Destiny?* Eugene, Oreg.: Harvest House, 1989. A wide variety of astrological principles and practices receive extensive Christian criticism.

————. *Can You Trust Your Doctor?: The Complete Guide to New Age Medicine and Its Threat to Your Family.* Brentwood, Tenn.: Wolgemuth & Hyatt, 1991. The most exhaustive Christian analysis of holistic health care and alternative medicine that I know of so far. Worth the investment.

Bishop, Steve, and Christopher Droop. *The Earth Is the Lord's: A Message of Hope for the Environment.* Bristol, England: Regius Press, 1990. A very brief introductory work explaining the basis for Christian earth-stewardship. But what do the authors mean by "cosmic Christ"? Extensive bibliography is worth the price of the book.

Burnett, David. *Clash of Worlds: A Christian's Handbook on Cultures, World Religions, and Evangelism*. Nashville, Tenn.: Oliver Nelson, 1992. Unreviewed. Examines major contemporary worldviews such as Islamic, secular, primal, Hindu, Chinese, New Age, and others, and shows why a biblical worldview is the most credible.

Burnett, David. *Dawning of the Pagan Moon*. Nashville, Tenn.: Oliver Nelson, 1992. Unreviewed. Understanding the roots, characteristics, and influences of Western paganism.

————. *Unearthly Powers: A Christian's Handbook on Primal and Folk Religions*. Nashville, Tenn.: Oliver Nelson, 1992. Unreviewed. Examines the worldviews, beliefs, and practices of modern day followers of primal religions, with a view to evangelizing the people of these faiths.

Campolo, Tony. *How to Rescue the Earth Without Worshipping Nature*. Milton Keynes, England: Nelson Word, 1992. Partially reviewed. Stretch your thinking with these fresh insights about Christian earth-stewardship.

Chandler, Russell. *Understanding the New Age*. Milton Keynes, England: Nelson Word, 1988. Full of information. Chandler's job as religious correspondent for the *Los Angeles Times* newspaper gave him access to many New Age and Christian leaders, whom he interviewed for the book.

Clark, David K., and Norman L. Geisler. *Apologetics in the New Age: A Christian Critique of Pantheism*. Grand Rapids, Mich.: Baker Book House, 1990. A scholarly defense of Christian belief against five kinds of pantheism and their New Age expressions.

Cole, Michael, et al. *What Is the New Age?* London, England: Hodder & Stoughton, 1990. Multiple authorship gives this book breadth of insight into topics such as New Age origins, conspiracy theory, spiritual powers, the real new age, and more.

Cooper, Tim. *Green Christianity*. London, England: Spire, 1990. Though the book virtually ignores the occult potential of New Ageism, it provides a critique of New Age earth-stewardship ideologies and makes a convincing case for Christian earth-stewardship. Cooper is a prominent figure in Britain's growing Green movement.

Culver, Roger B., and Philip A. Ianna. *Astrology: True or False?: A Scientific Evaluation*. Buffalo, N.Y.: Prometheus Books, 1988. May be the definitive scientific criticism of astrology from a secular viewpoint. Written by two professors of astronomy. Well researched and thought through.

Drane, John. *What Is the New Age Saying to the Church?* London, England: Marshall Pickering, 1991. This lecturer in religious studies at the University of Stirling, Scotland, interviewed leading New Agers for the book. Somewhat unsettling criticisms of Christian failure with New Age people.

Ellis, Roger. *The Occult and Young People*. Eastbourne, England: Kingsway, 1989. Clear warnings about occult power and practices from astral projection to witchcraft, and help for those involved in them.

Geisler, Norman L., and J. Yutaka Amano. *The Reincarnation Sensation*. Wheaton, Ill.: Tyndale, 1987. This biblical evaluation includes examination of the psychology and injustice of reincarnation; also, a look at Christian belief in it.

Gordon, Ian. *The Craft and the Cross*. Eastbourne, England: Kingsway, 1989. Autobiography. Insights about the New Age are woven throughout this fascinating account of Gordon's rise in the Masons, which he thought was compatible with Christianity, until ...

Groothuis, Douglas. *Unmasking the New Age*. Downers Grove, Ill.: InterVarsity Press, 1986. May be the best "get acquainted with the New Age" book on the market. Topics include "All is one, one is all"; human potential in psychology; New Age science and politics; Christian response.

———. *Confronting the New Age*. Downers Grove, Ill.: InterVarsity Press, 1988. A good companion book to *Unmasking*. Topics include New Age education, business, and music; visualization; three chapters on witnessing to New Age people.

———. *Revealing the New Age Jesus: Challenges to Orthodox Views of Christ*. Downers Grove, Ill.: InterVarsity Press, 1990. In-depth coverage of pagan, Gnostic, and New Age views of Jesus Christ. Other topics: the "lost years" of Jesus; Jesus the Essene, the Spirit, the Cosmic Christ. Very helpful bibliography.

Hoyt, Karen, et al. *The New Age Rage*. Old Tappan, N.J.: Revell, 1987. From eight Spiritual Counterfeits Project writers comes a careful exploration of the New Age, holistic health, quantum physics, transpersonal psychology, tantra, an appendix on Christian and New Age worldviews, and other relevant ideas and practices.

Korem, Dan. *Powers: Testing the Psychic and the Supernatural*. Downers Grove, Ill.: InterVarsity Press, 1988. A psychic detective finds a missing body; a mind reader knows your thoughts; a psychic points and the pencil moves. This investigative journalist and magician exposes how psychics fool us. The section on cold readings is worth the price of the book.

Lewis, C. S. *That Hideous Strength*. New York: Macmillan, 1972. Take a break. Want a novel that actually does what everyone (almost) thinks Peretti's tales are doing? A chilling good yarn. Was Lewis playing the prophet?

Logan, Kevin. *Close Encounters with the New Age*. Eastbourne, England: Kingsway, 1991. After spending time at Findhorn (Scotland) and Glastonbury (England), the author shares his observations about the esotericism of those places.

Maharaj, Rabindranath R., with Dave Hunt. *Death of a Guru*. London England: Hodder & Stoughton, 1978. Also published as *Escape into the Light*. Autobiography. A convincing Eastern mystical connection with the Western New Age is made in this young yogi's poignant search for meaning within Hinduism and his parallel struggle toward Jesus Christ.

Mangalwadi, Vishal. *In Search of Self: Beyond the New Age*. London, England: Hodder & Stoughton, 1992. This L'Abri Fellowship associate writes with refreshing insight from his background and experience as an Indian Christian. Endorsed by Os Guinness.

Martin, Walter. *The New Age Cult*. Minneapolis, Minn.: Bethany, 1989. Unreviewed. Written by one of Christianity's foremost investigators of cults and the occult.

Matrissiana, Caryl. *Gods of the New Age*. Basingstoke, England: Marshall Pickering, 1985. Autobiography. A fashionable Londoner enters the New Age and later becomes disillusioned and turns to Christ.

Michaelson, Johanna. *The Beautiful Side of Evil*. Eugene, Oreg.: Harvest House, 1982. Autobiography. The unmasking of psychic healing from someone who was a personal assistant to a psychic healer in Mexico, and her conversion to Christ.

Miller, Elliot. *A Crash Course on the New Age Movement*. Grand Rapids, Mich.: Baker Book House, 1989. Some autobiography. Chiefly a survey and critique of New Age ideology from the editor-in-chief of the *Christian Research Journal*. Topics include mysticism, general systems theory, New Age activism, and channeling.

North, Gary. *Unholy Spirits: Occultism and New Age Humanism*. Fort Worth, Tex.: Dominion Press, 1986. Also published as *None Dare Call It Witchcraft*. An intelligent look at things, from the crisis of Western rationalism, to Carlos Castaneda, to Edgar Cayce, to UFOs, to the end of the world(?).

Osborn, Lawrence. *Angels of Light?: The Challenge of the New Age*. London, England: Daybreak, 1992. Unreviewed. Foreword by Christian thinker Lesslie Newbigin, who commends the book as "necessary reading."

Pement, Eric, ed. *Contend for the Faith: Collected Papers of the Rockford Conference on Discernment and Evangelism*. Chicago, Ill.: Evangelical Ministries to New Religions, 1992. More than twenty contributors on a wide variety of subjects—discernment, worldview, apologetics, Islam, Buddhism, Mormonism, Jehovah's Witnesses, astrology, channeling, exit counseling, and much more—make this unique volume appropriate for your reference section. Limited print run.

Perry, Michael. *Gods Within: A Critical Guide to the New Age*. London, England: SPCK, 1992. Makes some good points at times, but the book clouds the borders between paranormal phenomena and Christian spiritual gifts, does not take a firm stand against visiting spirit mediums, and includes occultist Rudolph Steiner in a list of Christian oracles. Not recommended for young Christians or those already confused by the New Age. Does not seem to me to live up to its subtitle.

Pfeifer, Samuel. *Healing at Any Price?: The Hidden Dangers of Alternative Medicine*. Milton Keynes, England: Nelson Word, 1988. A good Christian appraisal of the twilight zone of holism and alternative medicine. Topics include reflexology, acupuncture, homeopathy, iridology, herbal medicine, and more.

Reisser, Paul C., Teri K. Reisser, and John Weldon. *New Age Medicine: A Christian Perspective on Holistic Health*. Downers Grove, Ill.: InterVarsity Press, 1987. A good introductory assessment of popular holistic practices. The chapters on energy and Chinese medicine are particularly helpful.

Rhodes, Ron. *The Counterfeit Christ of the New Age Movement*. Grand Rapids, Mich.: Baker Book House, 1990. This associate editor with the *Christian Research Journal* surveys New Age teaching about Jesus Christ. Discusses David Spangler, Elizabeth Clare Prophet, Matthew Fox, and others.

Seaton, Chris. *Whose Earth?* Westchester, Ill.: Crossway Books, 1992. Unreviewed. Foreword by Mike Morris, International Secretary of the Evangelical Alliance, who commends the book for "informed insights with radical proposals for action."

Sire, James. *Scripture Twisting*. Downers Grove, Ill.: InterVarsity Press, 1980. Reveals many ways in which the Bible can be taken out of context. New Age relevance.

Smith, LaGard F. *Out on a Broken Limb*. Eugene, Oreg.: Harvest House, 1986. A Christian response to Shirley MacLaine's New Age best-seller *Out on a Limb*. Shows the flaws of MacLaine's New Age beliefs and her misuse of Scripture.

————. *Crystal Lies: Choices and the New Age*. Ann Arbor, Mich.: Vine Books, Servant Publications, 1989. A plethora of Bible verses helps move the book along and helps readers make wise choices about their beliefs.

Taylor, Mike. *Ley Lines and the Christian*. Market Harborough, England: Diasozo Trust, 1992. Booklet. The soundest explanation of the subject that I know of. May challenge some Christians to give up beliefs not founded on the Bible.

Evangelization, Outreach, and Counseling Resources

Brooke, Tal. *Riders of the Cosmic Circuit*. Batavia, Ill.: Lion Publishing, 1986. Autobiography. This former Western disciple of Sai Baba writes to New Age seekers about his life, his assessment of leading gurus, and his conversion to Jesus Christ.

Buell, Jon A., and Quentin O. Hyder. *Jesus: God, Ghost or Guru?* Grand Rapids, Mich.: Zondervan/Probe, 1978. This Christian Free University Curriculum book is an apologetic for an orthodox view of Jesus Christ, with a response by F. F. Bruce. Will help New Agers to see other choices.

Enroth, Ronald, ed. *Evangelizing the Cults*. Ann Arbor, Mich.: Servant, 1990. Ten Christian contributors write chapters on Mormonism, Scientology, occult groups, Eastern religions, the New Age, and more in the context of how to share Jesus with such people.

Green, Michael. *You Must Be Joking: Popular Excuses for Avoiding Jesus Christ*. London, England: Hodder & Stoughton, 1976. Great material to use in conversations with New Agers who lean on typical objections to Christianity.

Halverson, Dean. *Crystal Clear: A Small Group Discussion Guide for Understanding and Reaching New Agers*. Colorado Springs, Colo.: NavPress, 1990. Just what the subtitle says. The nine sessions in this compact work will help you explore the significant characteristics of the New Age belief system and how to approach New Agers with understanding and sensitivity. Leader's Guide runs parallel to the sessions.

Koch, Kurt. *Christian Counseling and Occultism*. Grand Rapids, Mich.: Kregel Publications, 1972. Ought to be read slowly and carefully by any Christian involved in ministry to people who are thought to be influenced by occult phenomena. Hundreds of pastoral case studies cited. Principles for discernment given.

Lewis, C.S. *Mere Christianity*. New York: Macmillan, 1952. This lucid defense of the Christian faith can be given to New Agers to speak to them about the reality of God, Jesus, morals, forgiveness, and other cardinal Christian beliefs.

Martin, Walter. *Kingdom of the Cults*. Minneapolis, Minn.: Bethany, 1985. Rev. ed. Still the definitive work for nearly two dozen major cults. Also carries chapters on dealing with the language barrier and the psychological structure of cultism. Ought to be on the shelf for any Christian who needs a handy and dependable reference. Chapters on New Age–related topics include theosophy, spiritism, scientology, and Eastern religions.

McDowell, Josh. *Evidence that Demands a Verdict*. San Bernardino, Calif.: Campus Crusade for Christ, 1972. A good book for doing a series of Bible studies on the fact and meaning of the Resurrection.

Petersen, Jim. *Evangelism as a Lifestyle*. Colorado Springs, Colo.: NavPress, 1980. How to reach people in your world who have little or no understanding of Christianity. Identifies problems with traditional evangelism and offers solutions for communicating the gospel to a secularized world.

———. *Evangelism for Our Generation*. Colorado Springs, Colo.: NavPress, 1985. Very helpful material on worldview and understanding our times, and how these affect our evangelism. An appendix with a step-by-step evangelistic study of John's gospel.

———. *Church Without Walls*. Colorado Springs, Colo.: NavPress, 1992. Unreviewed. Foreword by Dr. Gene A. Getz, who writes that this "veteran missionary . . . has earned the right to speak out about why traditional church structures have outlived their functions and impede the gospel in today's world, and how forgotten New Testament ideas would help us correct this."

Richardson, Don. *Peace Child: An Unforgettable Story of Primitive Jungle Treachery in the Twentieth Century*. Ventura, Calif.: Regal Books, 1976. Autobiography. Shows how Don and Carol Richardson overcame unbelievable odds to communicate the gospel to a Stone Age Sawi tribe. A real faith builder for Christians who feel terribly up against it with New Age people.

Strohmer, Charles. *What Your Horoscope Doesn't Tell You*. American edition—Wheaton, Ill.: Tyndale, 1988; Milton Keynes, England: Nelson Word, 1991. I put myself on the other side of the typewriter while I was writing the book and asked, "What would have made sense to me from a Christian point of view when I was into the New Age, to help me see its dangers and get out of it?" Out of that came a weighty exposé of astrology, written for non-Christian spiritual seekers. It is a book you can put into their hands that will challenge them at their level and also offer the gospel. It has been very influential toward this end.

Christianity and the Modern World

The following books will assist readers who are interested in knowing more about the importance of worldview as it relates primarily to the cultural shift that is occurring in the West today, and how we as Christians should understand it and respond.

Guinness, Os. *The Dust of Death*. Downers Grove, Ill.: InterVarsity Press, 1973. A critique of the counterculture as it journeyed out of a rationalistic and technological wasteland into the promised land of radical politics, Eastern religion, psychedelic drugs, and the occult.

Newbigin, Lesslie. *Foolishness to the Greeks: The Gospel and Western Culture*. London, England: SPCK, 1986. A healthy dose of understanding for the problems we face in communicating with a modern Western world. The author is especially concerned with the problems represented by modern science, social structures, and political practices. Deeply thoughtful.

Niebuhr, H. Richard. *Christ and Culture*. New York: Harper & Row, 1975. Unreviewed. Analysis of the problematic relations of Christianity with culture. Sections include Christ against culture, the Christ of culture, Christ above culture, Christ as transformer of culture.

Peck, John. *Wisdom in the Marketplace.* London, England: Greenbelt, 1989. Penetrating and groundbreaking. This Christian philosopher and theologian helps us faithfully meet the radical questions that beset the modern world with the wisdom of God. The book is about more than building up ideas and making them work. It aims to assist the personal development of a biblical viewpoint that will become instinctive and govern actions in a spontaneous, godly manner.

Schaeffer, Francis, *Escape from Reason*. Downers Grove, Ill.: InterVarsity Press, 1968. A penetrating analysis of trends in modern thought. Starting with Aquinas and coming up through the Renaissance, the Reformation, and early modern science, the book shows what has led to modern people's despair and their blind existential leap into whatever they think will bring the answer to life's meaninglessness.

———. *The God Who Is There*. Downers Grove, Ill.: InterVarsity Press, 1968. Surveys the intellectual and cultural climate of the second half of the twentieth century, shows the relationship of the new theology to that climate, explains how historic Christianity differs.

———. *He Is There and He Is Not Silent*. Wheaton, Ill.: Tyndale, 1972. "This book," Schaeffer wrote, "deals with the philosophic necessity of God's being there and not being silent, in the areas of metaphysics, morals and epistemology." (These three books by Schaeffer make a unified base for much of the author's thought and work.)

Sire, James. *The Universe Next Door*. Downers Grove, Ill.: InterVarsity Press, 1976. Different worldview perspectives, including Eastern pantheistic monism and the new consciousness.

———. *Discipleship of the Mind.* Downers Grove, Ill.: InterVarsity Press, 1990. Unreviewed. Topics include introduction to worldview analysis, the nature of human nature, knowing and doing, the meaning of human history. Includes an appendix to Christian students and an amazing bibliography.

Walsh, Brian J., and J. Richard Middleton. *The Transforming Vision: Shaping a Christian Worldview*. Downers Grove, Ill.: InterVarsity Press, 1984. Unreviewed. Sections include what are worldviews?; biblical worldview; modern worldview; Christian cultural response.

Webber, Robert E. *The Church in the World*. Grand Rapids, Mich.: Zondervan, 1986. Unreviewed. A historical and theological survey of the church-world issue from New Testament times to modern day. Explores how Christians can have a redemptive influence on the world and guide decisions of government. Assesses Christian activists as diverse as Jerry Falwell, Tim LaHaye, Ron Sider, Richard Neuhaus, and Gustavo Gutiérrez.

Cassette Tapes

Charles Strohmer has produced the following two cassette tape courses on the New Age. These are not composed of assorted messages collected from various conferences, but were designed and taught as whole courses in an effort to provide continuity of thought throughout. These have an international flavor to them, and they bring more than twenty years of experience as an insider turned outsider to the subject. Each course uses biblical wisdom to evaluate the theories, beliefs, practices, and therapies of the New Spirituality. They answer the questions that most people are asking and bring perspectives we may have missed. They also help to equip the listener with effective communication skills. *The Gospel and the New Spirituality* has been chiefly about effective communication; both the courses below are designed for gaining a systematic and much more thorough understanding of New Age wisdom in particular, and a biblical response to it. Either course makes an ideal tool for use by individuals, Sunday school classes, and home Bible study groups or to stimulate small-group discussions and activities.

1. New Age Spirituality and Christian Belief
This popular in-depth course is one of a kind. It contains more than fifteen hours of systematic teaching on ten cassette tapes. It includes classes on the following:

- Principalities and powers
- Man as God
- Rebirth theory
- Spiritual evolution
- Mystical experience
- New Age occultism (3 classes)
- New Age wisdom in culture (2 classes)

- New Age wisdom in health care (2 classes)
- Communicating with New Agers (2 classes)
- Psychic powers and the paranormal
- Carl Jung and New Age psychology
- Charles Strohmer's testimony

2. A Crash Course on the New Age

This is not a shortened version of the above course. It stands on its own, consisting of six classes, five hours of teaching. The classes include the following:

- Common misunderstanding about the New Age
- What we are up against
- New Age occultism
- Holistic health care
- New Age wisdom in education and business
- Effective communication

To order in the United States:
For "New Age Spirituality and Christian Belief," send $39.95, or for "A Crash Course on the New Age," send $12.95 to:
Charles Strohmer, Tapes, P.O. Box 4325, Sevierville, TN 37864. Make check payable to C. Strohmer.

To order in Great Britain or elsewhere in Europe:
For "New Age Spirituality and Christian Belief," send £24.95, or for "A Crash Course on the New Age," send £8.95 to:
Manna Christian Centre, 147–149 Streatham High Road, London, SW16 6EG. Make check payable to Manna.

If you wish to write directly to Charles Strohmer from outside the United States and order your tapes that way, please send only an *International Money Order* in U.S. dollars only. (Each course comes in an attractive album and cover.)

Useful Organizations

Great Britain

Beacon Foundation, 3 Grosvenor Avenue, Rhyl, Clywd, LL18 4HA, Wales.
Helps professionals and churches monitor the occult problem in Britain. Will
assist in rehabilitation of victims of occult abuse.

Christian Information Outreach, 92 The Street, Boughton, Faversham, Kent,
ME13 9AP, England.
Offers films, tapes, books, research, etc. Newsletter.

Deo Gloria Trust, Selsdon House, 212–220 Addington Road, South Croydon,
Surrey, CR2 8LD, England.
Books, leaflets, research, etc.

United States

Christian Research Institute, P.O. Box 500, San Juan Capistrano, CA 92693.
Publishes a popular quarterly journal and a bimonthly newsletter. Offers
books, tapes, and many timely helps.

Evangelical Ministries to New Religions, P.O. Box 10279, Denver, CO
80210.
Research, conferences.

Jesus People USA (JPUSA), Eric Pement or John Trott, 4707 N. Malden,
Chicago, IL 60640.
Publishes *Cornerstone* magazine and offers counseling, lectures, and timely
research, as well as an extensive directory of evangelical and nonevangelical
agencies, cult, occult, and New Age research organizations (hundreds of
listings, international).

Spiritual Counterfeits Project, P.O. Box 4308, Berkeley, CA 94704.
Publishes noteworthy journal and newsletter. Offers a wealth of research at
your fingertips through their Access Line, phone (415) 540-5767, 10:00 A.M.
to 2:00 A.M. West Coast time only. Lectures and conferences.

ABOUT THE
AUTHOR

Charles Strohmer is an author, editor, seminar speaker, and ordained Christian minister. Before becoming a Christian in July 1976, he spent many years as a professional astrologer. He also practiced meditation and visualization with "spirit guides." After his conversion, he studied Christian spirituality under the late Dr. Francis Schaeffer's L'Abri ministry and took classes in Christian philosophy and world-view under English theologian and philosopher the Reverend John Peck. An American, he lived in Great Britain where his wife was a missionary for several years. He now resides in the Smoky Mountains of Tennessee.

The Gospel and the New Spirituality is his third book. His second, *Explaining the Grace of God*, was written as a teaching booklet for CIS and Third World nations. His first book, *What Your Horoscope Doesn't Tell You*, is having wide success in numerous translations. He has been a guest on radio and television, including the "700 Club" and the BBC, and his articles have been published in several magazines, including the *Spiritual Counterfeits Project Journal*. His work also takes him into many denominations on both sides of the Atlantic, speaking in churches, colleges, and mission organizations.

He is associated with the Trinity House Arts Group in Livonia, Michigan, is listed in the fourth edition of *Who's Who in Religion*, and is at work on his autobiography.